Wealth into Power
The Communist Party's Embrace of China's Private Sector

In *Wealth into Power*, Bruce J. Dickson challenges the notion that economic development is leading to political change in China or that China's private entrepreneurs are helping to promote democratization. Instead, they have become partners with the ruling Chinese Communist Party to promote economic growth while maintaining the political status quo. Dickson's research illuminates the Communist Party's strategy for incorporating China's capitalists into the political system and shows how the shared interests, personal ties, and common views of the party and the private sector are creating a form of "crony communism." Rather than being potential agents of change, China's entrepreneurs may prove to be a key source of support for the party's agenda. Based on years of research and original survey data, this book will be of interest to all those interested in China's political future and the relationship between economic wealth and political power.

Bruce J. Dickson received his PhD from the University of Michigan in 1994. He has been a professor of political science and international affairs at George Washington University since 1993, where he served as director of the Sigur Center for Asian Studies and the Asian Studies Program from 1998 to 2001 and as the director of graduate studies in the Political Science department from 2004 to 2006. He is the author of *Red Capitalists in China: The Party, Private Entrepreneurs, and Prospects for Political Change* (2003) and *Democratization in China and Taiwan: The Adaptability of Leninist Parties* (1997), as well as numerous articles.

D0924136

Wealth into Power

The Communist Party's Embrace of China's Private Sector

BRUCE J. DICKSON

George Washington University

CAMBRIDGE
UNIVERSITY PRESS

CAMBRIDGE UNIVERSITY PRESS
Cambridge, New York, Melbourne, Madrid, Cape Town, Singapore, São Paulo, Delhi

Cambridge University Press
32 Avenue of the Americas, New York, NY 10013-2473, USA

www.cambridge.org
Information on this title: www.cambridge.org/9780521702706

First published 2008

Printed in the United States of America

A catalog record for this publication is available from the British Library.

Library of Congress Cataloging in Publication Data
Dickson, Bruce J.
Wealth into power : the Communist Party's embrace of China's private sector /
Bruce J. Dickson.
p.   cm.
Includes bibliographical references and index.
ISBN 978-0-521-87845-6 (hbk.) – ISBN 978-0-521-70270-6 (pbk.)
1. China – Economic policy – 2000–   2. Entrepreneurship – Political aspects – China.
3. Capitalism – China.   4. Zhongguo gong chan dang.   I. Title.
HC427.5.D53 2008
338.951 – dc22   2007046993

ISBN   978-0-521-87845-6 hardback
ISBN   978-0-521-70270-6 paperback

For
Benita, Andrew, and Caitlin

Contents

Tables and Figure

FIGURE

Acknowledgments

When I first began to study the political impact of China's private entrepreneurs, I never imagined I would still be at it more than ten years later. My main interest has been the evolution of the Chinese Communist Party (CCP), in particular its ability to adapt to the social and economic reforms under way in China. The relationship between the CCP and the private sector has proven to be a valuable window on that larger issue, and this is the second book I have written on that research question. Without advice and encouragement from a variety of people over the years, this research would not have been possible.

First and most importantly, I want to thank Shen Mingming for his invaluable help on all phases of this project. He proposed the original idea of doing a survey, and together we came up with the basic research design of comparing the views of private entrepreneurs with the local party and government officials in their communities. Along with his staff at the Research Center for Contemporary China (RCCC) of Peking University, we worked out the details of the questionnaires, and then the RCCC implemented the survey twice, first in 1997–1999 and then again in 2004–2005. In addition, I want to thank Yang Ming, the RCCC's associate director, for his advice and support of the project from beginning to end.

The funding necessary for the research was provided with the generous support of the Smith Richardson Foundation, the United States Institute of Peace, and the Sigur Center for Asian Studies at George

xi

Washington University. For administering my grants over the years, I particularly want to thank Ikuko Turner of the Sigur Center.

This book was written during the 2006–2007 academic year when I was a visiting scholar at the Woodrow Wilson International Center for Scholars in Washington, D.C. The Wilson Center provided the ideal scholarly environment and gave me the luxury of staying focused on one project day in and day out, without having to divide my time between research, teaching, and administrative work. I wish to thank Lee Hamilton for creating the intellectual atmosphere of the center and Bob Hathaway and Mark Mohr of the Asia Program for being such generous hosts.

Many friends and colleagues have given feedback in different ways on various aspects of this work over the years. I wish to thank Bruce Gilley, Merle Goldman, David Goodman, Kent Jennings, Scott Kennedy, Pierre Landry, Eric Lawrence, Susan Lawrence, Cheng Li, Ken Lieberthal, Melanie Manion, Kevin O'Brien, the late Mike Oksenberg, Kristen Parris, Margaret Pearson, Liz Perry, Lee Sigelman, Dorie Solinger, Jon Unger, Paul Wahlbeck, Susan Whiting, and Marty Whyte. Kellee Tsai has been studying China's capitalists for several years, and I have learned much from her work and from her feedback on mine. Jie Chen, Minxin Pei, and David Shambaugh read the entire book manuscript and provided detailed comments and suggestions that improved the final product greatly. It would undoubtedly have been even better had I not ignored some of their best ideas.

Portions of this book were previously published in "Integrating Wealth and Power in China: The Communist Party's Embrace of the Private Sector," *China Quarterly*, no. 192 (December 2007), pp. 827–854, and are reprinted here with permission.

Over the many years of this research, a small army of talented graduate students has provided outstanding research assistance. For their help on this book, I want to thank Jeff Becker, Enze Han, Evans Leung, Amanda Peet, Injoo Sohn, Fred Vellucci, Logan Wright, Jonathan Yu, and Yuelin Zhu.

At Cambridge, I want to thank Lew Bateman for his enthusiastic support for this book from the proposal stage to its completion; Hal Henglein for his judicious copyediting; Helen Wheeler for shepherding the book through the production process; and Nancy Hearst for her expert eye during proofreading. Together, they made the process go as smoothly and as quickly as possible.

Finally, I want to thank my family for the many distractions they provided. They have suffered with envy from my annual trips to China, and we finally made the trip a family affair in 2006, the first trip for them in eight long years. The book may have been written faster if not for the many games, concerts, practices, appointments, snow days, and sick days we shared together, but the time saved would not have been worth the times lost. In loving appreciation, this book is dedicated to them.

Introduction

After three decades of rapid economic growth in China, many observers believe that continued economic reform, and privatization in particular, is leading to eventual political change. China's economic reforms are creating the independent sources of wealth, power, and influence that scholars have shown to be key factors in a country's democratization. These economic and social changes have created expectations of a coming political change in China. Just as Chinese consumers have grown accustomed to freedom of choice in the market, they are also expected to begin demanding the right to choose their political leaders. China's growing numbers of private entrepreneurs and urban middle class are also expected to push for the increased transparency and accountability that democracy provides.

However, neither the Chinese Communist Party (CCP) nor China's capitalists have been willing to follow this script. Instead of engaging in conflict and confrontation, China's political and economic elites are increasingly intertwined, cooperating on producing national development and colluding in accumulating personal wealth. The CCP has not been a passive actor in the process of economic and social change but instead has taken steps to prevent organized demands for political change emanating from outside the party. In so doing, China has become a prime example of how authoritarian governments can employ strategic action to survive indefinitely despite rapid economic and social development.[1] It has selectively accommodated some interests while suppressing others. In particular, it has limited the types of organizations that can exist, allowing the ones it feels can be beneficial to its policy agenda and suppressing those it deems a potential threat to its political power. It screens which individuals are elected or selected for political posts, thereby deciding who can be active in the political system. It carefully monitors the flow of information via the media and the Internet, and although dissenting views occasionally appear, they are normally quickly removed. China has promoted the flow of information and allowed the types of organizations that are conducive to economic development while simultaneously preventing the same tools to be used for political purposes. These efforts have raised the costs of collective action and lowered the prospects for immediate political change. Rather than being on the wrong side of history, as President Bill Clinton famously warned Jiang Zemin during the latter's visit to the White House in 1997, China may represent an alternative to the conventional wisdom that democracy and markets must go together. China's recent experience has been described as the "Beijing consensus" and shows how countries can be increasingly prosperous economically while remaining steadfastly authoritarian politically.

For their part, China's capitalists are being increasingly integrated into the political system. Many are members of the CCP, making them "red capitalists." But most red capitalists were already in the party before going into business and took advantage of their political connections to become economically successful. A growing number of capitalists also participate in China's formal political institutions from the grass roots to the national level, including legislative and executive posts, and even party committees. Their participation is not solely by their own initiative, however; the CCP screens and approves all those who are elected or appointed to political posts. It arranges their participation in order to accommodate their interest in greater participation, to elicit their continued support, and to make sure that those who gain

---

[1] Bruce Bueno de Mesquita and George W. Downs, "Development and Democracy," *Foreign Affairs*, vol. 84, no. 5 (September–October 2005), pp. 77–86. Sheri Berman makes a similar argument regarding political parties in Western democracies. Socioeconomic and cultural changes did not have the predicted impact on parties because parties were able to adapt in different ways; see Sheri Berman, "Life of the Party (Review Article)," *Comparative Politics*, vol. 30, no. 1 (October 1997), pp. 101–122.

access to the political system will not present a threat to the status quo. As a result, most capitalists in political posts are red capitalists. They are already integrated into the most important political institution in China – the CCP – before being appointed to other posts. Because of their close personal and professional ties and their shared interests in promoting economic growth, China's capitalists and communist officials share similar viewpoints on a range of political, economic, and social issues. In short, rather than being promoters of democratic governance, China's capitalists have a stake in preserving the political system that has allowed them to prosper. They do not pose an immediate threat to the CCP; indeed, they are among the party's most important bases of support.

This book will elaborate on this argument, relying primarily on original survey data with private entrepreneurs and party and government officials. In this chapter, I will begin with a look at the theoretical basis for linking economic development with democracy, compare some of the empirical findings from China, and then present a brief summary of the following chapters, where the relationship between the CCP and the private sector will be explored in greater detail.

EXPLANATIONS OF DEMOCRATIZATION

The Chinese Communist Party's support of the private sector has been an increasingly prominent part of its economic reform strategy. Similarly, its embrace of the private sector has been a key part of its efforts to adapt to China's changing economic and social environment. The CCP banned the recruitment of entrepreneurs into the party in 1989, but during the 1990s, many local party officials quietly co-opted entrepreneurs in violation of the ban. In 2002, the CCP revised its constitution to legitimize this informal practice. Both the informal co-optation and the formal endorsement of recruiting entrepreneurs were designed with two goals in mind: first, to seek cooperation between the state and private enterprises, which are responsible for most new growth and job creation, central elements of the CCP's claim to legitimacy; and second, to prevent entrepreneurs from becoming an organized opposition. As such, the practice of co-opting entrepreneurs has been an essential part of the CCP's strategy for survival. At the same time, the alliance between political and economic elites, symbolized by the growing number of "red capitalists," is bringing new interests and new people into the political system. What impact is this trend having on China's still nominally communist system?

In the following sections, I will look at the expectations of modernization theory, the link between capitalism and democracy, and the role of civil society in both undermining and supporting incumbent regimes.

Consequences of Modernization

The attention paid to private entrepreneurs as potential agents of political change in China is partially because of the resumption of interest in modernization theory that accompanied the "third wave" of democratization and the recognition of the link between markets and democracy.[2] The correlation between wealth and democracy is one of the most studied topics in political science. This relationship was first elaborated by Seymour Lipset and later replicated in numerous other studies. Although many scholars debated the direction and degree of causality, few denied the correlation between economic prosperity and political democracy.[3]

Modernization theory posited that support for democracy was the result of social and cultural changes brought about through economic modernization. Labor shifted from the primary sector (agriculture) to the secondary and tertiary sectors (industry and services), which was accompanied by the emergence of a politically powerful capitalist class; the population shifted from rural to urban areas; education levels rose; science and technology replaced tradition and superstition. These

---

[2] Seymour Martin Lipset, "Some Social Requisites of Democracy: Economic Development and Political Legitimacy," *American Political Science Review*, vol. 53, no. 1 (March 1959), pp. 69–105; Samuel P. Huntington, *The Third Wave: Democratization in the Late Twentieth Century* (Norman: University Oklahoma Press, 1991); Larry Diamond, *Developing Democracy: Toward Consolidation* (Baltimore: Johns Hopkins University Press, 1999).

[3] Lipset, "Some Social Requisites of Democracy," pp. 69–105; Seymour Martin Lipset, "The Social Requisites of Democracy Revisited: 1993 Presidential Address," *American Sociological Review*, vol. 59, no. 1 (February 1994), pp. 1–22; Huntington, *Third Wave*; Ronald Inglehart, *Modernization and Postmodernization: Cultural, Economic, and Political Change in 43 Societies* (Princeton, NJ: Princeton University Press, 1997); Diamond, *Developing Democracy*.

sociodemographic changes in turn led to changes in values; together, they created the foundations of stable democracies.[4] Despite the many critiques of modernization theory, the simple and intuitive logic linking economic and political change is too seductive for many scholars and policy analysts to ignore. The causal relationships, however, remain complex and controversial. Does economic growth lead to democracy, or do the political and legal institutions of democracy set the conditions for stable economic development? Do democratic values emerge before a democratic transition or as the consequence of living under democratic institutions?

Scholars routinely point out the fallacies of the modernization theory perspective, especially the simplistic notion that economic development and political change go together in a linear and deterministic way.[5] Nevertheless, some observers use the conceptual connection between development and democracy to predict political change in China in the near future. For example, Henry Rowen predicted that China would be democratic by 2015, at which time he projected that per capita income would reach $7,000 (in 1990 U.S. dollars, based on purchasing power parity). At this point, the increased demand for political liberties would push China toward democracy; five years later, using revised economic data, he pushed back his prediction by another five years to 2020.[6] The implication of his argument is that faster growth would shorten the time until China became democratic. Shaohua Hu is even more optimistic, anticipating that China will be democratic by 2011 because the obstacles to democracy, including a backward and stagnated economy, are breaking down.[7] Larry Diamond observed that economic development in China "is creating a

---

[4] In addition to the works of Lipset, Inglehart, and Diamond already cited, see also Gabriel Almond and Sidney Verba, *Civic Culture: Political Attitudes and Democracy in Five Nations* (Princeton, NJ: Princeton University Press, 1963); Robert A. Dahl, *Democracy and Its Critics* (New Haven, CT: Yale University Press, 1989).

[5] Adam Przeworski and Fernando Limongi, "Modernization: Theories and Facts," *World Politics*, vol. 49, no. 2 (January 1997), pp. 155–183; Ross E. Burkhart and Michael A. Lewis-Beck, "Comparative Democracy: The Economic Development Thesis," *American Political Science Review*, vol. 88, no. 4 (December 1994), pp. 903–910.

[6] Henry S. Rowen, "The Short March: China's Road to Democracy," *The National Interest*, no. 45 (Fall 1996), pp. 61–70; Henry S. Rowen, "The Growth of Freedoms in China," APARC Working Paper, Stanford University, 2001.

[7] Shaohua Hu, *Explaining Chinese Democratization* (Westport, CT: Praeger, 2000).

more complex, pluralistic, self-confident, resourceful society ... *sooner or later*, economic development will generate growing pressures (and possibilities) for China to make a definitive regime change to democracy."[8] In 2004, Bruce Gilley wrote that, "the amount of wealth in China is probably already sufficient to finance democratic transition." What is missing, he argued, is the courage of party elites to initiate democratization.[9] Ronald Inglehart and Christian Welzel offer a more nuanced argument based on a revised version of modernization theory. Classical modernization theory posits that political values necessary for a stable democracy emerge in response to economic development and the social and political changes that accompany modernization. According to Inglehart and Welzel, the most important value is the desire for self-expression, which they argue is a more reliable predictor of liberal democracy than interpersonal trust, membership in associations, and even per capita GDP. Over the past generation, Chinese have enjoyed increased freedom of choice in the economic realm while still being denied equivalent political freedoms, including, most of all, freedom of expression. Accordingly, Inglehart and Welzel predict that China will become democratic within 15–20 years (i.e., by 2025) in response to "growing societal pressure to liberalize."[10]

Democratization is not simply an automatic result of economic development and value change, however. Although they may facilitate the consolidation of democracy, they are less necessary for the transition to democracy. Adam Przeworski and Fernando Limongi tested some of the main elements of modernization theory using time series data from a wide range of countries and found that there was no simple correspondence between economic change and the timing of democratization.[11] The cases of postwar Germany and Japan, and "third

---

[8] Diamond, *Developing Democracy*, p. 265, emphasis added.
[9] Bruce Gilley, *China's Democratic Future: How It Will Happen and Where It Will Lead* (New York: Columbia University Press, 2004), p. 64.
[10] Ronald Inglehart and Christian Welzel, *Modernization, Cultural Change, and Democracy: The Human Development Sequence* (Cambridge: Cambridge University Press, 2005), quoted from p. 156.
[11] Przeworski and Limongi, "Modernization"; See also Burkhart and Lewis-Beck, "Comparative Democracy." A rejoinder by Carles Boix and Susan C. Stokes found a closer fit between economic growth and political change as predicted by modernization theory, but only for first-wave democracies (i.e., European and North American countries that democratized before the 20th century); see Carles Boix and Susan C.

wave" democratizers such as South Korea and Taiwan, show that democratic values are not necessary prerequisites for democratization but can emerge as a consequence of personal experience in a democratic system. Although Rowen approvingly quotes Przeworski and his colleagues as finding that above $6,000 per capita GDP (or $8,000 in 1998 dollars) "democracies are impregnable and can last forever," he ignores the more important finding that no level of economic development guarantees a democratic transition, and the possibility that any type of regime can survive above this threshold as long as it can maintain economic growth. Moreover, critics of these predictions based largely on economic development point out that despite the obvious trend of economic growth in China, liberalization or democratization is being inhibited by such factors as unclear property rights, the state's ambivalence over privatization, local protectionism, labor unrest, the heavy role of the state in economic development, and more importantly the common backgrounds and shared interests of the emerging private entrepreneurs and middle classes and state officials.[12]

Despite these criticisms, the insights of modernization theory are echoed in the beliefs of many Chinese: China is not yet ready for democracy because the level of economic and cultural development is still too low, its urban population is relatively small, and so on. Many are willing to accept claims by party leaders that a long period of development must precede democracy in China. Regardless of whether they have read Lipset, Inglehart, or Diamond, many in China accept the link between development and democracy.[13]

Stokes, "Endogenous Democratization," *World Politics*, vol. 55, no. 4 (July 2003), pp. 517–549.

[12] David Zweig, "Undemocratic Capitalism: China and the Limits of Economism," *The National Interest*, no. 56 (Summer 1999), pp. 63–72; David S. G. Goodman, "The New Middle Class," in Merle Goldman and Roderick MacFarquhar, eds., *The Paradox of China's Post-Mao Reforms* (Cambridge, MA: Harvard University Press, 1999); Zhaohui Hong, "Mapping the Evolution and Transformation of the New Private Entrepreneurs in China," *Journal of Chinese Political Science*, vol. 9, no. 1 (Spring 2004), pp. 23–42; Mary Elizabeth Gallagher, *Contagious Capitalism: Globalization and the Politics of Labor in China* (Princeton, NJ: Princeton University Press, 2005); Kellee S. Tsai, *Capitalism without Democracy: The Private Sector in Contemporary China* (Ithaca, NY: Cornell University Press, 2007).

[13] For a thoughtful and wide-ranging assessment of Chinese views toward democracy, see Suzanne Ogden, *Inklings of Democracy in China* (Cambridge, MA: Harvard University Asia Center, 2002).

Changes in Social Structure

Another tradition in political science has focused on how economic development, and in particular capitalism and industrialization, gives rise to new social classes, which in turn push for greater inclusion and influence in the political system. Comparative research has shown the important role that capitalists have played in political development, in some cases as agents of change, in others as a primary source of political support for the incumbent regime. Samuel Huntington found that one of the main threats to an authoritarian regime is the "diversification of the elite resulting from the rise of new groups controlling autonomous sources of economic power, that is, from the development of an independently wealthy business and industrial middle class."[14] Barrington Moore's oft-quoted phrase "no bourgeois, no democracy" has had tremendous influence on the link between capitalism and democracy and has often been interpreted to mean that capitalists are likely vehicles for democratization.[15] Moore argued that democracy arose in Europe when early capitalists pressured their monarchs to lift barriers to industrialization and trade and formed parliaments to oversee the crown and government. In this set of historical developments, the creation of sources of wealth independent of the state led to demands for greater participation by new elites to protect their private interests.

Capitalist development may be associated with democracy not because of inherently democratic qualities of capitalists but because of the structural changes it brings about, especially the weakening of the landed aristocracy and the expansion of the working class. But the case of China, like that of many late-developing countries, does not resemble the feudal states that Moore studied. During the reform era,

---

[14] Samuel Huntington, "Social and Institutional Dynamics of One-Party Systems," in Samuel P. Huntington and Clement H. Moore, eds., *Authoritarian Politics in Modern Society: The Dynamics of Established One-Party Systems* (New York: Basic Books, 1970), p. 20. See also Dietrich Rueschemeyer, Evelyne Huber Stephens, and John D. Stephens, *Capitalist Development and Democracy* (Chicago: University of Chicago Press, 1992).

[15] Barrington Moore, *Social Origins of Dictatorship and Democracy: Lord and Peasant in the Making of the Modern World* (Boston: Beacon Press, 1966), p. 418. Moore's phrase is equally quoted and misquoted: many authors misquote him as "no bourgeoisie, no democracy," which seems to be more grammatically correct. In fact, the copy editor of my *Red Capitalists in China* made this same "correction" in the text without my realizing it.

there has been no landed aristocracy for China's capitalists to struggle against; the CCP eliminated that class during the land reform of the 1950s. Nor was the emergence of the private sector in China the result of determined efforts by capitalists to wrest power and privileges from the state; rather, it was the result of the state's own initiatives. In fact, at the beginning of the reform era, there was no capitalist class in China; it only emerged after the party initiated wide-ranging economic reforms. Moreover, the private sector is populated by many who came out of the state sector. Most of China's "red capitalists" were in the party before taking the plunge into private business, and at least one-quarter of private firms were originally part of state-owned enterprises. Close personal and familial ties continue to link the public and private sectors. This is not a scenario that Moore had in mind. It is hard to speak of a clash between communist leaders and capitalist business owners in China when so many capitalists are deeply embedded in the party.

More recent studies have noted the complex and ambiguous contribution of capitalists to the transition from authoritarianism.[16] Capitalists may prop up an authoritarian regime because they benefit materially or because they are worried that political change will harm their economic interests. Their political activism is often limited to economic issues that directly affect their immediate interests and does not extend to broader political issues. Moreover, the literature on business associations in developing countries also emphasizes collective action efforts on economic and commercial matters while paying less attention to strictly political matters.[17]

In both first-wave democracies and late-developing countries, capitalists may push for their own inclusion in the political system but

[16] Leroy Jones and Il SaKong, *Government, Business, and Entrepreneurship in Economic Development* (Cambridge, MA: Harvard University Press, 1980); Guillermo O'Donnell and Philippe C. Schmitter, *Transitions from Authoritarian Rule: Tentative Conclusions about Uncertain Democracies* (Baltimore: Johns Hopkins University Press, 1986); Huntington, *Third Wave*; Rueschemeyer, Stephens, and Stephens, *Capitalist Development and Democracy*; Sylvia Maxwell and Ben Ross Schneider, eds., *Business and the State in Developing Countries* (Ithaca, NY: Cornell University Press, 1997); Edmund Terence Gomez, ed., *Political Business in East Asia* (London: Routledge, 2002).

[17] Jones and SaKong, *Government, Business, and Entrepreneurship in Economic Development*; Maxwell and Schneider, *Business and the State in Developing Countries*; Gomez, *Political Business in East Asia*.

generally do not favor wider expansion of political participation by other social classes. But once capitalists perceive that the regime is under challenge by broader elements of civil society, especially if this opposition is triggered by an economic downturn, businesspeople may turn from regime support (or at least political neutrality) to more overt opposition.[18] Even where capitalists have supported democratization, they have rarely been first movers. Instead, their role is more like king-makers: their support can tip the balance between the continuation of authoritarian rule and the transition to democracy. Where workers have been the primary agents of change, the shift of capitalists' support away from the state toward the democratic opposition has often been the tipping point needed for democratization to succeed.[19] Although businesspeople rarely initiate the push for democracy, they have been necessary allies for democratic movements initiated by the working classes. In countries as diverse as South Korea, the Philippines, Brazil, Peru, Ecuador, and Spain, democratization was facilitated when businesspeople and the broader middle classes shifted their support from the government to the opposition.[20] These comparative examples have created expectations for China's capitalists to also be agents of political change.

Even in countries where capitalists have supported democratization, they have not been natural or constant supporters. In a variety of late-developing countries, capitalists have been at best "contingent democrats," as Eva Bellin put it. Their support for democracy is a function of their level of dependence on the state and their fear of the social unrest that often accompanies political openings. In many late developers, capitalists depend on the state for their access to financing, technology, and markets; for protection from foreign competition; for keeping labor low-paid and quiescent; and for having lenient policies on environmental protection and safety standards. The more capitalists depend on the state to protect their material interests, the more likely they are to prefer "cozy collaboration with

[18] Stephan Haggard and Robert R. Kaufman, *The Political Economy of Democratic Transitions* (Princeton, NJ: Princeton University Press, 1995).

[19] Rueschemeyer, Stephens, and Stephens, *Capitalist Development and Democracy*.

[20] Huntington, *Third Wave*, pp. 67–68; O'Donnell and Schmitter, *Transitions from Authoritarian Rule*; Eva Bellin, "Contingent Democrats: Industrialists, Labor, and Democratization in Late-Developing Countries," *World Politics*, vol. 52, no. 2 (January 2000), pp. 175–205.

state elites, not public contestation and opposition" to ensure their economic success.[21] Similarly, if capitalists have strong concerns that democratization will threaten their bottom line, they are not likely to support it. In recent cases of democratization, however, the right to vote has been extended to the entire population, not just the preexisting political, economic, and social elites. Newly elected leaders in new democracies may try to mobilize popular support by promising to increase public welfare spending (which requires higher taxes, often levied on business), raise wages, and enforce tougher workplace safety and environmental regulations (which raise the cost of doing business). Political reformers may mobilize labor and other disadvantaged groups to challenge the status quo through strikes and protests. The fear of this scenario makes most capitalists opposed to democratization. Ironically, although the presence of a strong Communist Party is often an indicator of mobilized labor, the ruling Communist Party in China has been committed to keeping wages low and preventing the formation of independent unions. Both the CCP and the official All-China Federation of Trade Unions are decidedly pro-business. Under these conditions, China's private entrepreneurs have been strong supporters of the status quo and will likely continue to be.

Democracy is not the consequence of economic and social change but a political process driven by actors inside and outside the regime. In this regard, many foreign observers in academic and policy communities expect that the formation of a private sector will lead, directly or indirectly through the emergence of a civil society, to political change and ultimately democratization. The increased economic and political prominence of private entrepreneurs has received special attention from scholars and also Western media. These reports have paid careful attention to the CCP's embrace of capitalism and the potential for China's new economic elites to serve as agents of change either by subtly influencing the CCP from within or engaging in organized collective action against the state on economic and political issues. Others see private entrepreneurs as the leading edge of an emerging civil society that will eventually transform China's political system.[22]

---

[21] Bellin, "Contingent Democrats," p. 181.
[22] Kristen Parris, "Local Initiative and National Reform: The Wenzhou Model of Development," *China Quarterly*, no. 134 (June 1993), pp. 242–263; Gordon White,

American policymakers also expect that continued privatization and prosperity will eventually push China more rapidly toward democracy. This belief has been the basis for expanded economic and trade ties between the two countries: policymakers argue that as China gets more integrated into the international economic system, it will eventually conform to the new norm of democratic governance. According to this argument, American trade with China not only benefits American companies and consumers but also contributes to democratization in China.[23] This reasoning persists despite the absence of any direct link between increased trade and the onset of democratization.

In contrast, most empirical studies have shown that China's entrepreneurs are not strong supporters of democracy and democratization. Margaret Pearson found that entrepreneurs were not likely to initiate demands for democratization but might "lend support if others take the lead in pressuring for economic and political change."[24] According to Kellee Tsai, "only a fraction of the current generation of private entrepreneurs has both the ability and desire to confront the state in defense of their interests, and many of them have already found non-democratic means for promoting their interests."[25] Similarly, An Chen concluded that China's bourgeoisie "have a taken-for-granted personal stake in preventing regime change," largely because of their

---

"Democratization and Economic Reform in China," *Australian Journal of Chinese Affairs*, no. 31 (1994), pp. 73–92; Gordon White, Jude Howell, and Shang Xiaoyuan, *In Search of Civil Society: Market Reform and Social Change in Contemporary China* (Oxford: Oxford University Press, 1996); Baogang He, *The Democratic Implications of Civil Society in China* (New York: St. Martin's Press, 1997); Xiaoqin Guo, *State and Society in China's Democratic Transition: Confucianism, Leninism, and Economic Development* (New York: Routledge, 2003); Yongnian Zheng, *Will China Become Democratic? Elite, Class, and Regime Transition* (Singapore: Eastern Universities Press, 2004).

[23] This rationale has been skewered in James Mann, *The China Fantasy: How Our Leaders Explain Away Chinese Repression* (New York: Viking, 2007).

[24] Margaret Pearson, "The Janus Face of Business Associations in China: Socialist Corporatism in Foreign Enterprises," *Australian Journal of Chinese Affairs*, no. 31 (January 1994), pp. 25–46. See also Margaret Pearson, "China's Emerging Business Class: Democracy's Harbinger?" *Current History*, vol. 97, no. 620 (September 1998), pp. 268–272.

[25] Kellee Tsai, "Capitalists without a Class: Political Diversity among Private Entrepreneurs in China," *Comparative Political Studies*, vol. 38, no. 9 (November 2005), p. 1145.

corrupt and familial ties with the state.[26] The beneficiaries of the limited accountability of China's partially reformed authoritarian system have an incentive to preserve the status quo rather than promote political change.[27]

This is a twist on the pattern of other postcommunist countries undergoing economic and political reform. In these countries, Joel Hellman found that the beneficiaries of initial economic reform used the political process to block further privatization.[28] In China's transition economy, the winners in economic reform have supported further reform but have not supported political change, leading to what Minxin Pei calls a "trapped transition."[29] Successful entrepreneurs, and red capitalists in particular, have learned how to make the current system work for them. Although individual entrepreneurs may be outspoken supporters of political reform, on the whole China's private entrepreneurs, like capitalists in other countries, have generally been ambivalent about the need for and benefits of democratization, preferring the authoritarian regime in which they have thrived to the uncertainty inherent in a new and untried political system.[30]

The Emergence of Civil Society

The study of democratization has also created interest in the emergence of civil society and its political implications. Larry Diamond has defined civil society as "the realm of organized social life that is

[26] An Chen, "Capitalist Development, Entrepreneurial Class, and Democratization in China," *Political Science Quarterly*, vol. 117, no. 3 (Fall 2002), p. 412.

[27] More generally, studies have found a remarkably high level of political support among Chinese society. Despite reports of localized protests throughout the country, most Chinese claim that they support the current political system. See, for example, Wenfang Tang, "Political and Social Trends in the Post-Deng Urban China: Crisis or Stability?" *China Quarterly*, no. 168 (December 2001), pp. 890–909; Jie Chen, *Popular Political Support in Urban China* (Stanford, CA: Stanford University Press, 2004).

[28] Joel S. Hellman, "Winners Take All: The Politics of Partial Reform in Postcommunist Transitions," *World Politics*, vol. 50, no. 2 (January 1998), pp. 203–234.

[29] Minxin Pei, *China's Trapped Transition: The Limits of Developmental Autocracy* (Cambridge, MA: Harvard University Press, 2006).

[30] A rare alternative perspective is offered in Lu Chunlong, "Democratic Values among Chinese People: Analysis of a Public Opinion Survey," *China Perspectives*, no. 55 (September–October 2004), pp. 40–48.

voluntary, self-generating, self-supporting, and autonomous from the state and bound by a legal order or set of shared rules."[31] Robert Putnam identified civil society as the essential element of a well-governed democracy.[32] In the transitions from communism in Eastern Europe and the former Soviet Union, civil society played a prominent role in their "velvet revolutions."[33] As Martin King Whyte wrote, "To the extent that a civil society develops within a Leninist system, it will produce pressure on elites for democratic reforms. If the state actively represses civil society, elites may feel that they can conduct business as usual, but they may learn to their surprise and sorrow... that a nascent civil society nurturing and spreading protodemocratic views lies just below the surface of official controls."[34] Even in postcommunist countries, social movements have led "color revolutions"[35] to further promote the democratic cause.[36] The CCP is actively monitoring its social environment to preempt such an occurrence in China. The implication is clear: if a civil society emerges, the prospects for democratization in China will improve.

The search for signs of civil society in China is largely influenced by the expectation that it will naturally promote democratization. The historical and contemporary debates center on whether key elements of a civil society existed either in the past or the present. Did organizations

[31] Larry Diamond, "Rethinking Civil Society: Toward Democratic Consolidation," *Journal of Democracy*, vol. 5, no. 3 (July 1994), p. 5.
[32] Robert Putnam, *Making Democracy Work* (Princeton, NJ: Princeton University Press, 1993).
[33] Timothy Garton Ash, *The Uses of Adversity: Essays on the Fate of Central Europe* (New York: Vintage, 1990); Marcia A. Wiegle and Jim Butterfield, "Civil Society in Reforming Communist Regimes: The Logic of Emergence," *Comparative Politics*, vol. 25, no. 1 (October 1992), pp. 1–23; Vladimir Tismaneanu, *Reinventing Politics: Eastern Europe from Stalin to Havel* (New York: The Free Press, 1992).
[34] Martin King Whyte, "Urban China: A Civil Society in the Making?" in Arthur Lewis Rosenbaum, ed., *State and Society in China: The Consequences of Reform* (Boulder, CO: Westview Press, 1992), pp. 79–80.
[35] "Color revolutions" refers to social movements that became known for the color or flower that symbolized their protests, such as orange in Ukraine, roses in Georgia, and tulips in Kyrgyzstan.
[36] Charles H. Fairbanks, Jr., "Georgia's Rose Revolution," *Journal of Democracy*, vol. 15, no. 2 (April 2004), pp. 110–124; Adrian Karatnycky, "Ukraine's Orange Revolution," *Foreign Affairs*, vol. 84, no. 2 (March–April 2005), pp. 35–52; Henry E. Hale, "Democracy or Autocracy on the March? The Colored Revolutions as Normal Dynamics of Patronal Presidentialism," *Communist and Post-Communist Studies*, vol. 39, no. 3 (September 2006), pp. 305–329.

of various kinds exist that enjoyed relative autonomy from the state? Were they able to represent the interests of their members and the community at large? Were they able to influence government policy? Even advocates of a civil society perspective acknowledge that the degree of autonomy, representation, and influence varied considerably over time, in different areas of the country, and among different types of organizations. William Rowe claimed that the "balance between autonomy and state control was thus never clearly defined, but it was in practice the result of a process of continual negotiation."[37] Rather than seeing the rise of entrepreneurs as the vanguard of an autonomous civil society, Dorothy Solinger saw the result as being the merger of state and society, "a bonding and incipient interdependence between the bureaucrat and merchant."[38]

To best appreciate the implications of an emerging civil society in an authoritarian state like China, it is best to unpack the concept. There are different strands of thinking and political preferences within civil society, and they may be present in varying degrees at any given point in time. In their critique of Putnam, Michael Foley and Bob Edwards distinguished between a politicized realm of civil society, which pushes the state to make political changes, and a more apolitical realm, which is organized for social and economic pursuits but avoids political activities.[39] China scholars have made a similar distinction. In their search for signs of civil society in China, Gordon White, Jude Howell, and Shang Xiaoyuan described two separate dynamics that lead to the emergence of civil society. The political dynamic entails "resistance to state control on the part of groups and organizations with implicit or explicit political agendas."[40] This dynamic could be seen as early as the 100 Flowers movement and later in the Red Guards, the anti–Gang of Four protests in April 1976, the Democracy Wall movement of 1978–1979, and most vividly to foreign audiences in the 1989 demonstrations in Tiananmen Square. The political dynamic

---

[37] William T. Rowe, "The Problem of 'Civil Society' in Late Imperial China," *Modern China*, vol. 19, no. 2 (April 1993), p. 148.

[38] Dorothy J. Solinger, "Urban Entrepreneurs and the State: The Merger of State and Society," in Rosenbaum, *State and Society in China*.

[39] Michael W. Foley and Bob Edwards, "The Paradox of Civil Society," *Journal of Democracy*, vol. 7, no. 3 (July 1996), pp. 38–52.

[40] White, Howell, and Shang, *In Search of Civil Society*, p. 7.

gives rise to what Yanqi Tong calls the "critical realm" of civil society, a political sphere that is critical of the state and represents a challenge to it.[41]

But there is also a separate market dynamic that gives rise to a "noncritical realm" that is primarily concerned with economic affairs and leisure activities and less interested in changing the political system itself. With the rise of a market economy and the shift of economic and social power away from the state toward new economic strata (viz., the private sector) comes a clearer separation of state and society. Whereas the political dynamic has taken place within a relatively static institutional context, "the market dynamic contains the potential for creating new institutions and shifting the balance of power between the state and society in the latter's favor. To that extent, the market dynamic can be seen as constructing a material or structural basis for the development of civil society."[42] The state needs, and indeed encourages, this market dynamic and cannot suppress it entirely. Whereas the "critical realm" arising from a political dynamic is a direct threat, the "noncritical realm" resulting from the market dynamic creates a more complementary relationship between state and society, presenting costs and benefits to both. Rather than undermine an authoritarian regime, the economic realm of civil society may lead to greater support for the status quo and dampen demands for democratizing reforms. Social capital may be the basis for stable government and good governance, whether in a democratic or nondemocratic polity.[43] The potential for political change comes in the potentially complementary and reinforcing relationship between the political and market dynamics and the critical and noncritical realms they create.

The distinction between the political and economic realms of civil society also illuminates the political significance of capitalists' contingent political support. When the critical and noncritical realms do not join together in common cause against the state, the state has more leeway to repress the political dynamic while supporting

---

[41] Yanqi Tong, "State, Society, and Political Change in China and Hungary," *Comparative Politics*, vol. 26, no. 3 (April 1994), pp. 333–353.

[42] White, Howell, and Shang, *In Search of Civil Society*, pp. 7–8.

[43] Putnam, *Making Democracy Work*; Lily Lee Tsai, *Accountability without Democracy: Solidary Groups and Public Goods Provision in Rural China* (Cambridge: Cambridge University Press, 2007).

the market dynamic. The CCP is actively integrating economic elites into the political system while forcefully suppressing political activists. Several decades of economic reform and rapid growth have fueled a market dynamic in China and created a noncritical realm made up of entrepreneurs, professionals, high-tech specialists, and others, and most observers have noted the apolitical, even antipolitical, character of these groups. Private entrepreneurs rarely engage in political activities beyond those that directly affect their business interests, such as lobbying for preferred laws and regulations.[44] Some entrepreneurs have given material support to political activists and intellectuals promoting political reform, but they are the exception, not the rule. Most private businessmen did not support the 1989 demonstrations; many of those who did later regretted doing so because it led to a temporary retreat from Deng Xiaoping's reform and opening policies and damaged the business environment in China.[45] Nevertheless, many observers continue to expect that continued privatization will ultimately lead to a stronger and more autonomous civil society, which in turn will bring about political change. In assessing the political impact of China's entrepreneurs, however, we must keep in mind the different realms of civil society and recognize that civil society is not necessarily antagonistic toward the state.

Critics of the civil society approach often note that the concept was originally tied to the development of liberalism and bourgeois society in the West and may therefore be inappropriate in the Chinese context.[46] Even advocates of the civil society approach acknowledge that the degree of autonomy associated with a true civil society is mostly lacking in China, now as in the past. Scholars looking for an

[44] Scott Kennedy, *The Business of Lobbying in China* (Cambridge, MA: Harvard University Press, 2005).

[45] David L. Wank, "Private Business, Bureaucracy, and Political Alliance in a Chinese City," *Australian Journal of Chinese Affairs*, no. 33 (January 1995), pp. 55–71; Margaret M. Pearson, *China's New Business Elite: The Political Consequences of Economic Reform* (Berkeley: University of California Press, 1997); He, *Democratic Implications of Civil Society in China*.

[46] Frederic Wakeman, Jr., "The Civil Society and Public Sphere Debate: Western Reflections on Chinese Political Culture," *Modern China*, vol. 19, no. 2 (April 1993), pp. 108–138; Timothy Brook and B. Michael Frolic, eds., *Civil Society in China* (Armonk, NY: M. E. Sharpe, 1997). Baogang He, "Intra-party Democracy: A Revisionist Perspective from Below," in Kjeld Erik Brodsgaard and Zheng Yongnian, eds., *The Chinese Communist Party in Reform* (London: Routledge, 2006).

emerging civil society in China typically look for evidence of autonomy for individuals and especially groups. Most individuals and groups in China do not seek autonomy but rather closer embeddedness with the state. They recognize that to be autonomous is to be "outside the system" and therefore powerless. Instead they seek to be integrated into the current political system in order to better pursue their interests and maximize their leverage.

Although these concerns about the applicability of civil society to China may be valid, we must also keep in mind a key point: CCP leaders act as though they believe in the power of civil society and in the challenge it poses for continued party rule. They are fearful of a color revolution occurring in China and have taken steps to preempt such an occurrence.[47] They limit what types of social organizations can exist and what activities they can engage in. They retain close control over the media and the Internet to limit the free exchange of ideas and exposure of government misconduct. They embrace the noncritical realm of civil society – the capitalists in particular – while repressing those in the critical realm who would seek political liberalization and democratization. They depend on the political loyalty of those in the noncritical realm and have joined with them in the common goal of economic growth while simultaneously punishing those in the critical realm for allegedly threatening the political stability that is necessary for growth. It is not only scholars who are looking for signs of civil society in China; the CCP is watching, too.

THE CCP'S STRATEGY FOR SURVIVAL

The expectation that economic development will trigger democratization in China is based on two assumptions: first, that the CCP is a passive actor and not able to adapt to changes in its economic and social environment; and second, that China's capitalists would prefer a democratic system to the current regime, in which they have prospered. The first assumption is patently untrue: the CCP has been more adaptable than most observers acknowledge, but these adaptations are

---

[47] This is the key theme of David Shambaugh, *China's Communist Party: Atrophy and Adaptation* (Berkeley and Washington, DC: University of California Press and Woodrow Wilson Center Press, 2008).

designed to keep it in power by governing more effectively, not to make it more responsive or accountable. The CCP is confronted with a host of problems, including policy and personnel issues internal to its organization as well as social and political unrest, but it has been able to cope with those challenges, even if it has not solved them. The second assumption – that China's capitalists are inherently pro-democratic – is also deeply flawed. It is based on a misreading of Moore's analysis of the relationship between capitalist development and democracy and ignores the ambivalent and contingent support for democracy by capitalists in other late developers.

The CCP has adapted to the changing economic and social environment by using a survival strategy that has proven to be successful in a variety of other contexts: a combination of strategic co-optation and corporatist-style links with the private sector. It is co-opting the main beneficiaries of its economic reform policies, such as entrepreneurs, high-tech specialists, and other urban professionals. Even though the CCP had traditionally been suspicious of the political loyalty of these groups, and frequently targeted them in political campaigns, in recent years it has actively co-opted them in order to ensure their cooperation on economic development and to preempt their potential political opposition. This strategy of co-optation was politically controversial in the 1980s and 1990s and generated extensive inner-party debate. After 2001, however, it became official party policy when the party adopted Jiang Zemin's "Three Represents" slogan, in which the party claimed to represent not just the workers, peasants, and soldiers (the "three revolutionary classes" that had been the social base for decades) but also the newly emerging economic and social elites known as the "advanced productive forces."[48] Conversely, the CCP has also encouraged its members to "jump into the sea" of private business in order to generate support for economic reform within the party and to have party members show others how to "take the lead in getting rich."

A second key element in the CCP's survival strategy has been to create new institutional links to the changing economic and social

---

[48] The "Three Represents" refers to the CCP's claim to represent the advanced productive forces (i.e., the urban economic elites), the most advanced culture, and the fundamental interests of the overwhelming majority of the people in China. See chapter 3 for further discussion.

environment. For the private sector, this has meant state-sponsored business associations and a network of party cells that is characteristic of Leninist parties. These institutional links are designed to allow the party to monitor its environment as well as provide leadership over it. These links follow a corporatist logic: the state allows a limited number of associations to exist and provides leaders and budgetary support. However, China's capitalists have begun to create their own associations in addition to the official business associations. This complicates the CCP's corporatist strategy but has not led the party to abandon it.

In both these ways, the CCP's survival strategy entails the integration of wealth and power in China. Its strategy is designed to enhance different aspects of the party's legitimacy. Most importantly, the integration of economic and political elites has contributed to the sustained and rapid growth of the past generation. In order to modernize the economy, the CCP increasingly relies on the private sector as the main source of growth, jobs, and tax revenue. Because wealth accumulated outside the state's control is a potential threat to any authoritarian government, the CCP has attempted to use a combination of co-optation and corporatism to integrate itself with the growing private sector. Economic modernization is arguably the most important dimension of the CCP's claim to legitimacy, and the CCP increasingly relies on the private sector to achieve this modernization. But CCP rule is not based on growth alone.

A second aspect of the party's legitimacy is based on improving China's image in the world and by extension increasing national pride within the country. The phrase "wealth and power" alludes to the long-standing goal of making China a wealthy and powerful country, able to stand up against foreign encroachments and pressure and able to wield its own influence on the international stage. The large and sustained growth rates over the past three decades have gone a long way toward achieving that goal of wealth and power. As China has developed economically, it has also sought international acknowledgment of its economic achievements and greater political influence to match its aggregate wealth. The decision to have China host the 2008 Olympics is widely seen within China as international endorsement of its path to modernity. As rapid growth increases China's economic and political influence in the world, national pride in these accomplishments also increases, which in turn enhances another aspect of party legitimacy.

Although the CCP's strategy for survival has been successful so far, it has not been uniformly accepted. Conservative leaders in the CCP see the integration of capitalists into China's political system as a betrayal of party traditions and a threat to its long-term survival. They argue for a slowing of the economic reform process and a return to the party's commitment to the poor and disadvantaged classes, in particular workers and farmers, instead of the wealthy beneficiaries of economic growth. Outside the party, intellectuals labeled as China's "New Left" criticize the pro-business orientation of the party for increasing inequality, which is not only a threat to political stability but also a violation of basic social justice.

These criticisms expose an inherent tension in the CCP's strategy for survival: integrating wealth and power has generated rapid growth, but the means by which that growth has been accomplished have also created a host of domestic problems. The cozy relationship between economic and political elites is mutually beneficial but is also resented by those who have not benefited equally from the "reform and opening" policies. Many farmers and workers, the traditional base of support for the CCP, have become unemployed during the reform era as the goals of efficiency and profitability have replaced the "iron rice bowl" of lifetime job guarantees. Even those who have found jobs in the private sector have had to accept lower wages and benefits such as housing, medical care, and pensions.

Although the reform and opening policies have created enormous wealth, they have also created enormous disparities in the distribution of that wealth. During the Maoist era, China was one of the most equitable countries, but during the reform era it rapidly became one of the least equitable. Between 1980 and 2006, China's per capita GDP (in current US$) rose from $312 to $2013, but its Gini coefficient, the most used measure of income equality, also rose from around .3 to .47.[49] These are both remarkable increases in such a short period of

---

[49] International Monetary Fund, *World Economic Outlook Database*, October 2007, available at http://www.imf.org/external/pubs/ft/weo/2007/02/weodata/index.aspx, accessed January 25, 2008; Martin Ravallion and Chen Shaohua, *China's (Uneven) Progress against Poverty* (Washington, DC: World Bank, 2004); World Bank, *World Development Indicators*, online database available at http://web.worldbank.org/WBSITE/EXTERNAL/DATASTATISTICS/0,,menuPK:232599~pagePK:64133170~piPK:64133498~theSitePK:239419,00.html.

time. The strategy for creating rapid growth also generated inequality, corruption, pollution, and other sources of popular resentment that have increased the frequency and size of protests around the country. This instability threatens a third aspect of the CCP's legitimacy: its ability to maintain political order.

To address this imbalance, the CCP has adopted a broad range of populist policies and measures to counterbalance the emphasis on growth. By the time of the 16th Party Congress in 2002, it had become apparent that the pro-growth strategies of the Jiang Zemin era needed to be supplemented with more balanced and equity-oriented policies to raise incomes in rural and inland areas, where the benefits of post-Mao economic reforms were less evident. Under the leadership of Hu Jintao and Wen Jiabao, the CCP began income subsidies and lowered taxes in the countryside. It also increased the emphasis on charity work, mostly at the direction of local party and government offices and the official, corporatist-style business associations, in order to alleviate poverty. But the emphasis on growth continues. Hu and Wen are committed to rapid growth and the reliance on the private sector, but they also recognize that the elitist, pro-growth strategies of the 1990s must be supplemented with concerns for improving equity. They are so concerned about striking the proper balance between the often competing goals of growth, equity, and order that in February 2007 the media were ordered to stop reporting on favorable statements by Hu and other top leaders about the benefits of privatization. These populist policies, and the populist image Hu and Wen are trying to create for themselves, are designed to improve political stability, the third dimension of the party's legitimacy.

CRONY COMMUNISM

By tying its legitimacy to the trappings of wealth and power (economic modernization and the nationalistic pride it generates), the CCP has also tied itself to the private sector to pursue those goals. As a consequence, a cozy relationship has emerged between the CCP and China's capitalists that can be described as "crony communism." Like the forms of government–business relations in East and Southeast Asia and in post-Soviet Russia, "crony communism" refers to a system of interaction between economic and political elites that is based on patrimonial ties and in which success in business is due more to personal contacts in the official bureaucracy than to entrepreneurial skill or merit. But unlike those other cases, crony communism has several distinct features.

The key feature of crony communism in China is that *the CCP is the central actor.* Just as all aspects of the political system are under party control, so, too, is the party at the core of economic activities. It initiated the economic reforms that led to rapid and sustained growth and remains committed to ongoing marketization and privatization. Party and government officials have benefited from the rent-seeking opportunities that have proliferated under reform, and red capitalists have distinct advantages over non-CCP entrepreneurs. Party members who go into business (whom I refer to as *xiahai* entrepreneurs because *xiahai* is the Chinese euphemism for leaving the state sector and going into business) are often the beneficiaries of sweetheart deals in which they buy a factory or firm for a fraction of its true value. Some of them were party and government officials, some were managers of state-owned enterprises (SOEs), and others were rank-and-file party members, but regardless of their point of origin, they were able to convert their political power into economic wealth. Entrepreneurs who are co-opted into the party because of their business success gain admission to the political elite, allowing them to turn their wealth into power. In a different manner, the sons, daughters, and spouses of party and government officials are able to use their access to political power to create opportunities to amass tremendous wealth. According to an internal party and government report, 90 percent of Chinese millionaires are the children of high-ranking officials.[50] The CCP has not only been the instigator of economic growth; its members have been the main beneficiaries of it. China may not be "communist" in the sense that it is heading toward the communist utopia envisioned by Karl Marx, but it remains very much a Leninist system under the leadership of the CCP.

---

[50] This information is contained in a report by the Research Office of the State Council, the Research Office of the Central Party School, and the Chinese Academy of Social Sciences, as reported in Hong Kong's *Singdao Daily* on October 19, 2006, available at http://financenews.sina.com/ausdaily/000-000-107-105/202/2006-10-19/1509124173.shtml.

Crony communism is also distinctive because it is *decentralized*.
Much of the collusion between the communists and the capitalists
occurs at the local level. Unlike the form of crony capitalism that
was common in Southeast Asia, crony communism in China is not
dominated by the ruling family or central officials.[51] The beneficiaries of crony communism are widespread and extend far down into
the bureaucratic ranks. Central and local leaders may benefit directly
from bribes or indirectly from the opportunities given to their children
or spouses. Lower-ranking officials may benefit from their personal
business activities, investments, and of course from corrupt dealings
with other businessmen. Party and government officials not only benefit materially from economic growth, their career progress depends on
achieving high rates of growth. This gives them an additional incentive
to develop cozy ties with the private sector.

Crony communism is not only decentralized within the state but also
diffuse within the private sector. Unlike that of Russia, China's private
economy is not controlled by a small number of oligarchs.[52] China's
private sector is characterized by small- and medium-sized firms. Its
industries are not highly concentrated by international standards, and
even its large firms are not particularly large when compared with the
largest firms in other countries. The diffuse nature of the private sector
makes collective action difficult. So far, collective action by private
enterprises has been limited to lobbying efforts in which the firms have
large material interests at stake. With the partial exception of the 1989
demonstrations, when some entrepreneurs supported the students (but
most entrepreneurs were opposed to the protests or were neutral), they
have not been involved in broader social or political issues. Instead,
individual entrepreneurs have used their access to political power to
enrich themselves without pushing for broader political liberalization.

---

[51] Paul D. Hutchcroft, "Oligarchs and Cronies in the Philippine State: The Politics
of Patrimonial Plunder," *World Politics*, vol. 43, no. 3 (April 1991), pp. 414–450;
David C. Kang, *Crony Capitalism: Corruption and Development in South Korea and
the Philippine*s (Cambridge: Cambridge University Press, 2002); Richard Robison and
Vedi Hediz, *Reorganising Power in Indonesia: The Politics of Oligarchy in an Age of
Markets* (London: RoutledgeCurzon, 2004).
[52] Hellman, "Winners Take All"; David E. Hoffman, *The Oligarchs: Wealth and Power
in the New Russia* (New York: PublicAffairs, 2002); Andrew Barnes, *Owning Russia:
The Struggle over Factories, Farms, and Power* (Ithaca, NY: Cornell University Press,
2006).

The numbers of both private entrepreneurs and red capitalists continue to grow, making crony communism an *expansive* system. Some red capitalists are created through the privatization of SOEs: as they are divided up, sold off, and converted into private enterprises, usually via insider buyouts, their managers are similarly converted into private entrepreneurs, and because most SOE managers were already party members, most of these new owners instantly become red capitalists. Other red capitalists first established their own firms and as a result of their success and newfound elite status were co-opted into the party. The benefits of the reform and opening policies are also available to noncronies, but to a much more limited degree. Access to the economic arena has lower barriers to entry than the political arena: almost anyone can open a business, but a glass ceiling exists for those who do not have political protection, especially party membership. This gives ambitious entrepreneurs an incentive to join and support the crony communist system.

From the perspective of party and government officials with economic oversight responsibilities, most of China's capitalists lack the management capabilities and business acumen necessary to be independently successful. It is therefore their responsibility to assist the development of the economy as a whole as well as the improvement of individual firms. This gives crony communism a distinctly *paternalistic* quality. Local party leaders see party-building efforts as the key to both economic development and party leadership over the private sector. The party sponsors activities to improve firm management; in other words, the goal of party building is not only to monitor the private sector and preempt any political challenge but also to foster cooperative relations between the party and the private sector and improve the quality of China's capitalists.

Above all, crony communism in China is *symbiotic*: it is based on the mutual benefits of both the party and government officials and the capitalists. Each side of the relationship benefits from the interaction and lacks clear incentives to change the rules of the game.

Because crony communism is under party control, decentralized, diffuse, expansive, paternalistic, and symbiotic, it may also be *self-perpetuating*. Because beneficiaries are so diverse and numerous, it is hard to organize collective action to preserve benefits for early winners. Instead, capitalists have used the policy process to extend economic reforms and property rights but have not pushed for parallel political reforms. In contrast, the early beneficiaries of economic reforms in Russia used the political system to prevent further economic reforms, thus preserving the benefits for themselves.[53] The potential to become a crony dampens resistance: many entrepreneurs have joined the system by being co-opted into the party, and many others want to join. The challenge from noncronies is also limited by collective action problems: most are small scale, do not have existing organizations to use as vehicles for collective action, and lack the necessary incentive to lead a collective challenge. Both the communist officials and the red capitalists have the means and the incentive to block noncronies from overturning the crony communist system.

Ironically, the greatest challenge to crony communism is a consequence of its success. The benefits that accrue to cronies (officials and capitalists alike, and even noncronies in the private sector to a more limited extent) create resentment from the workers and farmers who do not have equal opportunities to get rich. The new populist policies championed by Hu and Wen are intended to dampen popular resentment against the communist cronies. Challenges from society are also limited by the CCP's political monopoly and lack of accountability, which make organized collective action difficult and personally dangerous for those who attempt to organize a challenge. Even in the absence of collective action, however, party leaders are worried that growing resentment and unrest could push China toward a "tipping point" that would pose a serious threat to the beneficiaries of reform.

In these different ways, the CCP is trying to combine the elitist pro-growth policies of the Jiang Zemin era with the populist goals of the Hu–Wen leadership. Balancing elitism and populism (in policy and personnel) may make crony communism self-regulatory and self-perpetuating. Party leaders have come to recognize that neither extreme of elitism or populism can be sustained. China's leaders have discovered what Karl Polanyi observed about capitalist development in Europe: a market economy left unfettered can devastate society.[54] Consequently, a "double movement" is necessary: the state needs to bring about social and political changes necessary to allow market

---

[53] Hellman, "Winners Take All."
[54] Karl Polanyi, *The Great Transformation: The Political and Economic Origins of Our Time* (New York: Farrar and Rinehart, 1944).

competition but at the same time must enact policies to protect society from the often tumultuous changes that the market brings with it. Constant shifting and fine-tuning is required; there is no stable equilibrium. Elitism creates resentment and unrest from real and perceived inequalities; populism undermines incentives for growth, especially for cronies. In previous years, the policy pendulum swung between periods of *fang* and *shou*; that is, between openness and repression.[55] Today, the pendulum still swings but not as far and not as fast. As Cheng Li has put it, there is a sort of "bipartisan consensus" that both growth and equity are needed, but how to achieve that elusive goal is still in question.[56] The emphasis on creating a "harmonious society" may be meant to placate nonbeneficiaries without jeopardizing the benefits enjoyed by cronies.

Summary

China's continued economic growth challenges the common assumption that a market economy leads to democracy and common prosperity. In the short run and for the foreseeable future, it seems more likely to lead to a continuation of authoritarian rule under the Communist Party, as top leaders look for ways to govern better but not necessarily more democratically. So far, economic development has led to continued authoritarian rule as the CCP finds ways to adapt itself to the new situation in China. It is doing so by incorporating the growing number of private entrepreneurs into the political system – by integrating wealth and power – and by adopting new policies to address the social tensions created by rapid growth.

PRÉCIS OF THE BOOK

This book analyzes the CCP's strategy of integrating wealth and power by focusing on its relationship with the growing private sector. Whereas most previous research focused on the different strategies by which entrepreneurs interact with the state (for instance, by David

---

[55] Richard Baum, *Burying Mao: Chinese Politics in the Age of Deng Xiaoping* (Princeton, NJ: Princeton University Press, 1996).

[56] Cheng Li, "The New Bipartisanship within the Chinese Communist Party," *Orbis*, vol. 49, no. 3 (Summer 2005), pp. 387–400. See also Bruce J. Dickson, "Beijing's Ambivalent Reformers," *Current History*, vol. 103, no. 674 (September 2004), pp. 249–255.

Wank, Scott Kennedy, Kenneth Foster, and Kellee Tsai), my study turns the relationship around and looks at the CCP's strategy for relating to private entrepreneurs and the consequences of that strategy. This is a complementary perspective and yields a similar conclusion: China's capitalists are increasingly being integrated into the political system and have little incentive or inclination to change the status quo, in which they have prospered. Similarly, the book is not concerned with what makes Chinese enterprises successful, competitive, or profitable. These are important issues but best left to economists and business management specialists. Instead, the book looks at the political impact of China's capitalists, in particular how their incorporation into the CCP and other formal political institutions creates greater support for the status quo rather than pressure for political change.

Whereas previous studies focused on one point in time, and in many cases a single city, the evidence for the argument presented here is drawn from surveys of private entrepreneurs and local party and government officials at two different points in time; in addition, interviews were conducted with some of the officials at the time the survey was implemented in their communities (see the appendix for details on the design of the survey). These data allow me to observe how both regional differences, especially in the level of economic development and privatization, and changes over time affect the relationship between the party and the private sector.

Chapter 2 provides a review of economic privatization in China, which includes indigenous private enterprises as well as privatized state-owned enterprises and township and village enterprises. The development of the private sector has been driven by a combination of central directives and local initiatives, as well as debates among CCP leaders about the proper pace and scope of economic reform in general and privatization in particular. Over time, the CCP has revised the legal and institutional framework for supporting the private sector, including property rights, financing, and marketing. The chapter also examines the changing social status of private entrepreneurs. In the early reform era, private entrepreneurs were viewed with suspicion by both state and society, and many of them had shady political and criminal backgrounds. Over time, a more ambivalent image emerged. On the one hand, they were seen as contributing to China's modernization and rewarded with prestigious public roles (ironically even being chosen as "model workers"). On the other hand, they were also blamed for contributing to growing inequality and corruption, politically salient issues that have threatened stability, especially in recent years. This ambivalent image was matched by equally ambivalent policies: while the third generation of leaders (symbolized by Jiang Zemin) pursued an elitist strategy of promoting economic interests, the fourth generation (symbolized by Hu Jintao) has pursued more populist policies designed to maintain the benefits of rapid economic growth while minimizing their social costs and potential political risks.

The analysis of the CCP strategy for integrating wealth and power begins in chapter 3, which looks at the CCP's relationship with individual private entrepreneurs. After a discussion of the general theoretical issues, in particular how new actors can change organizations and political systems, it then describes the CCP's evolving policy toward recruiting entrepreneurs into the party and the debate surrounding the policy. The CCP imposed a formal (but not fully effective) ban on the practice between 1989 and 2001. After lifting the ban, reports indicated lukewarm efforts by local officials tasked with implementing the policy and a tepid response from entrepreneurs to the CCP's invitation to join. However, my survey data indicate a steady increase in the number of entrepreneurs co-opted into the party in the years after the ban was lifted. Even so, the growth in the number of red capitalists has been primarily due to the privatization of state-owned enterprises, which has turned former state managers into private entrepreneurs. The chapter will show how the capitalists' relationship to the party is closely correlated with a variety of key business matters, including firm size, sales revenues, and access to capital.

Chapter 4 examines the institutional ties between the CCP and the private sector. The party uses a combination of "bridges and branches" – business associations and party organizations within individual firms – to link itself to the private sector. China's official business associations have always been seen as representing the state and their members, but my most recent survey data show declining support for the associations from their members and lower estimates of their ability to influence the local implementation of policy. These data question my original prediction that these business associations could sponsor collective action on behalf of their members but are more consistent with the findings of other scholars. Because the official business associations are not seen as effective means of raising issues or resolving disputes, a variety of privately organized business associations have emerged. Although they are generally seen as more effective than the official business associations, they have not engaged in collective action on broader political or public policy issues. Their emergence, however, does undermine a key component of the CCP's survival strategy: forging and maintaining corporatist links with the private sector.

Another form of institutional tie is the result of the CCP's party-building activities within the private sector. One of the hallmarks of a Leninist system is its network of party cells, but the CCP's party-building efforts have not kept pace with the rapid expansion of the private sector. Despite the party's determination to "carry out party work wherever there is economic work, and create party organizations wherever there are party members," neither the capitalists nor their workers have been enthusiastic about party building. The CCP has therefore followed a "grasp the large, release the small" strategy toward party building (as it has toward the reform of state-owned enterprises): it has concentrated its efforts on the largest firms, which are typically owned by red capitalists, and put less emphasis on the larger number of small- and medium-sized enterprises. Interviews with local officials also reveal that party organizations within private enterprises operate primarily as auxiliary units of the firm rather than as the focal point for political study and party leadership, which was the traditional role for party cells.

In order to assess the likelihood that China's capitalists will be agents of political change, we need to know about their political values and policy preferences. In chapter 5, I compare the views of private entrepreneurs and local party and government officials using original survey data from 1999 and 2005. These surveys show remarkably similar views on the business environment, satisfaction with economic and political reform, and beliefs about broader public policy issues. This convergence of views runs counter to the prevailing view that ongoing privatization and the incorporation of entrepreneurs into the political system make democratization more likely. So long as entrepreneurs support the status quo and hold policy views similar to those of party and government officials, they are not likely to be agents of change. Instead, their support may serve to maintain the CCP in power and limit opportunities for other political actors to mobilize opposition.

The integration of wealth and power not only involves bringing capitalists into the CCP but also having them participate in China's formal political institutions. Chapter 6 will therefore examine the CCP's strategy for nominating and appointing private entrepreneurs to local people's congresses and political consultative conferences and which entrepreneurs have been candidates in village elections. The desire to participate in politics is one of the main motivations for joining the party, and this chapter will show how party membership is one of the most important predictors of which entrepreneurs have gained access to the political system and how their political values influence their participation. The capitalists who have become politicians are more closely tied to the CCP and more supportive of the status quo. Their involvement in China's political institutions is therefore more likely to reinforce the party's commitment to economic reform than to increase pressure for greater political liberalization.

The CCP's embrace of the private sector has succeeded in creating rapid growth, but has also led to a variety of unintended and unwanted consequences. These "ripple effects" are the subject of chapter 7. The cozy relationship between local officials and businessmen has created popular resentment about the increasingly unequal distribution of wealth and the often corrupt means by which it is obtained. This resentment in turn has contributed to local protests against environmental degradation, the confiscation of farming land for industrial and commercial development without adequate compensation to the farmers who are displaced, and sweetheart deals during the privatization of state-owned enterprises, all of which are by-products of crony communism. The CCP has responded with a variety of populist measures to promote a "harmonious society," including mobilizing charitable contributions by wealthy capitalists. In charity as in other economic matters, the extent of giving is related to the relationship with the CCP: the more an entrepreneur is in the embrace of the party, the more likely he or she is to contribute to a variety of charitable activities.

Finally, chapter 8 summarizes the findings of the book and also looks at different scenarios for the future of the CCP and China's political system as a whole and the role of China's capitalists in shaping that future.

2

The Party's Promotion of the Private Sector

The process of economic privatization in China has been driven by a combination of local initiatives and central directives, as well as debates among CCP leaders about the proper pace and scope of economic reform in general and privatization in particular. Over time, the CCP has revised the legal and institutional framework for supporting the private sector, including property rights, financing, and marketing. In the early reform era, private entrepreneurs were viewed with suspicion by both state and society, and many of them had suspect political and criminal backgrounds. Over time, a more ambivalent image emerged. On the one hand, they were seen as contributing to China's modernization and rewarded with prestigious public roles (ironically even being chosen as "model workers"). On the other hand, they were also blamed for contributing to growing inequality and corruption, politically salient issues that have threatened stability, especially in recent years. This ambivalent image was matched by equally ambivalent policies: while the third generation of leaders (symbolized by Jiang Zemin) pursued an elitist strategy of promoting economic interests, the fourth generation (symbolized by Hu Jintao) has pursued more populist policies designed to maintain the benefits of rapid economic growth while minimizing their social costs and potential political risks.

The growth in China's private sector has been achieved through two separate paths. The first, which began at the start of the post-Mao reform era, was the indigenous development of individually owned (*getihu*) and private enterprises (*siying qiye*). The second path was the privatization of collective and state-owned enterprises, which began in earnest in the mid-1990s. Each was important for increasing the size of the private sector in terms of number of firms, employment, and output, but the rationale for each was different. This chapter will describe how the CCP promoted these separate paths of private sector development. Subsequent chapters will analyze the CCP's strategy for integrating private entrepreneurs into the political system; in other words, for integrating wealth and power.

INDIGENOUS DEVELOPMENT OF CHINA'S PRIVATE SECTOR

When the CCP came to power in 1949, it initially promised a united front strategy of cooperating with a wide range of noncommunist groups. Private entrepreneurs were designated the "national bourgeoisie" to distinguish them from the "bureaucratic capitalists" who had links to the old Nationalist government and whose property was confiscated by the new regime. In the early years of the PRC, the national bourgeoisie were treated with respect and given positions in the coalition government. They were an earlier version of "red capitalists," best represented by Rong Yiren, a member of a prominent capitalist family who became vice-mayor of Shanghai in 1957. In the post-Mao era, he was deeply involved in China's economic opening to the outside world as leader of the China International Trust and Investment Corporation and served in the ceremonial post of vice president from 1993 to 1997. In the 1950s, the phrase "red capitalists" referred to businessmen who cooperated with the Communist Party but were not members (Rong Yiren was secretly admitted into the CCP, a fact that was not revealed until after his death in 2005), whereas the current usage of the term, and the one used in this book, refers to capitalists who are also members of the CCP.[1]

This policy of collaboration was short-lived. In 1952, the CCP launched the Five Antis campaign against alleged economic crimes and tax evasion by large-scale entrepreneurs. In 1953, the government announced a new "general line for the transition to socialism" that

---

[1] The "Red Capitalist Club" in Beijing reflects this earlier usage of the term: it is decorated with photos from the 1950s, as well as Cultural Revolution–era kitsch.

called for the eventual socialization of industry and commerce. By 1956, the private sector had been eliminated and all significant industrial and commercial assets had been taken over by the state, with some compensation given to their former owners. Small-scale private trade in the rural areas was also abolished during the mid-1950s. For the remainder of the Maoist era (1949–1976), the state controlled all significant aspects of industry and commerce in China.[2] Even though private enterprises had been eliminated, their former owners and their families were subject to repeated and often harsh persecution during subsequent political campaigns launched by Mao.

As the post-Mao reform era unfolded, the private sector began to reemerge, initially comprising street vendors and very small-scale firms and later expanding to include much larger industrial and commercial enterprises. For most of the 1980s, the private sector was limited to individually owned enterprises. To avoid the appearance of ideologically proscribed "exploitation," these enterprises could only hire less than eight workers outside the family, although in practice many exceeded this limit.[3] Because of their quasi-legal status, many *getihu* had bad backgrounds. Some were actual criminals, whereas others were the victims of past political campaigns. In either case, they had a difficult time securing legitimate jobs. Although some opened their own businesses out of entrepreneurship, others did so out of sheer desperation. Because of their complicated backgrounds and reputations, the *getihu* had relatively low political and social status. By extension, the private sector that they were part of was also viewed with suspicion by other members of society as well as the state.[4]

---

[2] Dorothy J. Solinger, *Chinese Business under Socialism: The Politics of Domestic Commerce in Contemporary China* (Berkeley: University of California Press, 1984); Frederick C. Teiwes, "Establishment and Consolidation of the New Regime," in Roderick MacFarquhar, ed., *The Politics of China*, second edition (Cambridge: Cambridge University Press, 1997); Barry Naughton, *The Chinese Economy: Transitions and Growth* (Cambridge, MA: MIT Press, 2007), chapter 3.

[3] The limit of eight workers was based on Karl Marx's statement in *Das Kapital* that employing more than that number was to engage in exploitation; see Wu Jinglian, *Understanding and Interpreting Chinese Economic Reform* (Singapore: Thomson/South-Western, 2005), pp. 65, n. 44 and 182.

[4] For more details on the roles and backgrounds of *getihu*, see Thomas Gold, "Urban Private Business and China's Reforms," in Richard Baum, ed., *Reform and Reaction in Post-Mao China: The Road to Tiananmen* (New York: Routledge, 1991), pp. 84–103; and Susan Young, *Private Business and Economic Reform in China* (Armonk, NY: M. E. Sharpe, 1995).

The initial justification for allowing *getihu* was that they provided employment for the many youth returning to the cities from the countryside after the Cultural Revolution. Given the severe restrictions on their size, most *getihu* engaged in labor-intensive activities that involved little start-up capital. They did simple assembly work and opened repair shops, small restaurants, and similar operations that were not part of the centrally planned economy. They filled in niches that the centrally planned economy ignored, providing essential services to consumers that did not pose a challenge to the dominant public sector. In 1984, the CCP issued Central Party Document #1, which set limits on the number of workers able to be hired by private enterprises while acknowledging that many already exceeded the limit. This was the first mention of private ownership, but it was not fully legitimated or protected at this time. The document also emphasized that private investment in cooperative firms would be considered "socialist" and not capitalist. Throughout the post-Mao era, the CCP went to great lengths to argue that its economic reforms were consistent with socialism despite the growing reliance on market mechanisms.[5]

The announcement of a new dual pricing policy (one price for the planned economy and another for the market economy) in January 1985 had the unintended consequence of expanding the nonstate sector in industry and commerce. Higher prices in the market economy created incentives for individual and private firms to both compete against SOEs and meet consumer demands not filled by central planning. China adopted the strategy of reform "outside the system" to avoid the direct challenges of SOE reform and entrenched interests. According to Wu Jinglian, a prominent proponent of market reforms, the main obstacle to reform was "the Party-State, Inc.," which remained the core of the old and the new system, with vested interests in preserving the status quo.[6] It instead relied on the demonstration effect of successful regions and nonstate sectors to appeal to the self-interest of reform skeptics. In Barry Naughton's felicitous phrase, the strategy emphasized "growing out of the plan" instead of attacking the planned economy itself.[7]

---

[5] This is a central theme of Yan Sun's *The Chinese Reassessment of Socialism 1976–1992* (Princeton, NJ: Princeton University Press, 1995).

[6] Wu, *Understanding and Interpreting Chinese Economic Reform*, p. 86.

[7] Barry Naughton, *Growing Out of the Plan: Chinese Economic Reform, 1978–1993* (Cambridge: Cambridge University Press, 1995).

In April 1988, China's National People's Congress (NPC) added a new paragraph to Article 11 of the state constitution to give legal status to privately owned firms that employed eight or more workers. According to the revised constitution, "The state permits the private sector of the economy to exist and develop within the limits prescribed by law. The private sector of the economy is a complement to the socialist public economy. The state protects the lawful rights and interests of the private sector of the economy, and exercises guidance, supervision, and control over the private sector of the economy." The State Council subsequently issued regulations to put this into effect. However, many cadres continued to believe that private ownership in particular and capitalism in general were inappropriate for China's still nominally communist system. Opponents of reform blamed the economic crisis of 1988 and the political protests of 1989 on the reform strategy.

Following the tragic end of popular demonstrations in Tiananmen Square and elsewhere in China, capitalists were criticized for their alleged role in supporting the students, and the CCP adopted a ban on the recruitment of entrepreneurs into the party. The Fourth Plenum of the 13th Central Committee, which convened in June soon after the imposition of martial law, criticized "individual and private entrepreneurs who use illegal methods to seek huge profits and thereby create great social disparity and contribute to discontent among the public." Although some entrepreneurs did provide financial and material support for the demonstrators, most entrepreneurs were at best ambivalent about the popular demonstrations, and many were opposed to them.[8] This ban on recruiting private entrepreneurs into the party – and the circumvention of it by some local party leaders – was a prominent source of inner-party debate throughout the 1990s (see chapter 3). Later in 1989, the Fifth Plenum of the 13th Central Committee declared that some aspects of the private sector were "not beneficial" to socialism and should therefore be limited.

During these years, private property rights were not guaranteed under the law. Entrepreneurs were subject to harassment and even imprisonment for violating ill-defined laws and regulations concerning their business activities, and their factories and land could be

[8] David Wank, "Private Business, Bureaucracy, and Political Alliance in a Chinese City," *Australian Journal of Chinese Affairs*, no. 33 (January 1995), pp. 63–65.

confiscated without compensation. To protect themselves, many private entrepreneurs registered their firms as collective enterprises, which are essentially publicly owned enterprises under the control of local governments.[9] Firms that used this subterfuge were known as "red hat collectives": they were for all intents and purposes privately owned and operated, but they wore a politically correct "red hat." This gave some degree of protection to private firms, but the precarious nature of their political and legal status stifled business activity.

Registering as a collective firm provided not only political protection but practical benefits as well. At this time, private entrepreneurs did not have the legal standing to open a commercial bank account or sign binding contracts, but registering as a collective allowed them to do so. State-owned banks could not lend money to private firms, which encouraged some to register as collectives and forced others to turn to informal (illegal and often usurious) money lenders as an alternative.[10] Private firms were also taxed at a higher rate than collectives, another important motivation. Being a red hat collective was not without risks, however. Some local officials would seize the property of successful firms, leaving entrepreneurs with little recourse to protect their interests. The jobs and tax revenue provided by entrepreneurs did not always protect them from the predatory behavior of local officials.

The rapid expansion of the private sector began in 1992, following Deng Xiaoping's much heralded "southern tour." Frustrated by the slow pace of economic reform in the post-Tiananmen climate, Deng embarked on a tour of special economic zones and other prosperous cities in south China and lauded their dynamism and willingness to initiate reform-oriented policies despite the conservative political climate in Beijing. During his trip, he proposed that decisions on whether to permit the nonpublic sector to exist and grow should be based on "whether it promotes the growth of the productive forces in a socialist society, increases the overall strength of the socialist state, and raises

---

[9] Kristen Parris, "The Rise of Private Business Interests," in Merle Goldman and Roderick MacFarquhar, eds., *The Paradox of China's Post-Mao Reforms* (Cambridge, MA: Harvard University Press, 1999).

[10] Kellee S. Tsai, *Back Alley Banking: Private Entrepreneurs in China* (Ithaca, NY: Cornell University Press, 2002); Susan H. Whiting, *Power and Wealth in Rural China: The Political Economy of Institutional Change* (Cambridge: Cambridge University Press, 2001), pp. 144–146.

TABLE 2.1. *Growth in China's Private Sector, 1989–2004*

	1989	1994	1999	2004
Number of private enterprises (millions)	0.091	0.432	1.509	3.651
Number of workers and staff (millions)	1.430	5.695	16.992	40.686
Average registered capital (million RMB)	0.093	0.335	0.681	1.313
Average output value (thousand RMB)	107	264	509	631

Source: For 1989–1999: Zhang Houyi, "Kuaisu chengzhang de Zhongguo siying qiyezhu jieceng" (The Rapid Growth of China's Private Entrepreneurs), in Ru Xin, et al, eds., *2005 nian: Zhongguo shehui xingshi fenxi yu yuce* (Blue Book of China's Society 2005: Analysis and Forecast on China's Social Development) (Beijing: Shehui kexue wenxian chubanshe, 2005), p. 329; for 2004: Zhang Houyi, "Siying qiyezhu jieceng chengzhang de xin jieduan" (The New Era of Growth of Private Entrepreneurs), in Ru Xin, et al., eds., *2006 nian: Zhongguo shehui xingshi fenxi yu yuce* (Blue Book of China's Society 2006: Analysis and Forecast on China's Social Development) (Beijing: Shehui kexue wenxian chubanshe, 2006), p. 345 (averages calculated from numbers in sources).

living standards," not on whether it conforms with traditional ideology. Even so, he insisted that the development of the nonstate sector would not undermine socialism: "a market economy is not capitalism because there are markets under socialism too."[11] Once the national media began to report Deng's comments, enthusiasm for economic reform, and the opening of private firms in particular, exploded (see table 2.1). In the years after 1992, the number of private enterprises grew by 35 percent per year.

Along with the growth of the private sector came greater political and legal protection. The 14th Party Congress, in 1992, endorsed Deng's call for a resumption of economic reform. It adopted a new definition of China's economic system, replacing "planned commodity economy" with "socialist market economy system." The next year, the Third Plenum of the 14th Party Congress adopted the "Decision on Issues Regarding the Establishment of a Socialist Market Economy." Among other things, this decision encouraged diverse forms of ownership, including private, individual, and foreign-invested enterprises.

The 15th Party Congress, in 1997, marked further progress in the party's promotion of the private sector and Jiang Zemin's role as the leader of that policy. When Jiang was appointed the CCP's general

---

[11] Quoted in Wu, *Understanding and Interpreting Chinese Economic Reform*, p. 8, and David L. Wank, *Commodifying Communism: Business, Trust, and Politics in a Chinese City* (Cambridge: Cambridge University Press, 1999), p. 204.

secretary in 1989 in the wake of the Tiananmen demonstrations, he was initially hesitant to support Deng's preference for renewed reform. After Deng threatened to remove him from his post if he did not change his stand, Jiang became the champion of rapid growth for the rest of the 1990s.[12] The 15th Party Congress declared that although public ownership remained the mainstay of the economy, the nonpublic sectors were "important components of a socialist market economy"; accordingly, the CCP would "encourage and guide the non-public sector comprising self-employed and private businesses to facilitate its sound development." According to Wu Jinglian, "this removed ideological impediments and laid down the political foundation for the development of the nonstate sectors."[13] On the basis of these decisions, the NPC once again revised Article 11 in the state constitution in 1999. The new wording indicated the importance of the individual and private sectors to the socialist market economy, raising their status from being supplemental to the public sector to important in their own right.[14]

At the Fifth Plenum of the 15th Central Committee, in October 2000, the CCP went even further, announcing that "the healthy development of the self-employed and privately-owned businesses ... [will be] supported, encouraged, and guided."[15] This new terminology was less restrictive than the previous pledge in the state constitution to "guide, supervise, and control" and gave the private sector the same status as the public sector. On July 1, 2001, the 80th anniversary of the founding of the CCP, Jiang recommended that private entrepreneurs be allowed to join the CCP, ending a ban that he himself had announced in August 1989 immediately after the suppression of the Tiananmen demonstrations. But, in 2001, he claimed they were a new social stratum that were making significant contributions to the country's

---

[12] Joseph Fewsmith, *China since Tiananmen: The Politics of Transition* (Cambridge: Cambridge University Press, 2001), pp. 55–60.

[13] Wu, *Understanding and Interpreting Chinese Economic Reform*, p. 198.

[14] The exact wording of Article 11 as revised was: "The non-public sector of the economy comprising the individual and private sectors, operating within the limits prescribed by law, is an important component of the socialist market economy. The state protects the lawful rights and interests of the non-public sector comprising the individual and private sectors. The state exercises guidance, supervision, and control over the individual and private sectors of the economy." See Xinhua, March 16, 1999.

[15] This new policy was announced in the communiqué of the Fifth Plenum of the 15th Central Committee of the CCP; see Xinhua, October 11, 2000.

development and modernization and therefore deserved a place in the ruling party. To further symbolize the CCP's support of the private sector, the 16th Party Congress in 2002 revised the party's constitution to include the "Three Represents" slogan promoted by Jiang Zemin. The "Three Represents" claimed that the party not only represents its traditional supporters, the workers and farmers, but also the interests of the new "advanced productive forces" of urban economic and social elites, thereby justifying their inclusion in the party. Although often ridiculed as empty rhetoric, the "Three Represents" changed the party's strategy of co-opting entrepreneurs from an informal practice to a formal goal. This was the culmination of Jiang's elitist strategy of the 1990s, where the CCP pursued its goal of rapid economic growth by relying on coastal provinces and gave privileged access to the entrepreneurs who succeeded in getting rich first.[16]

Under the new leadership of Hu Jintao and Wen Jiabao, the CCP became more cautious in trumpeting the benefits of privatization but no less determined to continue the process.[17] Hu and Wen have attempted to put forth a more populist image for the party, emphasizing the interests of society at large, especially in the countryside, instead of Jiang's emphasis on urban economic elites.[18] Whereas Jiang focused on the advanced productive forces in his discussion of the "Three Represents," Hu focused on the third, the interests of the vast majority of the Chinese people. For example, in his speech on Party Day in 2003, Hu concentrated exclusively on the "Three Represents." But whereas Jiang had emphasized the advanced productive forces in his speech two years earlier, Hu used that phrase only once in passing. Instead, he focused on the "fundamental interests of the vast majority of the people," a phrase he repeated 13 times. In doing so, he did

---

[16] For more details on the origins and development of the "Three Represents," see Bruce J. Dickson, "Dilemmas of Party Adaptation: The CCP's Strategies for Survival," in Peter Hays Gries and Stanley Rosen, eds., *State and Society in 21st Century China: Crisis, Contention, and Legitimation* (New York: Routledge, 2004).

[17] Hu replaced Jiang as general secretary of the CCP in 2002, president in 2003, and chairman of the Central Military Commission in 2004. Wen was elected to the Standing Committee of the Politburo at the 16th Party Congress in 2002 and became prime minister in 2003.

[18] Bruce J. Dickson, "Beijing's Ambivalent Reformers," *Current History*, vol. 103, no. 674 (September 2004), pp. 249–255; Cheng Li, "The New Bipartisanship within the Chinese Communist Party," *Orbis*, vol. 49, no. 3 (Summer 2005), pp. 387–400.

not reject an important symbol of the Jiang era but reinterpreted it to signal a shift in priorities. Similarly, whereas Jiang promoted the goal of becoming a "relatively prosperous society" (*xiaokang shehui*) in his speech to the 16th Party Congress in 2002, under Hu and Wen the slogan was redefined to shift the focus away from rapid growth and prosperity toward equity, balanced development, and environmental concerns.[19] To further emphasize the new leaders' priorities, the CCP in 2005 adopted the goal of creating a "harmonious society" (*hexie shehui*), balancing the need to promote economic prosperity with the need to improve economic and social equity and political order.

This commitment to China's have-nots has been shown both symbolically and substantively. Premier Wen has frequently visited miners, SARS and AIDS patients, and victims of natural and man-made disasters, even developing a reputation for weeping in public to show his sympathy. Beyond this, the state boosted rural incomes through subsidies and income transfers and eliminated the grain tax, which constituted a small part of the state's budget but a large portion of peasant incomes. One immediate effect of these policy decisions was improvement in the quality of life in rural China, which in turn led to the return of migrant labor back to the countryside, creating labor shortages in some cities and putting upward pressure on wages and working conditions.

Several motives may have been behind this populist shift. First, Hu and Wen spent parts of their careers in some of China's poorest provinces. They did not make their careers in cosmopolitan Shanghai, as did many in Jiang's camp, and therefore had a better understanding of why some areas continued to lag behind. Second, as part of their succession strategy, they needed to distinguish themselves from Jiang. In the grand tradition of Chinese politics, they did not abandon the "Three Represents" slogan but redefined it. Third, Jiang's elitist

---

[19] For an analysis of Jiang's thinking on *xiaokang shehui*, see Joseph Fewsmith, "The Sixteenth National Party Congress: The Succession that Didn't Happen," *China Quarterly*, no. 173 (March 2003), pp. 1–16, esp. pp. 3–6; and Zheng Yongnian and Lye Liang Fook, "Elite Politics and the Fourth Generation of Chinese Leadership," *Journal of Chinese Political Science*, vol. 8, nos. 1 and 2 (Fall 2003), pp. 65–86, esp. pp. 77–78. For the shift of focus under Hu and Wen, see Dickson, "Beijing's Ambivalent Reformers"; and Li, "The New Bipartisanship within the Chinese Communist Party."

strategy led to growing inequalities and disenchantment, potentially threatening popular support for the CCP's policy priorities. A slight reorientation of the reform strategy therefore could restore some of the balance lost during the years of rapid growth. These three reasons are quite complementary and show why this new populist orientation has both political and practical benefits.

Nevertheless, Hu and Wen have not softened the CCP's commitment to the private sector. If the results of the 16th Party Congress are best seen as endorsing Jiang's policies of previous years, actions taken at subsequent party meetings presumably had the full support of Hu and Wen. The CCP followed up on its earlier pledge to support, encourage, and guide the development of the private sector at the Third Plenum of the 16th Central Committee, in 2003, which approved the "Decision on Several Issues Related to Perfecting the Socialist Market Economic System."[20] This document called for equal treatment of public and nonpublic enterprises regarding investment, financing, taxation, land use, and foreign trade. It said that "laws, regulations, and policies which constrain the development of the non-publicly owned economy" would be sorted out and revised, and "systemic barriers" into new markets, such as infrastructure and public utilities, would be eliminated. The meeting also approved "establishing a modern system of property rights with clear ownership, specific rights and obligations, strict protections, and smooth circulation,"[21] which would benefit both the public and private sectors.

The need to better protect property rights had been a perennial concern for private entrepreneurs, and the CCP committed itself to clarifying those rights. In 2004, Article 11 of the state constitution was again revised to say that the state protects the rights, interests, and legality of individual and private enterprises and that the state "encourages, supports, and guides" the development of the private sector. This phrase had been adopted by the CCP in 2000, but this was the first time such language had been included in the state constitution. But the momentum to put the private sector on a firmer legal foundation slowed in 2005 when Gong Xiantian, a law professor at Peking University, published an article criticizing the proposed property rights

---

[20] Xinhua, October 21, 2003.
[21] Xinhua, October 14, 2003.

law as mimicking Western capitalism but ignoring the socialist nature of China's economy.[22] With the ideological debate on the propriety of private property once again revived, plans to introduce property rights legislation to the NPC were postponed until 2007, when it was finally approved.[23] In short, private property protection was not included in the state constitution until 2004, 25 years after the start of the reform era, and not codified into law until three years later, in 2007.

Hu and Wen not only continued the earlier trend of promoting the private sector but included private entrepreneurs on their trips abroad. In 2003, five entrepreneurs from Wenzhou, the county in Zhejiang that was the model for private sector–led development, were part of Wen Jiabao's delegation to Ethiopia. Entrepreneurs were also part of Hu Jintao's delegation to the United States and Canada in 2005, and a total of 202 entrepreneurs went with Vice Premier Wu Yi to the United States in 2006. According to Shanghai's *Oriental Morning Post*, most of the entrepreneurs on these trips came from Shanghai, Jiangsu, and Zhejiang, especially Wenzhou.[24]

Additional indications of the more supportive attitude of the party toward entrepreneurs also emerged in later years. Party schools at the central and local levels began to offer special classes and programs for private businessmen. In April 2000, the Central Party School held a course on the market economy for around 70 entrepreneurs from Wenzhou.[25] Hu Jintao was president of the Central Party School at this time, offering an early indication of his support for cooperation between the party and the private sector. This was reportedly the first course of its kind sponsored by the Central Party School but this practice subsequently became routine. For example, in 2002, a group of 43 entrepreneurs from Shanghai spent a week at the Central Party School to study the "spirit of the 16th Party Congress" as well as senior management techniques, and in 2005 over 400 private entrepreneurs from Guangdong alone attended one of the four classes held throughout

---

[22] Joseph Kahn, "A Sharp Debate Erupts in China over Ideologies," *New York Times*, March 12, 2006.
[23] Edward Cody, "Chinese Lawmakers Approve Measure to Protect Private Property Rights," *Washington Post*, March 17, 2007.
[24] Li Jingrong, "Engaging Entrepreneurs in State-level Visits," China.org.cn, April 18, 2006 (http://www.china.org.cn/english/2006/Apr/165971.htm).
[25] Xinhua, July 1, 2000, in *World News Connection*, July 3, 2000.

the year.[26] These courses proved so popular that new travel agencies opened to charter the trips, charging approximately 6,800 yuan per person, including airfare and hotel accommodations. As of early 2006, more than 10,000 entrepreneurs from all over China had reportedly attended courses sponsored by the Central Party School.[27] Provincial party schools held similar courses, which typically focus on economics and business management and are similar to short courses offered by business schools for owners and senior managers.[28] But the party also brings groups of entrepreneurs to party schools to influence their political thinking. Although the CCP is fully committed to the private sector, it wants to ensure that the private sector remains committed to the party, and short courses at the party schools are seen as one means of cultivating support.

Individual entrepreneurs have also received a variety of honorary titles at the national and local levels. Awards such as "Entrepreneur of the Year" and "National Young Entrepreneur" are routinely given to businessmen to acknowledge their economic achievements and to link them to the state. More controversial has been the selection of entrepreneurs as "Model Workers," an award traditionally given only to workers and farmers, the traditional mass base of the party. As early as 1987, that award was given to Guan Guangmei, a woman from Liaoning who became rich and famous by leasing state-owned enterprises. She was also selected (as were two other entrepreneurs) as a delegate to the 13th Party Congress that year, the first time

[26] "Shanghai Entrepreneurs Sent to Central Party School for Political Training," *Ming Pao* (Hong Kong), November 29, 2002, in *World News Connection*, November 29, 2002; "Shanghai Private Entrepreneurs Participate in Study Program at Central Party School in Beijing," *Wen Wei Po* (Hong Kong), January 10, 2003, in *World News Connection*, January 17, 2003; Xinhua, December 26, 2005, in *World News Connection*, December 26, 2005.

[27] *South China Morning Post*, April 26, 2006.

[28] The Zhejiang provincial government organized a 12-day training program for 30 private entrepreneurs at Beijing's prestigious Tsinghua University. The Zhejiang government reportedly paid 420,000 yuan (approximately $50,000) for the program because the provincial economy depends primarily on the private sector, even though the 30 people selected for the program came from private enterprises with value-added output of over 100 million yuan and profits of more than 10 million yuan and presumably could have paid their own way. See Wu Zhong, "Lessons for Millionaires," *The Standard* (Hong Kong), November 14, 2005, in *World News Connection*, November 14, 2005.

since 1949 that capitalists were included in a party congress. After the CCP imposed its ban on admitting capitalists into the party in 1989, the party became more low-key in granting such prestigious awards to entrepreneurs. Once the party lifted the ban and adopted the "Three Represents" slogan as official policy, however, the practice resumed. In 2002, the Shaanxi provincial government selected a group of entrepreneurs as model workers, and other local governments followed suit. In 2005, the All-China Federation of Trade Unions (ACFTU) designated entrepreneurs for its national-level model worker award for the first time. Despite the irony of naming capitalists as model workers even though they had been persecuted in the past for exploiting labor, the model worker awards are among China's highest honors, and the CCP signifies its full support of the private sector by giving the awards to private entrepreneurs.[29]

An additional sign of the CCP's support for the private sector is its sponsorship of a group called Guangcai 49. Founded in March 2006 with a ceremony at the Great Hall of the People, the building in Beijing adjacent to Tiananmen Square where most high-profile official ceremonies are held, Guangcai 49 is a consortium of private entrepreneurs with the mandate of rescuing financially troubled private and state-owned enterprises. It operates under the auspices of both the CCP's United Front Work Department and the All-China Federation of Industry and Commerce (ACFIC), the national-level organization that is a main institutional bridge between the party and the private sector. Guangcai 49 is a novel experiment in the CCP's support for the private sector. Whereas the CCP's support for the private sector has been primarily political and rhetorical, Guangcai 49 represents a more direct involvement in the actual financing of private enterprises. It has powerful institutional backers, but its leadership is drawn from the business world, not the political realm. This space is advantageous to both the shareholders in Guangcai 49 and the CCP. It gives

---

[29] "Private Entrepreneurs Win Socialist Prizes," Xinhua, April 30, 2002; "Private Entrepreneurs Nominated Top Honor for China's Labor Class," Xinhua, April 16, 2005; "China Awards Nearly 3,000 Model Workers Including Rocket Superstar Yao Ming," Xinhua, April 30, 2005; Ching-Ching Yi, "New Paradigm for a New China," *The Standard*, April 30–May 1, 2005. The selection of entrepreneurs as model workers was not the only controversial selection in 2005; many also objected to giving the award to celebrities such as NBA all-star Yao Ming.

the shareholders a fair degree of autonomy, plus official backing to make their activities more credible. For the CCP, Guangcai 49 offers the opportunity to experiment directly in financial deals, which could potentially be quite lucrative and could be expanded to other groups if successful. At the same time, if Guangcai 49 proves to be less than successful – for example, if it gets caught up in the corruption scandals that seem to plague many business deals in China,[30] if the companies in which it invests fail, or if it creates controversy by its very existence – the CCP can easily shut it down.

Summary

The CCP's attitude toward the private sector changed from the restrictiveness of the 1980s to active promotion in the 1990s and beyond. Whereas private entrepreneurs were blamed for much of the turmoil of the 1989 demonstrations and accused of counterrevolutionary ambitions, by the mid-1990s they had become full-fledged partners in China's economic development. But as the full effects of the progrowth strategy of the 1990s – including unbalanced growth, increased corruption, and rising inequality – became apparent, the CCP shifted its rhetoric and its policies. Since the 16th Party Congress, in 2002, the CCP has promoted a more populist agenda while still striving to maintain rapid growth. Recognizing the sensitivity of the party's embrace of the private sector, the CCP reportedly ordered state-run media to stop publicizing Hu Jintao's favorable comments about privatization during the period before the annual meeting of the NPC in March 2007 and the 17th Party Congress in October 2007.[31]

---

[30] One hint of potential trouble in this regard concerns Yan Jiehe, a vice chairman of Guangcai 49's board and head of China Pacific Construction Group. In October 2006, the Nanjing Intermediate People's Court ordered Yan to "avoid extravagant spending and not use luxury cars" after he was not able to repay a 5 million yuan loan from the Bank of China. The court also reportedly prohibited Yan from leaving the country, ordered him to document the sources of his wealth (Yan ranked 16th among China's wealthy in 2006, according to Rupert Hoogewerf's annual list, the Hurun Report), and froze the assets of one of his companies. This order may have been the result of recent efforts to slow economic growth by cracking down on local infrastructure projects, which is where Yan made his fortune. See "Tycoon Yan Jiehe Ordered to Cut Back on 'Luxury' Spending," *China Daily* (http://www.chinadaily.com.cn/china/2006–10/19/content_712433.htm).

[31] Edward Cody, "Broadcast Media in China Put on Notice," *Washington Post*, February 27, 2007.

PRIVATIZATION OF COLLECTIVE AND
STATE-OWNED ENTERPRISES

The growth of the private sector was not only a result of the opening of indigenous private and individually owned enterprises. The privatization of public sector firms, both collective and state-owned, also contributed to the expansion of the private sector, especially beginning in the 1990s. In the following two subsections, the privatization of township and village enterprises (TVEs) and state-owned enterprises (SOEs) will be briefly summarized.

Township and Village Enterprises

China's township and village enterprises were an important component of the economic development in the early reform period. Between 1978 and 1996, "TVEs played the catalytic role in transforming the Chinese economy from a command economy to a market economy.... [T]he entry of TVEs provided competition to state-run industrial enterprises and drove the process of marketization forward in the entire economy."[32] Like *getihu*, TVEs were originally seen as a way of soaking up excess labor. In the countryside, the decollectivization of agriculture freed up millions of peasants from farming, but without new jobs in industry they would remain idle. During the 1980s, TVEs produced 10 million nonagricultural jobs in the countryside compared with only 2 million by SOEs.[33]

Township and village enterprises were supplements to SOEs, not competitors. In fact, they often subcontracted with SOEs in a mutually beneficial arrangement: SOEs would supply raw materials and equipment, and TVEs would supply the labor. As a result, TVEs were involved in labor-intensive industries, such as textiles and assembly work, where the barriers to entry – especially capital requirements – were low. This close relationship with SOEs also meant that the TVE phenomenon was particularly prominent in suburban areas or rural areas with easy access to urban suppliers, buyers, and markets. Most TVEs were concentrated in coastal provinces, which was and still is

[32] Naughton, *Chinese Economy*, p. 271.
[33] Shahid Yusuf, Kaoru Nabeshima, and Dwight Perkins, *Under New Ownership: Privatizing China's State-Owned Enterprises* (Palo Alto, CA, and Washington, DC: Stanford University Press and World Bank, 2006), p. 69.

also true of the private sector. In the late 1980s, Jiangsu, Zhejiang, and
Shandong accounted for half of all TVE output, even though they had
only 17 percent of the rural population.[34]

There were three main variants of TVEs:

- **Sunan model:** Township and village enterprises in southern Jiangsu
  (the region known as Sunan) were primarily owned and operated by
  local governments. According to Naughton, "Because of the longer
  history and greater capital resources in these areas, TVEs tend to
  be much bigger, more capital intensive, and more technologically
  sophisticated than TVEs in other parts of the country."[35] These
  collectively owned TVEs also tended to be more closed to outsiders,
  whether firms or labor, in order to preserve the collective benefits
  for the local communities.[36]

- **Wenzhou model:** Township and village enterprises in Wenzhou
  County in Zhejiang relied on private ownership from the beginning
  of the reform era (in fact, even during the Maoist era, Wenzhou was
  frequently accused of pursuing capitalist practices). Because private
  firms could not borrow from banks, the Wenzhou model was exem-
  plified by small-scale, labor-intensive operations that relied on both
  local and national markets. Wenzhou merchants were among the
  first to travel extensively around the country and the first to establish branches of the Wenzhou Chamber of Commerce to represent
  their interests in other cities.[37]

- **Pearl River Delta model:** Generally restricted to the Guangzhou
  area with easy proximity to Hong Kong, this model depended for
  its success on openness to foreign trade and investment. Many of
  the TVEs in the Pearl River Delta received investment from Hong

[34] Naughton, *Chinese Economy*, p. 279.
[35] Naughton, *Chinese Economy*, p. 282.
[36] Andrew G. Walder, "Local Governments as Industrial Firms: An Organizational Anal-
ysis of China's Transition Economy," *American Journal of Sociology*, vol. 101, no. 2
(September 1995), pp. 263–301; Jean C. Oi, "The Role of the Local State in China's
Transitional Economy," *China Quarterly*, no. 144 (December 1995), pp. 1132–1149;
Whiting, *Power and Wealth in Rural China.*
[37] Writings on the Wenzhou model include Yia-Ling Liu, "Reform from Below: The
Private Economy and Local Politics in the Rural Industrialization of Wenzhou," *China
Quarterly*, no. 130 (June 1992), pp. 293–316; Kristin Parris, "Local Initiative and
National Reform: The Wenzhou Model of Development," *China Quarterly*, no. 134
(June 1993), pp. 242–263; Whiting, *Power and Wealth in Rural China.*

Kong. They were also a main destination for migrant labor, who worked in the assembly factories that relied on foreign trade.[38]

Why did some localities adopt one TVE model or another? According to Susan Whiting, whether a region relied on collective or private ownership was largely path dependent: areas such as Sunan that began rural industrialization in the early 1970s had a preexisting stake in collective enterprises at the beginning of the reform era and actively defended those interests. In contrast, regions such as Wenzhou that did not receive much investment in rural industry in the Maoist era did not have vested interests in collective ownership and had little reserve capital to create new enterprises. As a result, private ownership was able to develop rapidly. Variations in local patterns of ownership had their origins in the Maoist era.[39]

Official restrictions on private ownership in the post-Mao era also encouraged local governments to create collectively owned TVEs. As Jean Oi has shown, the development of collectively owned TVEs followed a logic similar to Alexander Gershenkron's analysis of economic development in late-developing countries, where the challenge is not to mobilize labor or raw materials but capital.[40] In China, collective ownership allowed local governments to pool local savings far more than any individual could provide and also pool risk more than any individual would be willing to bear. The political rationale was twofold: first of all, collective ownership provided local officials with additional resources with which they could foster local development, enlarge their patronage, and strengthen their influence; secondly, prohibitions on private ownership in the early 1980s left little choice but to develop rural industrial enterprises under collective ownership. Only in areas such as Wenzhou, which was geographically isolated

[38] A vivid account of the links between Hong Kong and Chinese firms in the Pearl River Delta is in Anita Chan, Richard Madsen, and Jonathan Unger, *Chen Village under Mao and Deng* (Berkeley: University of California Press, 1992).

[39] Whiting, *Power and Wealth in Rural China*. Variations in local models of development are also analyzed in Kellee S. Tsai, *Capitalism without Democracy: The Private Sector in Contemporary China* (Ithaca, NY: Cornell University Press, 2007), chapter 6.

[40] Jean C. Oi, *Rural China Takes Off: Institutional Foundations of Economic Reform* (Stanford, CA: Stanford University Press, 1999), pp. 65–66; Alexander Gershenkron, *Historical Backwardness in Historical Perspective* (Cambridge, MA: Harvard University Press, 1962).

and not a beneficiary of central largesse, did private ownership lead economic development. In other words, the Wenzhou model was born of necessity, not a strategic decision by local leaders.

Privately owned TVEs faced discriminatory treatment in the 1980s: they were cut off from both official bank loans available to state-owned and collective enterprises and the types of tax incentives available to foreign investors. As a consequence, like private firms in the cities, private TVEs were constrained from expanding their scale of operations due to limits on obtaining new capital and had to rely on their own profits for new investment. During the economic retrenchment of 1988–1989, private TVEs were the first to be forced to close by local officials. One local official referred to private entrepreneurs as "underground snakes," showing the contempt commonly felt toward private entrepreneurs.[41]

Many TVEs were "red hat" collectives: they were registered as collectives but were essentially privately owned and operated, but exactly how many fit this description is not known.[42] Beginning in the 1990s, both the economic and political environments shifted in favor of the private sector. Many red hat collectives were able to take off their disguise and reveal the private firm lurking underneath, making formal what was already true in practice. By 2004, over 90 percent of TVEs were registered as privately owned. By then, the TVE phenomenon had run its course and TVEs were less important as economic actors on the national stage, although they undoubtedly remained important locally.

Township and village enterprises were very profitable in the beginning. These profits were made possible by state-set prices, not necessarily by efficient operations. As a result, TVEs provided local governments with new sources of revenue: profits from collectives and taxes from private TVEs. As more firms entered the market to get a share of these profits, they all faced increased competition, lower prices for their products, and sinking profit margins.[43] In addition,

---

[41] Oi, *Rural China Takes Off*, p. 74.

[42] Oi says that one county official estimated that 10–20 percent of firms registered as collectives were actually privately owned, but this was in the mid-1990s, when the subterfuge was less necessary, and therefore may underestimate the practice at its peak; see Oi, *Rural China Takes Off*, p. 133.

[43] Naughton, *Chinese Economy*, pp. 275–282.

urban consumers grew more discriminating in their tastes, demanding better-quality goods than TVEs were able to produce. Consumers in several cities were so unhappy with the cheap quality of Wenzhou shoes and other commodities that they burned the goods in protest. Soon after, Wenzhou merchants created local chapters of the Wenzhou Chamber of Commerce around the country to monitor and publicize the quality of Wenzhou goods sold in other markets. In this increasingly competitive environment, many firms did not survive. They either simply closed or more often merged with successful TVEs, which took over the assets, workers, and operation of insolvent ones.

As noted, the national policy environment shifted in favor of private ownership in the 1990s. Restrictions on the formation of private firms and the privatization of state-owned and collective enterprises began to relax, even to the point of assigning quotas to local governments for creating new private firms.[44] Over time, even TVEs in the Sunan region began to adopt the Wenzhou model. In addition to the change in central policy, local factors also encouraged local governments to privatize TVEs under their control. According to Shahid Yusuf, Kaoru Nabeshima, and Dwight Perkins, the initial privatization of TVEs was not a response to central directives but "was driven by the localities responding to pressures to improve firm efficiency and competitiveness."[45] Many TVEs were facing growing debt problems and needed to recapitalize. Privatization was one means of injecting new capital into existing firms. Relatedly, local governments were facing increasing budget constraints of their own and wished to rid themselves of debt-ridden and unprofitable TVEs.[46] The privatization of TVEs put the firms and the local state in a mutually dependent relationship, according to Susan Whiting: "the firm was dependent on the state to support the firm's claim on its assets, while the state was dependent on the firm to generate revenue."[47]

---

[44] Oi, *Rural China Takes Off*, p. 87.
[45] Yusuf, Nabeshima, and Perkins, *Under New Ownership*, p. 98. See also Hongyi Chen, *The Institutional Transition of China's Township and Village Enterprises: Market Liberalization, Contractual Form Innovation, and Privatization* (Aldershot: Ashgate, 2000).
[46] Sun Laixiang, "Ownership Reform in China's Township and Village Enterprises," in Stephen Green and Guy S. Liu, eds., *Exit the Dragon? Privatization and State Control in China* (London: Blackwell, 2005), pp. 90–110.
[47] Whiting, *Power and Wealth in Rural China*, p. 177.

Beginning in the mid-1990s, TVEs privatized on a massive scale and at a rapid pace. In a survey conducted by Hongbin Li and Scott Rozelle, 86 percent of TVEs in Jiangsu and Zhejiang underwent at least partial privatization (i.e., the transfer of at least some shares to private ownership), and 57 percent had been completely privatized by 1999.[48] Over time, privately owned TVEs also provided a growing share of the jobs in this sector: in 1985, they represented around 40 percent of TVE employment, in 1995 exactly half, but by 2003 over 90 percent of the TVE workers were employed in private firms.[49] However, before 1995, many TVEs had been red hat collectives, so it is hard to make accurate comparisons: some had been essentially privately owned and operated even before their formal "privatization." The consolidation of some TVEs and the privatization of others also meant that they were no longer a major producer of new jobs. Competitive pressures forced TVEs to become more efficient, leading to reductions in their labor forces.

Unlike privatization in other parts of the world, privatization in China was mostly via insider buyouts. Li and Rozelle found this to have economic benefits, for example by allowing experienced managers to continue operating the firms. But insider buyouts also presented local officials with new opportunities to engage in corruption, such as selling firms to friends and family, receiving kickbacks on sales, or shifting publicly owned assets to their own private ownership. Insider buyouts are prone to corruption due to "asymmetric information": TVE managers had a better understanding of the value of a firm and its assets than did local officials. As a result, as Stephen Green and Guy Liu dryly point out, "insiders are liable to underpay."[50]

In Zhejiang and Jiangsu, a common practice was "privatization with a tail," in which TVEs were sold at a discounted price and local governments were given a share of future profits. Buyers who anticipated strong future performance were willing to pay full price for the firms in order to keep all future profits for themselves. Those who were less optimistic received discounted sales prices but also agreed to

---

[48] Hongbin Li and Scott Rozelle, "Privatizing Rural China: Insider Privatization, Innovative Contracts, and the Performance of Township Enterprises," *China Quarterly*, no. 176 (December 2003), pp. 981–1005.

[49] Naughton, *Chinese Economy*, p. 286.

[50] "Introduction," in Green and Liu, eds., *Exit the Dragon?* p. 7.

share a portion of future earnings with the local government. According to various scholars, primarily economists, this model helped local governments gain a more accurate sense of the true value of their firms because accurate and fair assessments were difficult to obtain.[51] However, widespread reports of sweetheart deals, kickbacks, and asset stripping suggest that many of these "discounts" reflected corrupt ties between buyers and local officials, not simply an honest assessment of future earnings potential.

Even after the shift in national policy in favor of the private sector, virtually no bank loans were made to private TVEs. Although Wenzhou was the model of private ownership, only 5 percent of total lending to local industry by the Hualing Industrial and Commercial Bank in Wenzhou went to private firms. Moreover, they were usually small loans for short periods, often just six months.[52] In areas where the private sector was less developed than in Wenzhou, private TVEs faced even tighter restrictions on gaining access to bank loans. Although some firms registered as fake collectives or engaged in bribery of bank officials in order to gain access to loans from state banks, neither tactic was foolproof. Most private entrepreneurs were simply excluded from lending by the formal banking system and had to rely on reinvested profits or unofficial moneylenders, who typically charged much higher rates of interest on their loans. An ACFIC survey in 1994 found that the difficulty in obtaining credit was one of the greatest concerns of private entrepreneurs, and that concern continued in later years despite the growing official commitment to private ownership.[53]

After the mid-1990s, TVEs, especially collectively owned TVEs of the Sunan model, were of less importance to the creation of new jobs and new economic output. In many ways, they were the victims of their own early success: by showing how small-scale enterprises could enter markets with little capital or experience, they motivated others to

[51] Li and Rozelle, "Privatizing Rural China"; Sun, "Ownership Reform in China's Township and Village Enterprises," pp. 103–104; Naughton, *Chinese Economy*, pp. 291–292.

[52] Whiting, *Power and Wealth in Rural China*, p. 259. The situation did not improve much in later years; see Tsai, *Capitalism without Democracy*, pp. 177–178.

[53] Whiting, *Power and Wealth in Rural China*, pp. 262–263; see also Tsai, *Back Alley Banking*.

follow suit. As more and more firms entered the market, competition forced prices and profits to fall, which led to the consolidation and privatization of TVEs.

State-Owned Enterprises

The reform of state-owned enterprises (SOEs) was the third contributor to the growth of the private sector in China, but it followed different dynamics than the development of indigenous private firms and TVEs. First of all, the opening of individual and private firms and TVEs was done at the initiative of individual entrepreneurs and local officials. Changes in central policy more often caught up to what was already in practice at the local level. In contrast, SOE reform was initiated with central directives, although with local discretion in how the directives were implemented. Second, the most controversial and far-reaching elements in SOE reform – for example, the closing or sale of unprofitable firms – were delayed in part by the desire to avoid the massive layoffs that would follow. Whereas job creation was an explicit rationale for the existence of the private sector and TVEs, job preservation was an initial but in the end not insurmountable obstacle to SOE reform. Third, SOE reform was undertaken to cut the state's losses rather than maximize gains. Most SOEs were unprofitable and a drain on state resources, whereas private firms and TVEs produced new jobs and generated revenue for local governments. In all three areas, privatization had the same goals – better firm performance, more revenue, and more jobs – but the evolution of policy reflected very real differences in the economic and political aspects of private firms, TVEs, and SOEs.

Under the central planning system, SOEs were the mainstay of the economy. In 1978, at the beginning of the reform era, SOEs contributed 77 percent of industrial output; by 1996, that figure had dropped to only 33 percent as TVEs, private firms, foreign-invested enterprises, and other nonstate firms became more prominent.[54] The

---

[54] Information in this paragraph comes from Edward S. Steinfeld, *Forging Reform in China: The Fate of State-Owned Industry* (Cambridge: Cambridge University Press, 1998). Steinfeld compares different forms of SOE restructuring, including stock offerings, managerial incentives, and contracting arrangements, in the steel industry, none

main trigger for SOE reform was the chronic unprofitability of this sector. State-owned enterprises were often grossly inefficient, wasting energy and other inputs, employing far more employees than necessary, and producing goods for which there were no markets. In addition, SOEs were also responsible for the housing, medical, and educational expenses for workers and their families. As market competition increased, SOEs were unable to compete against private and collective enterprises that operated more efficiently and did not provide the full range of benefits that workers at SOEs enjoyed. Whereas the emergence of private firms and TVEs of different ownership types proved to be beneficial to economic growth and job creation, SOEs have been a perennial drag on the economy. As a whole, the SOE sector was the worst-performing sector, and efforts to make firms more profitable were generally unsuccessful.

Throughout the early reform era of the 1980s, SOE reform did not include or even envision privatization. Instead, the CCP remained committed to reliance on state-owned enterprises and central planning. Even through the mid-1990s, key Chinese leaders believed "ownership was not a decisive influence on SOE performance, and that privatization was to be ruled out."[55] Instead, early reforms were designed to give firms more incentives to be profitable but not change their form of ownership. These reforms included allowing firms to retain a larger share of their profits; the adoption of "dual track pricing," which allowed SOEs to sell their goods at a higher market-set price after fulfilling their state-set quota; giving managers more autonomy from the state and responsibility over their enterprises' operations, including decisions about what to produce and more discretion in hiring and firing decisions. But SOEs were constrained in their ability to be truly responsible for their own profits and losses, especially because of their inability to lay off surplus labor and the need to meet welfare needs (such as housing, medical care, and education) for employees.

In addition, "soft budget constraints" provided a safety net for firms that did not or could not turn a profit. Firms that operated at a loss simply requested additional state subsidies or loans from state banks.

---

of which proved successful. A larger World Bank survey reached similar conclusions. See Yusuf, Nabeshima, and Perkins, *Under New Ownership*.

[55] Yusuf, Nabeshima, and Perkins, *Under New Ownership*, p. 72.

These loans were not based on the firms' ability to repay, and in fact many were never repaid and were not expected to be repaid. They are commonly referred to as "policy loans" because they were given on the basis of policy decisions, not creditworthiness. Large firms had too many assets (sunk costs) and employed too many workers to be allowed to fail. This created a vicious cycle of pouring more and more money into perennially unprofitable firms. In contrast, collectives and especially private firms faced hard budget constraints: if they operated at a loss, they either had to cut their costs, find new investors, or close. State-owned enterprises had an advantage in this regard: many were protected from failure through continued state support, and they had no real incentive to become profitable. The continued poor performance of SOEs created a growing burden on state coffers. According to a World Bank study written by Yusuf, Nabeshima, and Perkins, even after nearly a decade of SOE reforms, by the late 1990s "nearly 40 percent of small and medium-size state-owned enterprises were insolvent... [and] almost half of all SOEs were running losses."[56] The Chinese government announced that the SOE sector *as a whole* was in the red in 1996 for the first time since 1949.[57] More importantly, continually pouring more money into SOEs presented a tremendous opportunity cost. Nonperforming loans to SOEs represented capital that otherwise could have been put to better use by private firms.

The poor performance of some SOEs was also the consequence of asset stripping, not simply the inefficient use of productive assets. Managers conspired to skim capital, labor, equipment, and technology from SOEs under their control to collective and private firms. All profits went to the subsidiary and all losses to the parent company, to the extent that some SOEs were essentially hollowed out and technically bankrupt, whereas their subsidiaries were profitable, at least on paper. According to X. L. Ding, this gave rise to the expression "the mother is poor, the kids are rich."[58] Workers in SOEs resented asset stripping because it harmed the financial health of their firms. Workers received bonuses when their firms made profits, but asset stripping

---

[56] Yusuf, Nabeshima, and Perkins, *Under New Ownership*, p. 13.
[57] Steinfeld, *Forging Reform in China*, p. 18, emphasis added.
[58] X. L. Ding, "The Illicit Asset Stripping of Chinese State Firms," *China Journal*, no. 43 (January 2000), p. 7.

made their firms look weaker than they really were, thus harming the material interests of the workers. Investigations into the behavior of managers and officials were often the result of pressure from the parent company's workers.[59]

In the 1990s, SOE reform changed its focus from improving incentives and managerial autonomy to corporate restructuring. The process of incorporation created new corporate forms, including limited liability shareholding corporations, limited liability firms, employee shareholding companies, and private firms.[60] The Company Law of 1994 was an important turning point in SOE reform. It offered for the first time a common legal framework for the incorporation of firms regardless of their form of ownership, putting them on an equal footing. Corporatization proved to be a popular and convenient concept: "the corporate form offered the promise of limited liability to the government; the local governments found that privatization was the only way to staunch the bleeding of small and medium state-owned and collective enterprises; [and] the listing of enterprises on the stock exchanges seemed like a convenient way to raise funds for restructuring."[61]

At the 15th Party Congress, in 1997, where the CCP declared that nonstate sectors were "important components of a socialist market economy," it also adopted a new policy toward SOE reform known as "grasp the big, release the small" (*zhuada fangxiao*). This was designed to get the state out of sectors where privately owned small- and medium-sized enterprises were already present and competitive and where SOE performance had been poor (for example, in textiles, building materials, food processing, services, and commerce). Between 1996 and 2001, nearly 50,000 small- and medium-sized SOEs went through restructuring, including public offerings, joint ventures, employee buyouts, leasing, and bankruptcy. According to a survey of industrial SOEs, 86 percent had undergone some degree of reform by the end of 2001, and 70 percent had been wholly or partially privatized. At the same time, the CCP intended to retain large firms under

---

[59] Ding, "Illicit Asset Stripping of Chinese State Firms," p. 19.
[60] Stephen Green and Guy S. Liu, "China's Industrial Reform Strategy: Retreat and Retain," in Green and Liu, eds., *Exit the Dragon?* pp. 15–41.
[61] Stoyan Tenev and Chunlin Zhang with Loup Brefort, *Corporate Governance and Enterprise Reform in China: Building the Institutions of Modern Markets* (Washington, DC: World Bank and International Finance Corporation, 2002), p. 24.

state ownership in strategic and "pillar" industries because the state has a continuing interest in controlling these sectors and protecting workers in those firms from massive layoffs (large SOEs can employ tens of thousands of workers). Some larger SOEs were merged into enterprise groups; more commonly, they were converted into shareholding companies, with some shares offered on the stock market but most shares controlled by the state. In 2005, the state retained an average 65 percent share of large SOEs.[62]

The fear of massive layoffs had postponed the most ambitious SOE reforms, but as SOEs were incorporated and restructured, large numbers of SOE workers lost their jobs. In the years after the 15th Party Congress in 1997, 36 percent of the state sector workforce was laid off; the figure rises to 50 percent if retirees are included, as many of them were forced into early retirement. Put differently, over 50 million urban workers lost their jobs as a result of SOE restructuring.[63] To compensate for the elimination of the "iron rice bowl," local governments created reemployment centers, health insurance companies, and a range of social services offered by mass organizations such as the Women's Federation, the ACFTU, and the Communist Youth League. These various organizations are funded and staffed by the state, making their effectiveness at serving the interests of laid-off workers questionable.[64]

As was the case for TVE privatization, the SOE restructuring process has been prone to corruption, including asset stripping, insider buyouts, and nepotism. Although it is hard to determine the actual value of SOEs in the absence of competitive bidding and a credit market, there is no question that many SOEs were sold at a fraction of their true value. Insider buyouts have often been the result of corrupt

---

[62] Yusuf, Nabeshima, and Perkins, *Under New Ownership*, p. 16; "Introduction," in Green and Liu, eds., *Exit the Dragon?* p. 4.

[63] Yusuf, Nabeshima, and Perkins, *Under New Ownership*, p. 79. Official estimates put the number of workers laid off between 1993 and 2003 at 28 million, but this is undoubtedly a low estimate. See also Dorothy J. Solinger, "Labour Market Reform and the Plight of the Laid-Off Proletariat," *China Quarterly*, no. 170 (June 2002), pp. 304–326; Dorothy J. Solinger, "Why We Cannot Count the 'Unemployed,'" *China Quarterly*, no. 167 (September 2001), pp. 671–688.

[64] Xiaobo Hu, "The State, Enterprises, and Society in Post-Deng China: Impact of the New Round of SOE Reform," *Asian Survey*, vol. 40, no. 4 (July–August 2000), pp. 650–656.

sweetheart deals as local officials sold firms to friends and family, resulting in huge losses to the state. Many corruption cases involved these kinds of asset stripping and insider buyouts. As Melanie Manion has shown, the Chinese state is more prone to investigate and punish cases of corruption that entail losses of revenue to the state as opposed to more routine squeezing of nonstate actors, which is more aggravating to more people but does not cost the state revenue.[65] Moreover, these insider deals have not improved the performance of the restructured or privatized firm. In their study of reformed SOEs, Yusuf, Nabeshima, and Perkins concluded that insider buyouts were less likely to restructure firms in order to make them more productive and profitable: "Restructuring of SOEs without relinquishing state control of the [large and medium-sized enterprises] has been tried, and the results have been fairly meager."[66] Moreover, these sweetheart deals create strong social and political resentment, undermining support for the economic reform agenda (see chapter 7 for more details on this issue).

The absence of clear property rights makes the ownership status of reformed SOEs murky. According to a 2002 survey of the private sector sponsored by the All-China Federation of Industry and Commerce, the Chinese Academy of Social Sciences, and other groups, 25.7 percent of private firms were former SOEs.[67] But the state can hold up to a 20–50 percent stake in a firm that is technically classified as private. The unclear ownership status of reformed SOEs is further obscured by the

---

[65] Melanie Manion, *Corruption by Design: Building Clean Government in Mainland China and Hong Kong* (Cambridge, MA: Harvard University Press, 2005). See also Yan Sun, *Corruption and Market in Contemporary China* (Ithaca, NY: Cornell University Press, 2004); Minxin Pei, *China's Trapped Transition: The Limits of Developmental Autocracy* (Cambridge, MA: Harvard University Press, 2006).

[66] Yusuf, Nabeshima, and Perkins, *Under New Ownership*, pp. 38, 113. Based on their study, the key to better performance seems to be whether the firm has received foreign investment. Reformed SOEs do best in electronic components, consumer products, and vehicles and vehicle parts, sectors where joint ventures are common. Private ownership has proven to be the most efficient, but only for joint ventures. Private firms that were not joint ventures did not outperform SOEs, but that may have been the result of institutional obstacles, especially the difficulty in accessing capital from Chinese banks. That may have also been why joint ventures did so well: the foreign partners provided the capital and technology, and the Chinese partners provided knowledge of the Chinese market and connections with Chinese officials.

[67] See http://www.acfic.org.cn/acfic/12_xw/xxzk/708_8.htm; Xinhua, November 13, 2003.

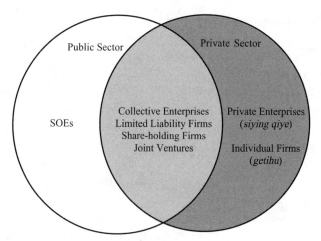

FIGURE 2.1. Forms of ownership in China

tendency to refer to the reform process as "restructuring" instead of
"privatization." As Naughton has noted, "Overall, because the process
is extremely dispersed and nontransparent, we do not have a very
detailed understanding of Chinese privatization."[68] The result is an
overlapping and often confusing mix of forms of ownership, as shown
in figure 2.1. This makes it difficult to determine the actual extent of
public and private ownership and control over a given firm. Although
managers of corporatized SOEs supposedly are appointed by their
boards of directors, in practice they are often chosen by the CCP's
Organization Department. This is especially true for large SOEs and
enterprise groups. In these firms, the general manager often also serves
as the secretary of the party committee.[69]

China remains committed to state ownership in key industries, such
as energy, telecommunications, public utilities, transportation, and sectors related to national security.[70] The government has tried to introduce some amount of competition in these sectors, but only among

---

[68] Naughton, *Chinese Economy*, p. 325.
[69] Tenev, Zhang, with Brefort, *Corporate Governance and Enterprise Reform in China*,
p. 23.
[70] In December 2006, China specified seven sectors that would remain under state control: the military industry, electric power generation and distribution, petroleum and
petrochemicals, telecommunications, coal, civil aviation, and shipping. See Xinhua,
December 18, 2006.

state-owned firms (such as provincial and regional airlines and various print media). In March 2003, the State Asset Supervision and Administration Commission (SASAC) was created to oversee the large SOE industrial groups, giving an "institutional presence to the government's industrial policy ambitions."[71] At the time of its creation, it controlled 196 firms representing almost half of China's state-controlled assets (approximately $833 billion; the rest were in noneconomic units, such as hospitals and schools). The desire to maintain state control over key industries is motivated in part by political motives – preventing private entrepreneurs from obtaining large amounts of wealth and control over scarce resources that could then be turned into political capital. As Green and Liu wrote, "Allowing small-scale private firms to prosper across an ever-larger economic space is politically rational because it generates jobs and fiscal revenues; allowing a small number of private citizens, a Chinese oligarch class, to grow politically influential through their ownership of limited natural resources and large-scale industrial assets is not."[72] Keeping a large fraction of the economy under state control also may placate those within the party who oppose privatization on ideological grounds.

The Size of the Private Sector

Making an accurate assessment of the size of the private sector and its contribution to the economy is difficult. As noted, the degree of state and private ownership and control can be hard to decipher and compare, even in firms with the same corporate classification. Another complicating factor was a change in the statistical reporting that occurred in the late 1990s. In the past, China's yearbooks included aggregate statistics on the number, employment, and output of all SOEs, collectives, and private firms. Since 1998, only firms "above a certain size" (i.e., over 5 million yuan in annual sales) have been included. Because SOEs on average are larger than collective and especially private firms, this policy change both underestimates the contribution of the private sector and prevents an accurate analysis of trends over time. In 2006, estimates of the size of China's aggregate economy increased by almost

---

[71] "Introduction," in Green and Liu, eds., *Exit the Dragon?* p. 9.
[72] Ibid., p. 2.

17 percent as statisticians realized that small and medium enterprises were underrepresented in official surveys. Nevertheless, rough estimates of the size and significance of the private sector all acknowledge that it has grown and will continue its predominance in generating new growth, jobs, and tax revenue.

As the CCP relaxed restrictions on private ownership and adopted more supportive policies, the private sector expanded rapidly. By 2005, China had over 4.3 million private enterprises, and the individual and private economy became the source of nearly all economic growth and new jobs. The Organisation for Economic Co-operation and Development's (OECD) "Economic Survey of China, 2005" reported that the private sector produced "well over half of GDP and an overwhelming share of exports." It also estimated a "fivefold rise in the output of domestically-owned private companies" between 1998 and 2003, compared with a 70 percent rise in the output of the state sector.[73] In 2005, the private sector contributed 50 percent of gross domestic product (GDP), and that was projected to grow to 75 percent by 2010. Between 2000 and 2005, it created 57 million jobs, including 80 percent of new jobs outside of agriculture; during that same time, the labor force in the state-owned sector shrank by 15 million. Tax revenue provided by private firms grew 40 percent per year between 2000 and 2005, whereas the state sector's contribution grew by only 7 percent.[74]

LOCAL SUPPORT FOR THE PRIVATE SECTOR

How well do the views of local officials follow this evolution in central policy? One way to measure changes on this issue is to compare the perceived importance of the private sector relative to the state-owned enterprises. In surveys completed in 1999 and 2005 (see the appendix for details on the survey project), local officials were asked to evaluate the importance of the private and state-owned enterprises in creating prosperity by giving a score between 0 (not important at all) to 10 (extremely important). In 1999, the state sector had a mean score

---

[73] Organisation for Economic Co-operation and Development, "Policy Brief: Economic Survey of China, 2005," *OECD Observer*, no. 251 (2005), pp. 1, 3.
[74] "Private Firms Powering China Economy," *China Daily* (online), September 22, 2006.

of 7.55 and the private sector 6.69; in 2005, their relative positions reversed, with the state sector's score falling to 5.94 and the private sector's score rising to 8.21. By taking the difference between each respondent's assessment of the importance of the private and state sectors, we get a measure of their relative importance.[75] If a respondent felt that the private sector was extremely important and the state sector was not important at all, the score for this combined measure would be 10; conversely, if the private sector was not important at all and the state sector was extremely important, the score would be -10; and if they were equally important, the score would be 0. In 1999, the average difference was -0.87 (in favor of the state sector). Most cadres attached greater importance to the state sector than to the private sector (52.17 percent), 26.52 percent gave them equal importance, and only 21.31 percent put more importance on the private sector. In all eight counties included in the 1999 survey, the average score was a negative number, showing the systematic preference for the importance of the state sector. In the 2005 survey, the situation was quite different. The mean score increased to 2.33 in favor of the private sector. More specifically, most local officials gave greater importance to the private sector than to the state sector (61.15 percent), 19.42 percent felt they were of equal importance, and only 19.42 percent believed the state sector was still the most important. In every county, the average score was now positive, and the counties with the highest per capita GDP also had the largest differences between their 1999 and 2005 scores. This indicates that the private sector was of growing importance not only in objective economic measures but also in the subjective views of local officials.

These results suggest several conclusions. First, the shift in support for the private sector has been clear and pronounced, even in just the years between 1999 and 2005, when these surveys were completed. The change in central policy is reflected in the change of views of local

---

[75] This measure was used by Melanie Manion to measure the "electoral connection" between township and village leaders on one hand and villagers on the other. See Melanie Manion, "The Electoral Connection in the Chinese Countryside," *American Political Science Review*, vol. 90, no. 4 (December 1996), pp. 736–748. I did not ask private entrepreneurs in my surveys to compare the importance of private firms like theirs with state-owned or collective enterprises, so I cannot compare entrepreneurs and officials on this issue.

officials. Second, this is not just rhetorical support by local officials dutifully repeating the central line but varies according to local economic conditions. The more prosperous the county, the more likely are local officials to place more importance on the private sector. I would expect these trends to strengthen in the years to come. On the other hand, variation in the relative importance of the private sector is not explained by characteristics specific to the cadres themselves: in a multivariate analysis (not shown here), the level of their appointment (that is, whether they were county or township/village level cadres), the length of their tenure in office, and their age, gender, and level of education were all statistically insignificant factors. On this question at least, it is context more than individual attributes that makes the difference.

CONCLUSION

As the private economy expanded in post-Mao China, so did the rhetoric needed to legitimize it. In the early reform era, much effort was made to square the private sector and the reform process as a whole with the socialist nature of the economy. At that time, the private sector was small and clearly subordinate to the planned economy. It was composed of small-scale enterprises owned and operated by individuals with problematic political and social backgrounds, and it operated on the margins of the economy. Over time, the private sector and the size of individual firms began to grow. Individual firms may have remained relatively small compared with SOEs, but in the aggregate the private sector became increasingly important in the economy, producing new growth, new jobs, and additional tax revenue for local governments. Only gradually did the emphasis on socialism fade as a criterion for the legitimacy and acceptability of the private sector.

The CCP was ambivalent about the role of the private sector for most of the reform era. Whereas private entrepreneurs were blamed for much of the turmoil of the 1989 demonstrations and accused of counterrevolutionary ambitions, by the mid-1990s they had become full-fledged partners in China's economic development. Throughout the 1990s, the CCP pursued a decidedly pro-growth and pro-business strategy, relying on urban economic elites in the coastal areas of China. As the following chapters will show, the CCP has actively integrated

China's capitalists into the political system by recruiting them into the party, appointing them to prominent political posts, and consulting with them on a range of policy matters. At the same time, since 2002 it has tried to balance the need to maintain rapid rates of growth with the need to restore balance to the patterns of growth and the manner in which wealth is distributed.

3

Co-opting the Capitalists

The expansion of the private sector described in chapter 2 has led to predictions that privatization will inevitably bring about political change in China and ultimately democratization. Expectations that China's capitalists will be agents of political change are based on two assumptions. The first is that the CCP is a passive actor, but as this chapter will demonstrate, it has actively integrated large numbers of private entrepreneurs into the party. The second is that China's capitalists have political beliefs and policy preferences significantly different from those of the state and will therefore promote a democratic opening; this will be explored in later chapters.

Throughout the reform era, the CCP abandoned its earlier goal of promoting class struggle for the key task of promoting economic modernization. Consequently, it undertook a determined and extensive effort to recruit new members with new sets of skills into the party. The change in goals necessitated a change in criteria for recruiting new members and appointing new personnel to key posts in the party and government at all levels. Party leaders recognized that the kinds of people who joined the party when waging revolution and class struggle were the focus of the party's agenda were ill suited to the more pragmatic efforts to develop the economy and raise living standards. Although the co-optation of new members is a key dimension of the policy of inclusion that allows Leninist parties to adapt and is also an important factor for promoting organizational change in a variety of organizations, it also leads to tensions within the organization between the proponents and opponents of change.

This chapter will begin by describing the logic of co-optation, its intended and unintended consequences, and the controversies it can generate within the organization. It will then describe the CCP's evolving policy toward recruiting entrepreneurs into the party and the debate surrounding this policy. The CCP's recruitment strategies to target intellectuals and entrepreneurs led to sharp criticism by those who felt that co-opting these former "class enemies" into the CCP was undermining the party's integrity and betraying the interests of its traditional base, the workers and farmers. The CCP imposed a formal (but not fully effective) ban on recruiting entrepreneurs between 1989 and 2001. After lifting the ban, reports indicated lukewarm efforts by local officials tasked with implementing the policy and a tepid response from entrepreneurs to the CCP's invitation to join. However, my survey data indicate a steady increase in the number of entrepreneurs co-opted into the party in the years after the ban was lifted and an increasingly coherent and predictable strategy for which entrepreneurs the party seeks to recruit. This illustrates the decentralized and expansive nature of crony communism in China: local officials began co-opting entrepreneurs even before the formal ban was lifted, but the practice was informal and uneven: not all officials supported the practice, and even after the ban was lifted, the recruitment of entrepreneurs into the CCP was not uniformly implemented. Even so, the growth in the number of "red capitalists" (entrepreneurs who are also party members) has been primarily a result of the privatization of state-owned enterprises, which has turned former state managers into private entrepreneurs.

THE POLITICAL LOGIC OF CO-OPTATION

Organizations have two main strategies for coping with environmental change: co-opting new personnel and creating new links with other organizations (the subject of chapter 4). These strategies allow the organization to be better integrated with its environment and better informed of changes occurring therein. Co-optation allows the organization to add new skills, experiences, and resources (such as political support) that may enhance its performance and increase its chance of survival. But co-optation can also threaten the organization if these co-opted actors do not share its goals. The organization may receive needed support but as a consequence be diverted from its original mission.[1] Therefore, the co-optation decision may be contested within the organization. Other organizational goals, such as self-preservation and self-replication, can become paramount, limiting the organization's ability to adapt successfully to new challenges. Opponents of adaptation may point to party traditions and established norms as more legitimate grounds for resisting change than sheer self-interest.[2]

The experience of authoritarian parties, and Leninist parties in particular, is consistent with this dilemma posed by co-optation. As they abandon class struggle for the sake of economic modernization, these parties typically switch from an exclusionary to an inclusionary, or co-optive, recruitment policy.[3] Organizations co-opt those they depend on, who possess resources they require, or who pose a threat to the organization. In the post-Mao period, the switch from class struggle to economic modernization as the key task of the party has made the party dependent on the technocrats and entrepreneurs who make the economy grow. Former class enemies and counterrevolutionaries are now brought into the party because they have the skills desired by party leaders to accomplish their new policy agenda. This may lead to the rejuvenation of the party but may also lead to long-term degradation if the interests of these new members conflict with party traditions. As the party tries to adapt by co-opting new members, supporters of party traditions resist "assimilating new actors whose loyalty to

[1] Philip P. Selznick, *TVA and the Grass Roots* (Berkeley: University of California Press, 1949); Jeffrey Pfeffer and Gerald B. Salancik, *The External Control of Organizations: A Resource Dependence Perspective* (New York: Harper and Row, 1978), pp. 164–165; Kathleen Thelen, "How Institutions Evolve: Insights from Comparative Historical Analysis," in James Mahoney and Dietrich Rueschemeyer, eds., *Comparative Historical Analysis in the Social Sciences* (Cambridge: Cambridge University Press, 2003), pp. 208–240.

[2] Michael T. Hannan and John Freeman, *Organizational Ecology* (Cambridge, MA: Harvard University Press, 1991), pp. 67–68; Pfeffer and Salancik, *External Control of Organizations*, p. 82.

[3] Samuel P. Huntington, "Social and Institutional Dynamics of One-Party Systems," in Samuel P. Huntington and Clement H. Moore, eds., *Authoritarian Politics in Modern Society: The Dynamics of Established One-Party Systems* (New York: Basic Books, 1970); Ken Jowitt, "Inclusion," in *New World Disorder* (Berkeley: University of California Press, 1992).

the organization (as opposed to its ostensible goals) is in doubt."[4] This is precisely the dilemma posed by admitting technocrats and entrepreneurs into the CCP: they are committed to economic growth, but more orthodox leaders question their support of communism and loyalty to the CCP. Those who are more concerned with self-preservation than adaptation resist the arrival of former enemies into their midst. As will be shown, resistance by some party leaders to admitting capitalists into the party continued through the run-up to the 17th Party Congress in 2007.

But the concerns of defenders of party traditions about the potential threat posed by entrepreneurs are not totally self-interested. Samuel Huntington notes that the main threat to an authoritarian regime is the "diversification of the elite resulting from the rise of new groups controlling autonomous sources of economic power, that is, from the development of an independently wealthy business and industrial middle class."[5] The creation of autonomous sources of wealth weakens one of what Andrew Walder calls "the institutional pillars" of a communist system: state control over the economy, resulting in organized dependence; that is, the dependence of society on the state for economic security (such as jobs, housing, and food) as well as political protection.[6] As economic reform creates alternative paths toward career mobility and acquisition of wealth (through education and entrepreneurship), dependence on the state is reduced, and the power of the state and its ruling party is similarly diminished. Thus, the fears of party conservatives are not totally self-serving or illusory.

Despite the inherent risks and the controversies it engendered, the CCP embarked on a strategy of co-optation in order to facilitate its goal of economic modernization and to help reconcile the state with

---

[4] Patrick H. O'Neil, "Revolution from Within: Institutional Analysis, Transitions from Authoritarianism, and the Case of Hungary," *World Politics*, vol. 48, no. 4 (July 1996), pp. 579–603, quoted from p. 585.
[5] Huntington, "Social and Institutional Dynamics of One-Party Systems," p. 20.
[6] Andrew G. Walder, "The Decline of Communist Power: Elements of a Theory of Institutional Change," *Theory and Society*, vol. 23, no. 2 (April 1994), pp. 297–323; Andrew G. Walder, "The Quiet Revolution from Within: Economic Reform as a Source of Political Decline," in Andrew G. Walder, ed., *The Waning of the Communist State: Economic Origins of Political Decline in China and Hungary* (Berkeley: University of California Press, 1995). The other institutional pillar is the party's Leninist style of organization.

society after the vagaries of the late Maoist era. The co-optation of private entrepreneurs began as an informal practice in some localities, even though it was officially banned between 1989 and 2001.[7] Over time, however, the propriety of the ban came into question as the party increasingly relied on the private sector to produce high rates of growth, the party's main task in the post-Mao era. Even after the ban was lifted in 2001, it remained controversial among some in the party who felt it betrayed the party's traditions and its long-term interests, as we will see.

THE DEBATE OVER CO-OPTING ENTREPRENEURS IN CHINA

Beginning in the mid-1980s, entrepreneurs were co-opted into the party in large numbers. According to regular surveys of the private sector by the CCP's United Front Work Department, the ACFIC, and related organizations, 13.1 percent of private entrepreneurs were CCP members in 1993, 17.1 percent in 1995, 19.8 percent in 2000, 30.2 percent in 2002, and by 2006 the number had grown to 32.2 percent.[8] In contrast, less than 6 percent of the total population (and approximately 7.5 percent of the adult population) belong to the CCP. The much higher concentration of party members among private entrepreneurs shows the growing integration of wealth and power in China.

The presence of newly wealthy entrepreneurs in the party irritated some party veterans, who felt their contributions to the revolution were being betrayed by the party's new commitment to economic growth.

---

[7] Relations between local government and the private sector in terms of "adaptive informal institutions" are discussed in Kellee S. Tsai, *Capitalism without Democracy: The Private Sector in Contemporary China* (Ithaca, NY: Cornell University Press, 2007), esp. chapter 2.

[8] See *Zhongguo siying jingji nianjian, 1996* (China's Private Economy Yearbook, 1996) (Beijing: Zhongguo gongshang lianhe chubanshe, 1996), p. 162; *Zhongguo siying qiye fazhan baogao (1978–1998)* (Report on the Development of China's Private Enterprises, 1978–1998) (Beijing: Shehui kexue wenxian chubanshe, 1999), p. 164; *2002 nian Zhongguo siying qiye diaocha baogao* (2002 Report on China's Private Enterprises); *2006 nian Zhongguo diqici siying qiye chouyang diaocha shuju fenxi zonghe baogao* (Comprehensive Report on the Data Analysis of China's 2006 Seventh Survey of Private Enterprises), report available at http://www.chinapec.com.cn/websites/news/newscontent.asp?id=1922, accessed September 11, 2007. The survey data for 1993–2002 are available through the Universities Service Centre of The Chinese University of Hong Kong.

This is reminiscent of the frustration felt by revolutionary veterans in the early 1950s, when the CCP switched from waging war to running the government and had to recruit new people with new kinds of skills to perform new tasks. Then as now, those who had committed many years of loyal service to the party were displeased with the sudden emphasis on expertise and the reliance on new personnel who had not demonstrated their commitment to the party's ultimate goals. The recruitment of entrepreneurs into the party in the 1980s was also a very potent symbol of the adoption of market-oriented policies and the decline of communist ideology in post-Mao China.

Fearing that bourgeois influences were spreading into the party, the CCP banned the new recruitment of private entrepreneurs into the party in August 1989, following the crackdown on demonstrators in Tiananmen Square and elsewhere around the country; entrepreneurs already in the party could no longer hold official positions.[9] Party leaders were angered by the support given to student demonstrators by entrepreneurs, most prominently Wan Runnan of Beijing's Stone Group, one of the pioneers in China's computer and information technology field.[10] Urban *getihu* formed "flying tiger brigades" of scooters and motorcycles, shuttling information and supplies to the demonstrators. In September 1995, the Central Organization Department repeated that the party would not admit private entrepreneurs "because they are capitalists bent on exploiting the labor force."[11] Yu Yunyao, deputy director of the CCP's Central Organization Department, said even debating the advantages and disadvantages of recruiting entrepreneurs was irresponsible.[12] In April 1999, he reiterated that local departments must adhere to the rule that private entrepreneurs are not allowed to join the party, even though some local officials were in favor of lifting or at least modifying the ban.[13]

---

[9] This was first reported in *South China Morning Post*, August 29, 1989, in Foreign Broadcast Information Service (hereafter FBIS), August 29, 1989, and later confirmed in *Zhenli de zhuiqiu*, November 11, 1994, in FBIS, January 12, 1995.

[10] Scott Kennedy, "The Stone Group: State Client or Market Pathbreaker?" *China Quarterly*, no. 152 (December 1997), pp. 746–777.

[11] Press digest of the Central Organization Department, as reported in *China News Digest*, September 17, 1995.

[12] Zhongguo xinwenshe, September 6, 1995, in FBIS, September 8, 1995, p. 16.

[13] See Yu's talk on party building while on an inspection tour of Fujian in *Fujian dangjian* (Party Construction in Fujian), April 1999, pp. 8–10.

Even when the ban was in place, however, local party committees found ways to circumvent it. Some local party committees classified private enterprises as collective or joint stock enterprises, thereby allowing them to recruit their leaders while remaining in technical compliance with the central ban.[14] The head of the organization department in an unspecified city in Shandong defended the practice of recruiting entrepreneurs, who have proven their innovativeness, administrative skills, and ability to produce wealth, which he claimed are the main criteria for party membership. "While maintaining party member standards, active recruitment into the party of outstanding people from among the owners of private enterprises can highlight the timeliness of the socialist market economy, and can make full use of the role of party members as vanguards and models in leading the masses along the path of common prosperity." Shenzhen even created special party branches for entrepreneurs who joined the party.[15] But co-optation was also done in violation of the ban: most of the co-opted entrepreneurs in the 1999 survey, and those in the 2005 survey who joined before the ban was lifted, owned firms that were formally registered as private, not shareholding or collective enterprises. These actions are consistent with the overall emphasis on economic modernization: rather than be bound by ideological propriety, local party committees sought to maintain their influence by co-opting successful entrepreneurs into the party.

Criticism of this trend was especially prominent in the journals representing the party's orthodox positions, such as *Zhenli de zhuiqiu* (The Pursuit of Truth) and *Zhongliu* (Mainstream). These articles argued that the presence of wealthy people in the CCP contradicted the allegedly proletarian nature of the party and created confusion

---

[14] Interviews in Zhejiang, summer 1997. See also Susan H. Whiting, *Power and Wealth in Rural China: The Political Economy of Institutional Change* (Cambridge: Cambridge University Press, 2001), p. 165. Classifying private enterprises as collectives (known as "red hat" enterprises) was not done solely, or even primarily, to allow party recruitment; rather it was done for the mutual benefit of entrepreneurs and local officials. See the discussion in chapter 2 and Kristen Parris, "The Rise of Private Business Interests," in Merle Goldman and Roderick MacFarquhar, eds., *The Paradox of China's Post-Mao Reforms* (Cambridge, MA: Harvard University Press, 1999).

[15] Quoted in *Zhenli de zhuiqiu*, November 11, 1994, in FBIS, January 12, 1995, pp. 24–25; the article went on to criticize this viewpoint. The information about Shenzhen is in Zhongguo xinwenshe, June 8, 1994, in FBIS, June 9, 1994, p. 51.

regarding the party's identity and policies.[16] *Zhongliu* reported that up to half of new party members in the towns and rural districts of coastal China were private entrepreneurs and that many party cells were headed by entrepreneurs. It warned that, "Private businessmen cannot accept the party's principles and policies. ... They only want to join the party to influence the adoption and implementation of local policies. They hope to enroll more private businessmen into the party to strengthen their own role."[17]

Leftists in the party decried the dangers inherent in the rise of the private sector while paying lip service to the correctness of the policy itself. One widely circulated report known as the "10,000 character statement" (*wanyan shu*) received a good deal of media attention in 1996, in part because of suspicions that it was written to reflect Deng Liqun's thinking on the matter. Deng Liqun, a former secretary to Liu Shaoqi, was a leading voice of Leninist orthodoxy and one of the few remaining conservative party elders. As such, his views carried more weight than the small number of his supporters would otherwise warrant. The report noted the rapid rise in the private sector and in return the decline of the state sector, which accelerated in the 1990s. The increase in private wealth led to increases in corruption, decadent lifestyles, and a fascination with all things foreign, especially symbols of the United States, leading the author of the report to conclude that such people "are likely to betray the interests of the motherland and directly undermine China's security." Private entrepreneurs were alleged to have broader political ambitions that posed a threat to the party. Already they had established newspapers and business associations to assert their viewpoints. But the real threat to the party, according to this report, came from the budding alliance between entrepreneurs and "bourgeois liberals." Entrepreneurs were allegedly subsidizing the research and publications of intellectuals (this accusation was presumably based on the actions of Wan Runnan, head of the Stone Group, who fled China in 1989 because of his outspoken support of the Tiananmen demonstrations and who funded the Stone

---

[16] See, for instance, "Lun dangyuan daitou zhifu yu dailing qunzhong gongtong zhifu" (On Party Members Taking the Lead in Getting Rich and Leading the Masses to Common Prosperity) *Zhenli de zhuiqiu* (July 1998), pp. 13–20; "Has a New Capitalist Class Been Formed in Our Country at Present?" *Zhenli de zhuiqiu* (May 2001), FBIS, July 3, 2001.

[17] Jasper Becker, "Capitalists Infiltrating Party, Article Warns," *South China Morning Post*, July 14, 2000.

Social Development Institute, a short-lived public policy think tank that advocated ambitious political reforms).[18] Although most capitalists avoided debates over political reforms, some supported public policy research by scholars and critical intellectuals. For example, in the late 1990s, private businessmen provided the financing for two major collections of articles favoring more ambitious political reforms, *Political China: Facing the Era of Choosing a New Structure* and *Liberation Literature, 1978–1998*.[19] This alliance between the critical and noncritical realms of civil society would then set the stage for challenging the CCP's continued rule in China.[20] "Once the conditions are mature, they will 'completely destroy' the communist party with the backing of the international bourgeoisie and openly use bourgeois dictatorship to replace proletarian dictatorship." In short, class struggle was alive and well, despite the party's decision in 1978 to abandon it as the focus of the party's work for the sake of economic development: "If our party cannot correctly understand and handle classes and class struggle, we may not be able to hold on to state power."[21]

Even though the report's identification of the negative and largely unintended consequences of economic reform was largely accurate, its interpretation of the implications of those trends was highly debatable. It put a more sinister spin on efforts by foreign countries who hoped to use increased trade and privatization to bring about a civil society, the rule of law, and eventually a change of regime. Cao Siyuan, one of China's leading liberal economists and advocates of political reform, denounced the report's message and conclusions in an article originally published in an internally circulated party journal but later banned from being reprinted.[22] He accused them of rejecting

---

[18] Kennedy, "Stone Group," pp. 761–762.

[19] See Merle Goldman, *From Comrade to Citizen: The Struggle for Political Rights in China* (Cambridge, MA: Harvard University Press, 2005), pp. 141–152.

[20] On the distinction between the critical and noncritical realms of civil society, see Yanqi Tong, "State, Society, and Political Change in China and Hungary," *Comparative Politics*, vol. 26, no. 3 (April 1994), pp. 333–353. Similar distinctions are made in Michael W. Foley and Bob Edwards, "The Paradox of Civil Society," *Journal of Democracy*, vol. 7, no. 3 (July 1996), pp. 38–52, and Gordon White, Jude Howell, and Shang Xiaoyuan, *In Search of Civil Society: Market Reform and Social Change in Contemporary China* (Oxford: Oxford University Press, 1996).

[21] *Yazhou zhoukan* (January 14, 1996), pp. 22–28, in *Summary of World Broadcasts* (September 16, 1996), pp. S1/1–9.

[22] His article was later published in the Hong Kong newspaper *Ming Pao*, August 16, 1996; a translation is available in *Summary of World Broadcasts* (September 3, 1996).

the entirety of the post-Mao policies of reform and opening and risking another Cultural Revolution by calling for the renewed emphasis on class struggle. Others turned the leftists' argument around and warned of the political dangers of *not* recruiting them into the party: as the number of private entrepreneurs grew, they were developing economic force and social influence and could turn into a dissident force if the party did not ally with them.[23] Although all sides in the debate acknowledged the rise of private entrepreneurs, there was sharp disagreement on the implications for the party and what it should do in response.[24]

The rationale for banning the new recruitment of private entrepreneurs into the CCP was straightforward and in large part understandable. Private entrepreneurs had been officially labeled (and during the Maoist years were persecuted) as exploiters of the working class, not members of it. Because the CCP presented itself as the vanguard of the working class and the champion of its interests, allowing exploiters of labor to join the party would be inconsistent with the party's original mission and detrimental to its integrity. This reasoning was sound ideologically but increasingly problematic politically. As the party shifted its work from class struggle to economic modernization, it came to rely more and more heavily on the private sector to achieve its economic goals. The private sector has been the primary source of economic growth, new jobs, new investment, and technological innovation throughout the reform era. As a result, the party's attitude toward the private sector has evolved from initial tight restrictions in the 1980s, to permitting its growth (especially after Deng's "southern tour" of 1992), and eventually promoting it by the end of the 1990s (as detailed in chapter 2). No longer seen as pariahs in China's still nominally communist system, private entrepreneurs had become partners in the party's efforts to modernize the economy and improve living standards. Advocates of co-opting entrepreneurs into

[23] Lu Ruifeng et al., "Shenzhen shi siying qiye dang de jianshe wenti yu duice" (Problems and Counter-measures in Party Building in Shenzhen's Private Enterprises), *Tequ lilun yu shixian* (December 1995), pp. 35–39.

[24] The debate between proponents and opponents of economic reform, particularly with regard to the expansion of the private sector, is described in Ma Licheng and Ling Zhijun, *Jiao feng: Dangdai Zhongguo sanci sixiang jiefang shilu* (Crossed Swords: A True Record of Three Rounds of Ideological Liberation in Contemporary China) (Beijing: Jinri Zhongguo chubanshe, 1998). The four *wanyan shu* are summarized in chapters 11–14, and responses by other scholars are presented in chapter 15.

the party argued that they were succeeding by dint of their own expertise and by following the party's policies of reform and opening and
should not be "punished" for their success by being excluded from the
party.

Despite this evolving policy climate, the ban on recruiting entrepreneurs into the CCP remained in place. Co-opting entrepreneurs and
other new social strata into the party was not only designed to benefit
the party by tapping new sources of support but was also intended
to preempt a potential source of opposition. Jiang Zemin reportedly
acknowledged in January 2001 that the party was considering lifting
the ban on entrepreneurs in order to prevent them from aligning themselves with the pro-democracy political activists.[25] A handbook of the
CCP's Central Organization Department said bluntly, "We cannot
afford to lose this camp."[26] Along these same lines, Wang Changjiang
of the Central Party School argued that if the party did not embrace
the vast majority of the Chinese people, they would seek to organize
themselves outside the political system. Inclusion was intended, at least
in part, to prevent organized opposition to the party and to maintain
political stability and party leadership. As noted, this is precisely one of
the motivations behind co-optation: to preempt a potential challenge
or threat outside the organization. The opposition to entrepreneurs
in the party also demonstrated part of the logic of co-optation: those
who want to uphold the original goals of the organization resist the
inclusion of these potential enemies into the organization.

Party leaders struggled to find an ideological basis for allowing entrepreneurs into the party, however. The campaign to promote the
"Three Represents" theory of the party's role became a vehicle to legitimize the inclusion of entrepreneurs in China's political system, and
into the party in particular. The slogan was nearly overlooked when it
was first outlined by Jiang Zemin in February 2000 during an inspection tour of coastal cities, but he then described it in more detail in May
2000 at the Central Party School, and in July 2001 he unveiled it publicly in his speech marking the 80th anniversary of the founding of the
CCP.[27] Instead of simply representing the interests of China's workers

---

[25] Kyodo News International, January 15, 2001.

[26] Cited in Bruce Gilley, *China's Democratic Future: How It Will Happen and Where
It Will Lead* (New York: Columbia University Press, 2004), p. 66.

[27] For Jiang's original statements on the topic, see Xinhua, February 25, 2000, in FBIS,
February 29, 2000, and Xinhua, May 15, 2000, in FBIS, May 16, 2000; his July 2001

and farmers, this new theory asserted that the party should represent the developmental needs of the advanced social productive forces,
the promotion of advanced culture, and the fundamental interests of
the greatest majority of the people. This is a very expansive definition of the party's role, much wider than simply representing China's
proletariat. It was reminiscent of Nikita Khrushchev's announcement
in 1961 that the Soviet Union had become an "all people's party,"
not simply a dictatorship of the proletariat. Not surprisingly, Jiang's
"Three Represents" was harshly criticized by party conservatives for
betraying the party's traditions and promoting the interests of capital
at the expense of labor. This in fact has been the leitmotif of the entire
post-Mao reform effort but it had not been enshrined in party doctrine
so explicitly before. The "Three Represents" theory thereafter became
the focus of intense efforts by party theorists and the media to define
a new role for the party.

After years of intense debate, Jiang Zemin publicly recommended
lifting the ban on entrepreneurs in his July 1, 2001, speech on the occa-
sion of the 80th anniversary of the founding of the CCP. In review-
ing the consequences of the reform and opening policies, he noted
that private entrepreneurs, freelance professionals, scientific and technical personnel employed by Chinese and foreign firms, and other
new social groups had emerged. "Most of these people in the new
social strata have contributed to the development of productive forces
and . . . are working for building socialism with Chinese characteristics." While claiming that the workers, farmers, intellectuals, service-
men, and cadres would remain the "basic components and backbone
of the party," Jiang claimed the party also needed "to accept those
outstanding elements from other sectors of the society."[28]

The party's orthodox leftists immediately rebuked the proposal in a
series of open letters. They not only challenged the ideological propriety of admitting capitalists into a communist party but also attacked

Party Day speech is in Xinhua, July 1, 2001, in FBIS, July 1, 2001. For an excellent
introduction to the theory, and the controversy it triggered, see Susan V. Lawrence,
"Three Cheers for the Party," *Far Eastern Economic Review* (October 26, 2000).

[28] Jiang's speech was carried by Xinhua, July 1, 2001, in FBIS, July 1, 2001. See also
John Pomfret, "China Allows Its Capitalists to Join Party: Communists Recognize
Rise of Private Business," *Washington Post*, July 2, 2001; Craig S. Smith, "China's
Leader Urges Opening Communist Party to Capitalists," *New York Times*, July 2,
2001.

the personal leadership style of Jiang Zemin. They accused him of violating party discipline by making such a significant recommendation without getting formal approval from the party's Central Committee or Politburo. They even compared him to Mikhail Gorbachev and Lee Teng-hui, leaders who are widely criticized in China for betraying their parties' interests.[29] Jiang Zemin responded to these attacks by ordering *Zhenli de zhuiqiu* to cease publication and putting *Zhongliu* under the stricter editorial control of *Guangming Daily*, the party's paper targeted toward intellectuals.

Despite continued opposition from leftists, the CCP reportedly planned to admit 200,000 entrepreneurs as new party members before the 16th Party Congress scheduled for fall 2002. Over 100,000 private entrepreneurs reportedly applied to join the party in the weeks immediately after Jiang's speech, and the party's Central Organization Department ordered localities to immediately implement Jiang's recommendation.[30] Jiang also reportedly directed the CCP to designate 10 provinces as experimental sites for admitting entrepreneurs into the party. As will be shown, however, these initial expectations of a tremendous upsurge in co-opted entrepreneurs were not realized.

To symbolize their official integration into China's political elite, private entrepreneurs were for the first time among the delegates to the 16th Party Congress in November 2002, although none were selected to the Central Committee, whose members comprise the top 200 or so party leaders. Several businessmen were elected to the Central Committee, but they were heads of SOEs or reformed SOEs, not private enterprises. The most well known of this group was Zhang Ruimin, the chairman of the board and CEO of the Hai'er Group, China's leading manufacturer of household appliances, and one of the first Chinese brands to make a mark in foreign markets (many of the minifridges commonly found in college dorms are made by Hai'er). He was not strictly speaking a private entrepreneur but the director of a conglomerate that was largely state owned, with some units at least nominally privately owned. Because alternate members of the Central Committee are listed in the order of the number of votes they received, we know that Zhang ranked 144th on the list of 158 alternate

---

[29] A text of the letter identified with Deng Liqun was translated by FBIS, August 2, 2001.
[30] *Ming Pao*, July 23, 2001 (Internet version), in FBIS, July 24, 2001.

members of the Central Committee. At the 17th Party Congress in 2007, he was reelected and ranked 156th of 167 members. The first private entrepreneur to even be nominated as a candidate for the alternate Central Committee was Zhou Haijiang, president of the Hodo Group in Jiangsu, but in the end he was not elected. This was generally interpreted as a signal that delegates to the Party Congress were still not ready to embrace the private sector, despite the supportive policy changes in recent years.

Despite the shift in official policy, resistance to integrating private entrepreneurs into the party and the political system in general continued to exist. In May 2007, Liu Fuyuan, a former director of the Macroeconomic Research Academy of the National Development and Reform Commission, called on the CCP to expel all members who did not truly believe in Marxism. In a paper entitled "Strategic Choices for the Communist Party of China," Liu criticized the decline of Marxism as a guide to party policy and a requirement for party membership. Opening the party to all segments of the population, as mandated by the "Three Represents" policy, threatened the future of the party as well as the country.[31] Although such viewpoints are rarely expressed publicly anymore, they clearly continue to fester just below the surface.

THE CCP'S STRATEGY FOR RECRUITING PRIVATE ENTREPRENEURS

Although recruiting entrepreneurs was a contentious issue among central leaders, it has proven to be advantageous for both local officials and entrepreneurs. For officials, it allows them to co-opt potential opposition, to establish links with the private sector and promote growth, and to create personal ties to wealthy and successful entrepreneurs. Local party committees may seek a connection with local economic elites to share in the fruits of their success and identify themselves with the people who are bringing prosperity to the local community. Because achieving high rates of economic growth is an essential criterion for evaluating local officials, they have an obvious incentive to cooperate with private entrepreneurs, who produce the

[31] Josephine Ma, "Party Told to Winnow Out Non-Marxist Members," *South China Morning Post*, May 5, 2007.

most growth, jobs, and tax revenue. Entrepreneurs are willing to provide capital to build roads, schools, and hospitals and provide jobs,
things local party committees are often unable to do because the center provides less capital for local investment. Local entrepreneurs have
the resources the local party needs. Relatedly, party committees may
co-opt local economic elites in order to have some influence over their
community investments and to share in the public acclaim they generated (see chapter 7). On a more personal level, as more and more party
officials are themselves getting directly involved in business operations,
they are building close ties with private entrepreneurs and support their
admission into the party.

The expectation that there would be a surge of new red capitalists following Jiang Zemin's speech on July 1, 2001 did not seem
to happen. Despite pilot programs implemented by the Organization
Department in a number of cities, little new recruitment reportedly
occurred. According to the Central Organization Department, only
894 entrepreneurs joined the party out of a total of 2.42 million new
members in 2004.[32] One reason for this apparent lack of new recruitment was that many local cadres did not support the new policy. They
dragged their feet in carrying it out, found reasons that disqualified
entrepreneurs from joining the party, or accepted applications from
entrepreneurs but failed to act on them. In Hebei's county H, the head
of the local industrial and commercial bureau complained that many
entrepreneurs were not enthusiastic about joining the party.[33] Worse,
they often demanded favorable policies, especially concerning taxes,
and had other types of demands for the government to consider as well,
but made few contributions in return. The bureau head described them
as having a "harmful influence." In several other sites included in my
survey, however, local cadres blamed the lack of guidance from higher-
level party committees for the difficulties in recruiting entrepreneurs.
Although some said higher-level committees placed a lot of importance
on this issue, others said they received no guidance despite requests for
clear directions on the standards of recruitment in the wake of the 16th
Party Congress in 2002.

---

[32] Xinhua, May 23, 2005.
[33] The eight sites of the survey are identified only by the province and a letter in order
to protect their identities.

The party center was slow to provide clear signals on what crite-ria should be used in deciding which entrepreneurs to admit into the party. According to Wang Changjiang of the Central Party School, "When the party expands its social foundation to various social strata and groups, it doesn't mean that all the people in these strata and groups can join the party.... What we want to absorb are the out-standing elements of these strata and groups. Possessing the political consciousness of the working class and willingness to fight for the party's program constitutes the common characteristics of these out-standing elements and also the qualifications they must meet in order to join the party."[34] In a journal for party cadres, he argued that "since the elements [i.e., party members] influence the nature of the party to some extent, we cannot just throw open the doors of the party and welcome everyone.... *Allowing entrepreneurs into the party is not the same as saying that any entrepreneur can join the party.*"[35] Other party media repeated this warning. According to *People's Daily*, "We allow the worthy people in the new social strata to join the party. However, this does not mean that we keep our doors wide open in an unprincipled manner. Still less should we drag into the party all those who do not meet our requirements for party membership."[36] *Qiushi* advised against "using erroneous methods to measure the new criteria for party membership, such as admission based on economic strength, on the amount of donation to society, and on personal reputation."[37] These more objective criteria – as opposed to the more abstract con-siderations of supporting the party's program and "standing the test of time" – were undoubtedly the ones used by many local committees in recruiting from the new social strata. But the alternative standards suggested by these authoritative statements – not too strict, not too lax – were difficult to translate into action.

Some local cadres complained that the standards of admission were too high. In Hunan's county C, officials complained that the high stan-dards prevented the party from recruiting entrepreneurs, even though many wanted to join. Only 11 of 307 red capitalists in this county

---

[34] *Liaowang*, August 13, 2001, in FBIS, August 22, 2001.
[35] *Zhongguo dangzheng ganbu luntan* (Beijing), January 6, 2002, in FBIS, Febru-ary 4, 2002; emphasis added.
[36] *Renmin ribao*, September 17, 2001, in FBIS, September 17, 2001.
[37] *Qiushi*, November 16, 2001, in FBIS, November 29, 2001.

were co-opted between 2001 and 2004; most of the rest had joined the party before the conversion of their firms from SOEs into private enterprises. In the other Hunan site, city J, local officials said many private entrepreneurs had applied for party membership but few had been approved because the process was "very strict and had not been opened up." Only two or three had joined since the 16th Party Congress. The officials of city J favored simplified and shortened procedures, while still maintaining high standards, to accommodate the entrepreneurs' wish for a quick decision. The head of the Organization Department in Hebei's county S said that no entrepreneurs joined after the 16th Party Congress "because the investigations were extremely strict." These reports show that the controversy surrounding admitting entrepreneurs into the party remains. As a head of the local industrial and commercial bureau in Zhejiang noted, even after two years of investigation and research after the 16th Party Congress in 2002, there was still no clear resolution (*mingque de shuofa*) on this issue.

In some individual cases, the CCP has decided that it is best to have some prominent entrepreneurs outside the party. For example, Yin Mingshan is one of the wealthiest and most politically influential of China's new private entrepreneurs. He was one of China's first billionaires, the first entrepreneur to be appointed to a provincial-level leadership position in the Chinese People's Political Consultative Conference (in Chongqing), and regularly consulted with leaders in Beijing. But his applications to join the party were repeatedly rejected. "I've applied, but the Communist Party said, you stay on the outside and work for us there," he said in an interview. "That way you can make a bigger difference."[38] In Shandong, the head of a county Self-Employed Laborers Association was also told that he should not formally join the CCP in order to convey a degree of independence, even though he was allowed to attend party meetings.

Another reason for the lack of new recruitment was that the entrepreneurs themselves might have lost interest in joining the party.[39]

---

[38] Peter Harmsen, "Capitalism Is on the Rise in China – but Not in the CCP," Agence France-Presse, June 18, 2005, reprinted in *Taipei Times*, June 18, 2005.

[39] Henry Chu, "Chinese Capitalists Cool to Party Invite," *Los Angeles Times*, August 3, 2002; Allen T. Cheng, "The Reformer Who Came in from the Cold," *South China Morning Post*, February 27, 2004.

As the party's commitment to the private sector grew and became more credible (as described in chapter 2), the benefits of party membership became less obvious. Most local officials interviewed during the course of the implementation of the survey repeatedly claimed that most entrepreneurs were only concerned with their economic interests and were not interested in joining the party.

Growing Numbers of Red Capitalists

Regardless of the controversy surrounding the issue, the number of red capitalists continued to grow, as noted, from 15 percent in 1988 to 35 percent in 2004. In part, the growth of both the private sector and the number of red capitalists resulted from the privatization of formerly state-owned enterprises. Approximately 25 percent of private enterprises were originally state owned. As these SOEs are converted into private enterprises, their former managers (most of whom were party members) become owners of private firms, instantly increasing the number of red capitalists.[40]

Because my surveys targeted relatively large-scale enterprises, a larger percentage of respondents were red capitalists than is the case for private entrepreneurs in general. Exactly half of the respondents in the 2005 survey were party members, up from almost 40 percent in the 1999 survey. Although it may seem implausible that exactly half of the respondents were party members, there was tremendous variation among the eight counties, ranging from 28 percent to 74 percent (in the 1999 survey, the range was similar: 22 percent to 78 percent). The percentage of entrepreneurs who were already party members before they went into business (a group I refer to as *xiahai* entrepreneurs) increased sharply from 25 percent to 34.2 percent. This is consistent with the point that the expanding number of red capitalists is mostly

---

[40] Respondents in my two surveys were not asked if they previously worked as an SOE manager. According to a 2002 survey of the private sector sponsored by the All-China Federation of Industry and Commerce, the Chinese Academy of Social Sciences, and other groups, 25.7 percent of respondents in private firms were former managers of SOEs, and the heads of 50.7 percent of them were party members. The report on this survey attributed most of the growth in red capitalists to the privatization of SOEs. See http://www.acfic.org.cn/acfic/12_xw/xxzk/708_8.htm, and Xinhua, November 13, 2003.

the result of the privatization of SOEs. The percentage of those who were co-opted into the party after going into business also increased but not as dramatically: from 13.1 percent in 1999 to 15.7 percent in 2005, an approximately 20 percent increase.[41] A more detailed analysis of patterns of recruitment will be presented later in this chapter.

Among the six counties in Zhejiang, Shandong, and Hebei, there is a negative relationship between the level of development and the percentage of red capitalists, with the two poorest counties having the highest proportions of red capitalists. This suggests that the need to co-opt entrepreneurs is highest where the level of development is lowest; conversely, where prosperity is already high, the need to co-opt entrepreneurs is reduced. Also, where the private sector is large, the pool of potential recruits is larger, allowing the party to be more selective. The two counties in Hunan act as a control group: in these areas, the level of development is low, the size of the private sector is small, the proportion of red capitalists is also low, and unlike in most other counties, the entrepreneurs who do not want to join the party substantially outnumber those who do. If the CCP's strategy of embracing the private sector remains in place, a greater proportion of private entrepreneurs will become red capitalists as the private sector begins to grow in Hunan, both through the conversion of SOEs and collective enterprises into private firms and the selective co-optation of other entrepreneurs into the party.

Although some locales faced difficulties recruiting entrepreneurs into the party, other areas were much more successful. Of the co-opted entrepreneurs, 31.5 percent joined between 2002 and 2004, the years after the ban on entrepreneurs joining the party was lifted.[42]

---

[41] This growth is consistent with Kellee Tsai's 2002 survey, in which 14.3 percent of her respondents were co-opted into the party, which is right between my 1999 and 2005 figures. See Tsai, *Capitalism without Democracy*, p. 101.

[42] In contrast, a 2002 survey of 3,635 private firms sponsored by the ACFIC found a much lower rate of recruitment: 30 percent were party members, but only 0.5 percent had joined after Jiang's July 1, 2001, speech. Even though the survey was conducted midyear in April–July 2002, and therefore only included a short period after Jiang's speech, the low percentage of newly recruited red capitalists is remarkable and not consistent with my survey conducted several years later. See chinanews.com.cn, February 19, 2003, cited in Minxin Pei, *China's Trapped Transition: The Limits of Developmental Autocracy* (Cambridge, MA: Harvard University Press, 2006), pp. 93–94.

In most of the counties, this growth was steady. In only one of the survey sites was there a sudden and sharp increase. In Zhejiang's district H (at the time of the 1999 survey it was a county-level city but by 2005 had become an urban district), half of the co-opted entrepreneurs there joined the party between 2002 and 2004. But this is also the site with the smallest percentage of co-opted entrepreneurs: only 6.1 percent, compared with 46.3 percent *xiahai* entrepreneurs. With the private sector accounting for 92 percent of employees and 60 percent of GDP (according to local officials), it was clearly overdue to start recruiting private entrepreneurs into the party. The head of the party's Organization Department said that about one-third of private firms in his district were run by party members, and most of these were the result of the reform of SOEs. According to him, entrepreneurs who open their own firms "seldom become party members and are not interested in becoming party members." He was only partially right: of the eight sites in the survey, this one had the smallest percentage of co-opted entrepreneurs, but half had joined after the 16th Party Congress and over half of the non-CCP entrepreneurs in the sample wanted to join the party. Local officials in most other survey sites reported that private entrepreneurs showed an increased interest in joining the party even though few of them had been admitted because of stringent standards.

Of the nonparty members in the entire survey, 50.3 percent reported they were interested in joining the party, and of them 30.9 percent had applied to join. To put it differently, 75 percent of the entrepreneurs in this survey, who represent the economic elites of their communities, were either in the party or wanted to be (compared with 66.7 percent in the 1999 survey). That indicates a strong and positive response consistent with the intended results of the CCP's new recruitment strategy but inconsistent with anecdotal reports of a much more limited impact. Remembering that the survey targeted relatively large-scale enterprises, the strong response may also indicate part of the party's strategy: it is more open to wealthy entrepreneurs who own large firms than smaller enterprises, which generate fewer jobs and tax revenue. More importantly, the response is inconsistent with efforts by Hu Jintao and Wen Jiabao to promote a more populist image for themselves and the CCP, in contrast with the elitist orientation of the party under Jiang Zemin. The remarkably precise and low number of private entrepreneurs who reportedly joined the party in 2004 – 894 – may simply have reflected the new rhetoric rather than the current reality: under Hu and Wen, the CCP wanted to downplay the idea that it was beholden to private economic interests.

The growth in recruitment of entrepreneurs into the party, legitimated and even mandated by the center, is reflected in changing attitudes among survey respondents. As seen in table 3.1, there was a dramatic drop in the percentage of local officials who believed entrepreneurs should not join the CCP, from 22.4 percent in 1999 to only 9 percent in 2005. Moreover, there was a notable difference between county-level cadres on the one hand, and township and village cadres on the other: in both surveys, it was the latter group that was most in favor of recruiting entrepreneurs. In part, this may be because of the closer proximity of these officials to the entrepreneurs and therefore their familiarity with them. But it is also because township and village officials were most likely to believe that private entrepreneurs could provide the kinds of skills the party currently needed. In both surveys, over 70 percent of them believed the CCP needed the entrepreneurs' skills, compared with less than 50 percent of county-level officials, who are physically more removed from the entrepreneurs and responsible for a wider range of responsibilities than township and village officials.

Entrepreneurs have somewhat different responses on the question of the party's relationship with the private sector. Among all groups of entrepreneurs, there is little difference over time in the percentage who believe entrepreneurs should not join the party. The group most likely to support entrepreneurs joining the party are – not surprisingly – the ones who are not yet in the party but would like to join. The group least likely to be supportive are those who do not want to join the party. However, on the related question of whether they provide the skills the CCP needs, there is a slight decline over time in the percentage of entrepreneurs of all types who agree. But even with these declines, all groups of entrepreneurs are more likely to believe the party needs their skills than do local party and government officials.

Assessing the CCP's Strategy for Co-optation

To understand the CCP's strategy for co-opting entrepreneurs, we need to consider both *where* the CCP recruited entrepreneurs and which specific entrepreneurs it sought to recruit. Given its primary goal of

TABLE 3.1. *Changing Attitudes toward Entrepreneurs Joining the CCP*

	1999	2005
Private entrepreneurs should not be allowed to join the CCP (percentage who agree):		
Cadres	22.4	9.0
County	27.4	10.0
Township/village	15.3	7.6
Entrepreneurs	12.0	11.0
Xiahai entrepreneurs	8.7	11.3
Co-opted entrepreneurs	10.9	9.8
Want to join CCP	7.9	9.0
Do not want to join CCP	17.4	13.4
Private entrepreneurs have the skills the CCP currently needs (percentage who agree):		
Cadres	58.2	59.9
County	49.3	45.2
Township/village	72.3	70.7
Entrepreneurs	87.4	83.8
Xiahai entrepreneurs	89.4	84.0
Co-opted entrepreneurs	87.5	87.4
Want to join CCP	88.6	85.9
Do not want to join CCP	84.6	79.0
Party members frequently have advantages in business (percentage who agree):		
Cadres	44.4	48.4
County	46.5	48.8
Township/village	41.7	49.9
Entrepreneurs	43.5	49.6
Xiahai entrepreneurs	37.3	57.1
Co-opted entrepreneurs	51.5	56.6
Want to join CCP	59.0	58.2
Do not want to join CCP	32.9	26.7

promoting economic growth, we would expect that the CCP would focus on the areas where the economy is growing most rapidly, the private sector is largest,[43] and the party's presence in the private sector

---

[43] In the 2005 survey, the size of the private sector in 2003 and the growth of the private sector between 2000 and 2003 (the only years for which I have data for these eight counties) is highly but negatively correlated: −.84. For this reason, including both in the statistical analysis makes them both insignificant. In the analysis here, I use the size of the private sector.

is relatively weak. Within those areas, it would target the owners of large-scale enterprises. These large firms are particularly important to the local economy because they contribute more tax revenue to local coffers; they are also most suitable for party-building efforts because they employ more workers. As shown in table 3.2, the survey data support these expectations. (NB: in this analysis, *xiahai* entrepreneurs are excluded because I am interested in which private entrepreneurs the party recruited, and by definition *xiahai* entrepreneurs were already in the CCP before opening their private enterprises.)

First of all, co-opted entrepreneurs were more likely to live in communities with fast-growing economies and a large private sector. The coefficients for *per capita GDP* and *per capita GDP growth* indicate that the level of development and the rate of growth have opposite effects on where the party recruits entrepreneurs. The statistically significant and negative coefficient for level of development indicates that being in a prosperous county makes it slightly less likely that an entrepreneur will be recruited into the party. The two counties in Zhejiang, both prosperous, had below average percentages of co-opted entrepreneurs, whereas the two poorest (Shandong's city Q and Hebei's county S) were above average. In contrast, the *rate* of growth had a positive and significant impact on the probability of recruitment: entrepreneurs were more likely to be recruited in counties with relatively rapid economic growth (relative to other counties in the sample) between 1999 and 2003. In addition, living in a county with a large private sector (measured by the share of *nonstate firms in the county*) relative to SOEs and collective enterprises also made it more likely that private entrepreneurs would be co-opted.

The CCP also targeted areas with low proportions of party members working in the private sector. This is shown by the negative and statistically significant coefficient for *CCP in private sector in county (percent)*.[44] The negative coefficient indicates that co-opted entrepreneurs were more likely to be in counties where the number of party members among all the people working in the private sector was relatively low. In counties that already had large proportions of party members in the

---

[44] Percentages for the size of the private sector, CCP members in the county, and CCP members in the private sector in that county are based on aggregate data provided by local organization departments, not the survey data. Unfortunately, I do not have comparable data for all eight counties in the 1999 survey.

TABLE 3.2. *Determinants of Party Recruitment among Private Entrepreneurs in China (probit regression coefficients, with robust standard errors in parentheses)*

	1999	2005
Contextual Factors		
Level of development	−.059	−.093***
(per capita GDP, 1,000 yuan)	(.040)	(.019)
Rate of growth (previous five years)	−.003	.012**
	(.002)	(.004)
Size of private sector	−	1.846***
(nonstate firms in county [percent])		(.400)
CCP in private sector in county (percent)	−	−.073**
		(.028)
CCP members in county population (percent)	−	.222*
		(.101)
Firm Characteristics		
Sales revenue (log)	.090	.152***
	(.064)	(.039)
Individual Characteristics		
Age (years)	−.004	−.022*
	(.015)	(.010)
Gender	.048	.389*
	(.356)	(.162)
Level of education	.378***	.381***
	(.109)	(.087)
Getihu background	−.126*	.002
	(.059)	(.134)
Years in business	.068*	.052***
	(.027)	(.018)
Years in county	.030**	.016**
	(.011)	(.007)
CYL member	.773**	.491**
	(.250)	(.155)
Constant	−3.192**	−4.066***
	(1.032)	(.857)
N	293	654
Chi²	44.99***	113.70***
Pseudo R^2	.249	.192

*$p < .05$; **$p < .01$; ***$p < .001$.

private sector, local officials presumably had less need to co-opt more entrepreneurs.

The impact of *CCP members in the county* is positive and statistically significant for the 2005 data. This means that entrepreneurs are less likely to be co-opted in counties where a relatively small percentage of the population belong to the party. This could be due to the party's recruitment strategy if it did not want entrepreneurs to be such a large share of the local party membership.[45] In areas that already have a large number of party members, adding entrepreneurs would be less noticeable. There may in fact be a rough quota on what percentage of local party membership can be made up of entrepreneurs. This would be consistent with the populist shift associated with Hu Jintao and Wen Jiabao after the 16th Party Congress.[46]

In addition to these contextual factors, the size of the enterprise matters to the CCP: all else being equal, the larger the *sales revenue* of a firm,[47] the more likely its owner is a party member.[48] Why should this matter? The main reason is the importance of large firms to the local economy: larger firms produce more tax revenue and provide more

---

[45] Alternatively, it could simply be because the local party organization lacked sufficient personnel to handle party recruitment work in general. My thanks to Jie Chen for pointing out this possibility.

[46] These results may be skewed by one of the counties in Hunan, which according to the aggregate data provided by the local Organization Department had the highest percentage of party members working in the private sector but the lowest percentage of party members among the county population as a whole and a below average percentage of co-opted entrepreneurs.

[47] Sales revenue is analyzed using its natural log because most firms are bunched together at the low end of the scale: the mean value is 12.46 million yuan, with a standard deviation of 47.33 million (which indicates the skewed distribution of sales revenue), and the median is 2 million. Fixed assets or the number of workers in a firm could also be used to measure the size of the firm, but in these surveys both are so highly correlated with annual sales that they are not truly independent variables. Using either sales, fixed assets, or the number of workers as the measure of firm size yields similar results; including more than one makes both or all of them statistically insignificant.

[48] It could also be true that larger firms are a consequence, not just a cause, of being co-opted. After all, a main motivation for joining the party are the economic benefits that are believed to come from party membership. In order to sort this out, I would need to know how large the firm was before the owner joined the party, but I do not have that information. An indirect test is to see if the firm's sales were larger the longer the entrepreneur had been in the party. When age, education, and gender are controlled for, however, the number of years in the party was not related to the size of the firm's sales.

jobs. There is also a practical reason. As will be shown in chapter 4, in its efforts to improve party building in the private sector, the CCP first focused on the largest firms, and it soon discovered that party building was easier and more successful when the firm was owned by a party member. Red capitalists are far more likely to have party organizations in their firms, have workers who have been recruited into the CCP, and would prefer to hire party members. In other words, red capitalists facilitate party building.

Other factors that influenced the CCP's co-optation strategy are consistent with the party's general criteria for recruiting new members: the CCP prefers young, male, and highly educated candidates for membership. In fact, as recruiting entrepreneurs became a regular part of the task of party building, the pattern of which entrepreneurs the party recruited became more like the general demographic criteria. The party prefers young entrepreneurs to older ones: annual reports of overall party recruitment results highlight that approximately three-quarters of new members were 35 years of age or younger and had at least a high school education. The same is true for private entrepreneurs. In the 1999 survey, 65 percent of them joined the party when they were 35 or younger, but 77 percent did so in the 2005 survey. Men were about one-third more likely than women to be co-opted in the 1999 survey but almost twice as likely in the 2005 survey. In overall party recruitment, men are about four times more likely to join the party than women, so the odds are better for women if they are successful entrepreneurs. The odds of an entrepreneur being recruited were better than one in three for those with a college degree, about one in four for those with a high school degree, but less than one in eight for those with a middle school education or less. Education standards for women may be higher than for men: in the 2005 survey, 88.9 percent of female entrepreneurs co-opted into the party had college degrees, compared with only 36.7 percent of men. With limited spots allotted to women, they may face higher educational requirements. Membership in the Communist Youth League (CYL) remains the fast track to party membership, as shown by its large and statistically significant coefficient. Of the co-opted entrepreneurs, 88.7 percent had been in the CYL in the 1999 survey and 83.9 percent in the 2005 survey. Ironically, most of the non-CCP entrepreneurs (56.2 percent and 64.3 percent in the 1999 and 2005 surveys, respectively) had also been in the CYL. In the case of entrepreneurs, the CCP also prefers those who have roots in the community: the longer the entrepreneurs had been in business and the longer they had lived in their current county, the more likely they were to be co-opted into the party.

Several factors that did not have a significant impact on whether an entrepreneur had been co-opted merit attention. First, the sector in which the enterprise operated did not matter: whether the firm was engaged in agriculture, industry, or commerce and services had no significant impact on whether its owner was co-opted when other variables were controlled for (these variables are not included in the table to simplify the presentation). Second, whether the respondent was (or had been) a *getihu* did not have a significant effect on whether he or she was co-opted into the CCP in the 2005 survey, whereas it was a significant negative factor in the 1999 survey. In the past, this designation had carried a stigma, but that is no longer the case. As the distinction between *geti* and other types of private enterprises blurred, the negative connotation also diminished.

The CCP is also selective about whom it attempts to recruit: only 31 percent of non-CCP entrepreneurs in the 2005 survey reported that the CCP had approached them about joining the party, up from 25 percent in the 1999 survey. This is consistent with the new policy of reaching out to private entrepreneurs and also with the call to be selective about who among the advanced productive forces is allowed to enter the party. But the party's invitation is influential: it doubles the chances that entrepreneurs will want to join the CCP. Of those who claim they want to join the party, only about half actually apply to do so. One of the factors encouraging entrepreneurs to apply is having the party approach them. This removes some of the uncertainty of whether it is worth the trouble to apply. It doubles the chances that entrepreneurs who want to join the CCP actually apply to do so: 76.77 percent of those approached by the party apply for membership, compared with only 37.33 percent of those who were not invited to join.

Among the entrepreneurs who are not yet party members, which ones does the party invite to join? Not surprisingly, the same pattern found among co-opted entrepreneurs holds true for others the party approaches: according to the 2005 survey, local party recruitment efforts are more likely to target men with higher levels of education and larger firms (measured in terms of sales revenues and workforce) than others. This shows a more strategic approach to recruiting entrepreneurs than in the late 1990s. The 1999 survey did not reveal any significant effect of education or firm size on the likelihood that the local party would approach the entrepreneur. The lifting of the ban on entrepreneurs, and the interest shown by the central party apparatus in recruiting them, have made criteria for recruiting entrepreneurs more consistent with overall recruitment criteria. As noted earlier, however, the criteria are apparently more strict when it comes to entrepreneurs, indicating that the basic demographic characteristics are necessary but not sufficient criteria for admitting entrepreneurs into the party.

Although membership in the CYL and most business associations did not have a significant impact on whom the local party invited to join, there was one exception: in both surveys, the party was more likely to contact entrepreneurs if they were members of the local Industrial and Commercial Federation (ICF, in Chinese Gongshanglian, the local chapter of the All-China Federation of Industry and Commerce [ACFIC]). Membership in the ICF increased the chances that the party would approach an entrepreneur by 50 percent in the 1999 survey and doubled the chances in the 2005 survey. Unlike the Private Entrepreneurs Association (PEA) and the Self-Employed Laborers Association (SELA, the official association for *getihu*), for which membership is mandatory for licensed entrepreneurs, membership in the ICF is voluntary and subject to approval by the association. Its members are typically owners or managers of large enterprises, which is itself an important factor in the party's recruitment strategy. Membership in the ICF signifies membership in the local economic elite, which is the group of entrepreneurs the CCP is targeting. The role of business associations in party building will be examined in chapter 4.

Motivations for Joining and Not Joining the CCP

Why do private entrepreneurs want to join the CCP? The most apparent reason is economic benefits: in the 2005 survey, 51.3 percent of co-opted entrepreneurs and 54.3 percent of those who wanted to join the CCP said a main motivation was the economic benefits to themselves or their firm.[49] Good political connections are always useful in business, and especially so in China, where the market economy is still

[49] These were open-ended questions that allowed respondents to state any reasons they had for wanting to join the party. Their responses were then coded into categories.

not fully developed and is subject to political intervention. According to the head of the Organization Department in Hebei's county H, many entrepreneurs saw the benefits of party membership for their firms and sought to join the CCP, but the number that actually joined the party remained small because of the political demands of party membership. Party membership gives entrepreneurs easier access to loans, official discretion in granting licenses and permits, discretion in enforcing worker safety and environmental regulations, and protection from competition and unfair policy implementation. At the same time, being co-opted also means that they can avoid the negative consequences of autonomy: party committees may deny such benefits to entrepreneurs who remain aloof. Party membership not only provides discernible benefits but may also allow entrepreneurs to avoid the interference of party and government organizations in their business affairs. By joining the party, and especially by taking an active role in local party affairs, entrepreneurs may gain better protection from economic competitors and easier access to material resources and financial and tax benefits than would be the case if they were outside the party.

Membership in the party, and in particular whether an entrepreneur joined the party before or after going into business, is an important correlate of the characteristics of private firms in these samples. As shown in table 3.3, firms owned by party members have higher sales revenues, more workers, and higher levels of fixed assets than those owned by nonmembers. Not surprisingly, most red capitalists, and those who want to be, agree that party members have advantages in business. Those who do not want to join the party are half as likely to share this viewpoint (see table 3.1). This may in part be simply sour grapes, but it also indicates that the CCP's growing support for the private sector benefits even nonparty entrepreneurs.

Membership in the CCP also represents inclusion in the political elite in the community and the country at large. According to local officials, some entrepreneurs seek party membership because it is an essential criterion for selection for other political positions. Among the entrepreneurs, 10.3 percent of co-opted entrepreneurs and 8.3 percent of those want to join the CCP mentioned their desire to participate in politics. Similarly, some others gave a very practical reason for joining: responses such as "the CCP is the ruling party in China," "everything is under the party's leadership," and "of course you would join the party" implicitly acknowledge that the party is the only game in town,

TABLE 3.3. *Characteristics of Surveyed Private Enterprises, 1999 and 2005*

	1999	2005
Annual sales (million RMB)		
All entrepreneurs	3.5	12.5
Xiahai entrepreneurs	5.3	18.6
Co-opted entrepreneurs	3.4	13.6
Want to join CCP	3.1	7.2
Do not want to join CCP	2.6	8.5
Number of workers		
All entrepreneurs	41.8	74.4
Xiahai entrepreneurs	75.4	95.5
Co-opted entrepreneurs	38.6	91.4
Want to join CCP	27.5	55.5
Do not want to join CCP	28.9	54.5
Fixed Assets (million RMB)		
All entrepreneurs	2.3	7.0
Xiahai entrepreneurs	4.3	10.3
Co-opted entrepreneurs	2.1	6.7
Want to join CCP	1.7	4.5
Do not want to join CCP	1.6	5.0

an important measure of legitimacy.[50] They may not like the party, but they accept it as the ruling party and seek to join it rather than challenge it. Moreover, the desire to be "within the system" is stronger than the desire for autonomy in China, where autonomy from the state often means weakness in the political system. The example of Lu Guoqiang, an entrepreneur in Zhejiang, illustrates this well. After a long-running dispute with a township official who Lu accused of being corrupt and discriminatory, Lu ran against the official in a local election and won by a landslide. After winning the election, Lu chose to join the party and then recruited other entrepreneurs to join also. "I could not fight the party outside the system, so I decided to help change the system from within." But what animated Lu were not the political ideals of democracy and liberty but the tangible goals of economic well-being:

[50] Other common reasons for joining the CCP fall under the category of support for the party. Although many of these are undoubtedly sincere, responses such as "the party is the reliable implementor of the three represents," "being a party member is glorious," and "everybody loves the party" are likely sarcastic.

"We want more business people to join because we want to reform the party. We want to make it not only as free-enterprise as possible, but also more transparent and less corrupt."[51]

Not all entrepreneurs want to join the party: in the 2005 survey, 25 percent were not party members and did not want to be. The most common reason for not wanting to join the party, given by 22.2 percent of this group, was that whether one was a party member or not made little difference for the enterprise. This is consistent with the observation in table 3.1 that entrepreneurs who did not want to join the party were less than half as likely as other entrepreneurs to believe that party members had advantages when it came to business (26.7 percent compared with 57.3 percent). Because material benefits were the most common reason for wanting to join the party, it therefore makes sense that those who do not see the economic advantages of party membership would not want to join the CCP. Another common reason for entrepreneurs not wanting to join the CCP was that they were too busy to join (18.1 percent), which is consistent with party membership making little difference: if it provided substantial benefits, they would undoubtedly find the time to apply. A third common reason (16.6 percent) was that entrepreneurs felt they lacked the qualifications for membership, and indeed they did: almost all of them were over 35 and had less than a high school education. These objective standards provide clear signals to potential applicants about who is and is not likely to be admitted.

Other reasons given for not wanting to join the CCP suggest a certain degree of alienation. Several respondents reported they disliked the CCP because it was corrupt, too monolithic, did not allow enough freedom for its members, and had a poor reputation. Others felt that being a party member was too demanding, both in terms of criteria for admission and standards expected of those in the CCP. This is an intriguing finding because as studies on institutional change have found, "Actors who are aggrieved but not coopted are an important source of pressure for institutional change."[52] Although their numbers

---

[51] Cheng, "The Reformer Who Came in from the Cold."
[52] Marc Schneiberg and Elisabeth Clemens, "The Typical Tools for the Job: Research Strategies in Institutional Analysis," *Sociological Theory*, vol. 24, no. 3 (September 2006), p. 218, quoted in Thelen, "How Institutions Evolve," p. 232.

are small – around 3 percent of all respondents and 12 percent of those who did not want to join the CCP – their views may be shared by others who were less outspoken.

Although men are roughly split between those who want to join the party and those who do not, about two-thirds of women who are not party members do not want to be, and this was true for both the 1999 and 2005 surveys. Among CCP members in general, men outnumber women more than four to one, and this proportion has been roughly stable since before the start of the reform era. Party membership is the first step for more formal political participation in China, but the political arena in China, as elsewhere, discriminates against women, which helps reduce the desirability of party membership among women. With men overwhelmingly favored in party recruitment, few influential and prominent positions available to women, and party membership of less immediate benefit for their firms, women are much less likely than men to be interested in joining the party.

Local officials, however, point to other reasons why private entrepreneurs may not be interested in joining the party. The most prominent one is that they did not want to be committed to the political activities expected of party members, such as political study meetings (7 percent of entrepreneurs agreed, saying the party was too demanding). They would also be held to a higher standard of behavior in their personal and professional lives. For example, the head of the national tax office in Shandong's city Q noted that red capitalists have a stronger inclination to pay their taxes and abide by the law (put differently, they may be under greater scrutiny and feel compelled to be tax-paying and law-abiding). Problems of tax evasion are more common among entrepreneurs who are not in the party. This problem is particularly common in small- and medium-scale enterprises, whose owners are much less likely to be party members than those of larger firms. Susan Whiting cites estimates from the State Council Development Research Center and the State Administration of Taxation that up to 70 percent of private entrepreneurs evaded taxes, underpaying by up to 50 percent. Similarly, Ole Bruun's case study of private entrepreneurs in Chengdu found that tax collection from the private sector was made difficult by the absence of standards for evaluating taxes owed by firms, giving local officials the opportunity to rely on "serious discrimination" in their approach to tax collection. David

Wank's study in Xiamen found that tax evasion was so widespread that those charged with the crime were more guilty of poor political connections than wrongdoing (a sentiment widely held elsewhere in China).[53]

From the perspective of local officials in the survey sites, many entrepreneurs are not interested in joining the party because they are not interested in politics at all. Some local cadres complained that many private entrepreneurs showed little interest in joining the CCP, which made recruitment difficult despite the new mandate to bring the "advanced productive forces" into the party. Those who are interested in politics prefer to belong to people's congresses or political consultative conferences (as will be discussed in chapter 6) and want to join the CCP primarily to gain access to these other political institutions. According to local officials, many entrepreneurs believed that being a delegate to the local party congress was not as good as being in the people's congress or political consultative conference. Delegates to party congresses could only vote for new leaders during the congress and had no influence afterward. In contrast, membership in people's congresses and political consultative conferences gave them the opportunity to take part in the deliberations over policy (*canzheng yizheng*) on an ongoing basis. According to the head of the combined PEA/SELA in Hunan's county C, entrepreneurs who join people's congresses and political consultative conferences also request to join the party, but the rest are not interested. According to the head of the ICF in Zhejiang's district H, red capitalists have a relatively low political status compared with party and government officials and delegates to people's congresses and political consultative conferences. Local party elites are concentrated in the party and government bureaucracies and in the party school, putting entrepreneurs on a "second line." This results in less interest in joining the party, especially if they are concerned primarily with advancing their economic interests, not the political process. In other words, party membership is seen by some as detrimental because it imposes new demands on their busy

---

[53] Whiting, *Power and Wealth in Rural China*, p. 183; Ole Bruun, *Business and Bureaucracy in a Chinese City: An Ethnography of Private Business Households in Contemporary China* (Berkeley: University of California, Institute of East Asian Studies, 1993), p. 122; David L. Wank, *Commodifying Communism: Business, Trust, and Politics in a Chinese City* (Cambridge: Cambridge University Press, 1999), p. 73.

schedules and their conduct and by others as a stepping-stone to other forms of political participation but not something desirable for its own sake.

Finally, private entrepreneurs are reluctant to join the CCP because they would face increased pressure to create party organizations within their firms. As will be explained in the next chapter, many entrepreneurs do not want the CCP to have a permanent presence in their firms and see party membership as opening the door to more direct monitoring of their business practices by the CCP.

CONCLUSION

Despite the controversy surrounding the propriety of inviting capitalists into the communist party, the CCP's policy of co-optation and cooperation has evolved from an informal and technically illegal practice to a formal policy. The growing ties between the party and the private sector are the foundation of crony communism in China. The main beneficiaries of economic reform have been red capitalists, who operate the largest firms, and the local party and government officials with whom they interact and on whom they depend. The number of red capitalists continues to grow, both through the privatization of SOEs and the co-optation of successful entrepreneurs into the party. Over time, the recruitment of entrepreneurs into the party has become routine, and the criteria used are the same as for party recruitment in general: the party prefers well-educated, male, and relatively young people as new members. In addition, the party targets the largest entrepreneurs for recruitment, a twist on the "grasp the large, release the small" strategy used for SOE reform. As will be seen in the next chapter, this same emphasis on large firms is also the basis for party-building efforts in the private sector. In its relations with the private sector, the CCP focuses on the economic elites at the local level and is less interested in the larger number of small and medium-sized enterprises. This integration of wealth and power is in the mutual interest of both communist officials and private entrepreneurs. The officials rely on the private sector to produce growth, jobs, and tax revenue, and the entrepreneurs rely on contacts within the party to improve their business prospects. This symbiotic relationship is what allows crony communism to perpetuate itself.

Just as co-opted capitalists help to perpetuate crony communism in China, and by extension the CCP's hold on power, those who do not want to join the CCP may be most likely to challenge it. Because they do not see the economic advantages of party membership and in some cases are critical of the party and its policies, they have less stake in perpetuating the system as it is and greater motives to seek a change. However, it is also true that most of those who preferred to remain outside the party were content to focus on the needs of the firm and not be engaged in politics at all. The apolitical nature of most Chinese capitalists can also help perpetuate the status quo by keeping them in the "noncritical realm" of civil society. As long as capitalists do not become politically active or support those who are in the "critical realm" of civil society, the CCP's strategy of embracing the private sector will maintain the active support of most capitalists and preempt a political challenge from others.

4

Bridges and Branches

The CCP's Institutional Links to the Private Sector

As the party gradually allowed the scope of the private sector to grow, it also created institutional means to manage and monitor private firms. It relied primarily on its traditional party-building practices: united front groups to organize entrepreneurs in different types of private firms and party branches within individual enterprises. These practices have had limited success. Although most private entrepreneurs belong to one or more of the official business associations, they have less confidence in their ability to serve members' interests than in the past, and party officials have less confidence in the ability of business associations to provide party leadership. Similarly, the CCP has been able to establish branches in a larger percentage of firms, especially large-scale enterprises, but they do a better job of supporting business operations than leading political work.

Local party-building efforts reveal a strong element of paternalism, one of the defining characteristics of crony communism. Local officials believe that entrepreneurs lack the business acumen and management skills to be successful, so it is the responsibility of the party to improve the performance of private firms. As the CCP's policy toward the private sector moved from "guide, supervise, and control" to "support, encourage, and guide," party-building efforts likewise shifted their focus from the party's political and ideological goals to the enterprises' business and management needs. Party-building efforts have accordingly changed from political study and recruitment of new members to also include training on basic business practices and seeking out new business opportunities.

Just as the slogan "grasp the large, release the small" has defined the CCP's policy for SOE reform, it is also an apt metaphor for its party-building efforts more generally. As shown in the last chapter, the CCP has privileged the owners of large firms in its strategy of co-optation. This chapter will also show that the creation of party organizations within private firms has focused primarily on large firms. Only when local officials have established party organizations in all or almost all large firms do they turn their attention to small and medium-sized enterprises. These practices demonstrate that as the party continues to integrate wealth and power, it first embraces the wealthiest entrepreneurs and the largest enterprises. Although Hu Jintao and Wen Jiabao have tried to move away from the elitist, pro-growth economic policies of the 1990s, they have continued the elitist approach to party building.

This chapter will begin by looking at the corporatist logic behind the CCP's organization of official business associations and then assess the efficacy of these associations in representing both the state's and their members' interests. Next, it will look at the work of building party branches in the private sector. Although more firms have party branches than in the past, these branches face the same challenges confronting party-building efforts as a whole: how can traditional party organizations remain relevant amid tremendous change in the economic and social environment?

THE CORPORATIST LOGIC OF CHINA'S BUSINESS ASSOCIATIONS: THE PARTY'S BRIDGE TO THE PRIVATE SECTOR

A key aspect of the party's embrace of the private sector has been organizational links that tie private firms to the state. It has rejuvenated old united front groups and created new organizations to both integrate the party with the private sector and also incorporate new groups into the political system. In doing so, it has followed a corporatist logic.[1]

---

[1] Margaret M. Pearson, "The Janus Face of Business Associations in China: Socialist Corporatism in Foreign Enterprises," *Australian Journal of Chinese Affairs*, no. 31

The concept of corporatism is a familiar one in comparative politics and describes a system of interest representation in which interests are vertically organized into peak associations to limit and institutionalize the participation of key groups in the policy process.[2] Corporatist arrangements may be dominated by the state in an authoritarian political system, a variant known as state corporatism, or they may provide greater autonomy and influence for the groups themselves in a more pluralist setting, a variant known as societal corporatism.

The emerging corporatist elements in China's political system provide a rationale for the more harmonious relations between state and society in the reform era. The corporatist model points out that the relationship between state and society is based on achieving consensus and common goals rather than being a zero-sum struggle for power. As Douglas Chalmers notes, "Corporatism has much in common with socialism's understanding of society after the end of class conflict." A harmony of interests is possible without the total transformation of society.[3] Similarly, Alfred Stepan identified the universal appeal of corporatism to elites facing "a perceived threat of fragmentation" and who reject both the liberal ideals of individualism and checks and balances and the Marxist ideals of class conflict "because they are seen as legitimizing conflict."[4]

Corporatist structures are consequently emerging in China as a substitute for coercion, propaganda, and central planning to maintain party hegemony. As Jonathan Unger and Anita Chan argue, corporatism is "a mechanism through which the state's grip could be lessened" but not released altogether. "The more the economy decentralizes, the

(January 1994), pp. 25–46; Jonathan Unger and Anita Chan, "Corporatism in China: A Developmental State in an East Asian Context," in Barrett L. McCormick and Jonathan Unger, eds., *China after Socialism: In the Footsteps of Eastern Europe or East Asia?* (Armonk, NY: M. E. Sharpe, 1996); Gerry Groot, *Managing Transitions: The Chinese Communist Party, United Front Work, Corporatism, and Hegemony* (New York: Routledge, 2004).

[2] Philippe C. Schmitter, "Still the Century of Corporatism?" in Philippe C. Schmitter and Gerhard Lehmbruch, eds., *Trends toward Corporatist Intermediation* (Beverly Hills, CA: Sage, 1979).

[3] Douglas A. Chalmers, "Corporatism and Comparative Politics," in Howard J. Wiarda, ed., *New Directions in Comparative Politics* (Boulder, CO: Westview Press, 1985), p. 62.

[4] Alfred C. Stepan, *The State and Society: Peru in Comparative Perspective* (Princeton, NJ: Princeton University Press, 1978), p. 58.

more corporatist associations get established as substitute control mechanisms."[5]

The "Regulations on the Registration and Management of Social Organizations," issued in draft form in 1989 and finalized in 1998, established the corporatist strategy of the CCP.[6] Neither the state nor the social organizations use corporatist terminology to describe the links between them. But as Philippe Schmitter has pointed out, corporatist structures may exist even in the absence of awareness of corporatism in the state's doctrine. The regulations reveal familiar elements of corporatism: every organization must register with the government and be sponsored by a state organizational unit. The state's sponsoring unit is responsible for its daily affairs, which can include providing officers and a budget. Social organizations have a representational monopoly, at least at their level. In any jurisdiction, there can be only one organization for each profession, activity, or interest. When more than one exists, the state typically requires them to merge or to disband. Some local social organizations belong to peak organizations, but others have limited horizontal or vertical links to other similar organizations. This representational monopoly is one of the weaker aspects of the corporatist strategy in China. For instance, in the burgeoning software industry, there is a growing multiplicity of organizations, many with overlapping memberships and areas of interest and activity. And although they must continue to have a state sponsor, they use this embeddedness in the state to work on behalf of their members.[7]

Most studies that explore the relationship between the state and social organizations begin by trying to determine if the organizations are simply agents of the state or if they are the agents of their members. In other words, how much autonomy do these new social organizations enjoy? The issue of autonomy is a key factor in understanding whether the state's corporatist strategy is working or if a civil society may be emerging. But most studies conclude that social organizations have a dual role: they simultaneously represent the interests of the state

---

[5] Unger and Chan, "Corporatism in China," pp. 105, 107.
[6] Tony Saich, "Negotiating the State: The Development of Social Organizations in China," *China Quarterly*, no. 161 (March 2000), pp. 124–141.
[7] Scott Kennedy, *The Business of Lobbying in China* (Cambridge, MA: Harvard University Press, 2005).

and their own members, although the balance between these roles varies considerably, depending on the organization, the attitude of local officials, the issue involved, and the broader political context. As Margaret Pearson described them, they are "Janus faced": they are supposed to represent not only the state but also their members.[8] The issue of autonomy is therefore something of a red herring: as is true in many developing countries, particularly in Asia, these organizations want to be autonomous enough to have some leeway in their activities but embedded enough to be effective. The leaders and members of these organizations see no inconsistency in this arrangement: both elements are necessary for organizations to be successful.

Is China a corporatist system? Most scholars do not argue that China has a full-blown corporatist system, only that there are corporatist elements emerging in the course of economic reform. Corporatism is an ideal type; it does not define a political system, but corporatist elements are present in a variety of contexts. Democratic countries such as Britain and the Netherlands, bureaucratic authoritarian countries such as Brazil and Argentina, military regimes such as Peru and South Korea, one-party regimes such as Mexico and Taiwan, and communist countries such as Poland, the Soviet Union, and most recently China have been described as corporatist. The corporatist model does capture core elements of China's political system, especially concerning its political economy. The state has created or licensed associations for independent entrepreneurs, owners of private enterprises, enterprises with foreign investment, organized labor, Catholic and Protestant churches, writers, scientists, and other functional interests. These associations are noncompetitive, and when two or more exist, the state forces them to merge or makes one or more disband. Membership is compulsory; for example, members in business associations are often enrolled when they receive their business license. The leaders of these associations are often officials from the party or government offices responsible for regulating or managing them, and association offices are often in party and government compounds.

These corporatist elements have very much in common with the key aspects of a Leninist system. A Leninist system is based on the ruling party's monopoly on legitimate political organization. The state

---

[8] Pearson, "The Janus Face of Business Associations in China."

may create mass organizations to link state and society, and these organizations are typically staffed and budgeted in large part by the state. A Leninist party also prevents the spontaneous formation of new organizations, especially where an official one already exists, and the presence of organizations outside of its control is a challenge to its authority. During its early years as a ruling party, what Ken Jowitt calls periods of transformation and consolidation, the party uses these organizations as "transmission belts" to send authoritative decisions to lower levels of the organizations.[9] The party grants leaders of these organizations a degree of leeway to manage their organizations and the people they nominally represent but prevents interests and preferences from working their way back up through the organization to influence state policy. During the later period of inclusion, these same organizations become channels for interest representation so that these interests can be incorporated into the party. As the party loses its ability to monitor the activities of these organizations and sanction the behavior of their members, and society more generally, the stability of the Leninist system itself is also weakened.[10]

Corporatist trends are nevertheless affecting several key factors of China's political system. An important variation on corporatism as practiced in China is that corporatist groups are usually sanctioned and controlled by local party and government authorities and not always vertically organized into peak associations whose primary interaction is with the central state. This has exacerbated the decentralization of political and economic authority. Just as corporate associations no longer act as transmission belts, local governments do not act as loyal agents of the center.[11] Relatedly, as a result of these newly created

[9] Ken Jowitt, "Inclusion," in *New World Disorder: The Leninist Extinction* (Berkeley: University of California Press, 1992), pp. 88–120.

[10] Andrew G. Walder, "The Decline of Communist Power: Elements of a Theory of Institutional Change," *Theory and Society*, vol. 23, no. 2 (April 1994), pp. 297–323; Andrew G. Walder, "The Quiet Revolution from Within: Economic Reform as a Source of Political Decline," in Andrew G. Walder, ed., *The Waning of the Communist State: Economic Origins of Political Decline in China and Hungary* (Berkeley: University of California Press, 1995).

[11] Wang Shaoguang, "The Rise of the Regions: Fiscal Reform and the Decline of Central State Capacity in China," in Walder, *Waning of the Communist State*; Huang Yasheng, *Inflation and Investment Controls in China: The Political Economy of Central–Local Relations during the Reform Era* (Cambridge: Cambridge University Press, 1996); Jae Ho Chung, "Reappraising Central–Local Relations in Deng's

institutional links, the party's traditional concern with party building as a means of linking state and society and monitoring compliance with party policy has atrophied.[12]

Both state and societal corporatism are monopolistic forms of group politics and therefore are structurally similar. Yet their origins and dynamics are fundamentally different. State corporatism is generally associated with authoritarian regimes, whereas societal corporatism is "more an evolution – perhaps a corruption – of liberalism."[13] Societal corporatism is not compatible with a Leninist system because the former requires the types of autonomous and politically active groups that the latter refuses to tolerate. The notion of state corporatism is less threatening to the regime: instead of autonomy, corporate groups are embedded in the state, where they can be manipulated, their leaders replaced, and their finances controlled. Leninist parties seek to prevent autonomous groups, and for good reason. The Eastern European experience shows that the rise of civil society has a significant – and in some cases decisive – impact on the collapse of communism, as do political and social movements commonly referred to as "color revolutions" in postcommunist countries.[14]

A more promising approach may be to apply Stepan's typology of inclusionary and exclusionary poles within state corporatism. The distinction between the two poles concerns whether the state incorporates

China: Decentralization, Dilemmas of Control, and Diluted Effects of Reform," in Chien-min Chao and Bruce J. Dickson, eds., *Remaking the Chinese State: Strategies, Society, and Security* (London: Routledge, 2001).

[12] Bruce J. Dickson, *Red Capitalists in China: The Party, Private Entrepreneurs, and Prospects for Political Change* (Cambridge: Cambridge University Press, 2003), chapter 2; Stig Thogersen, "Parasites or Civilisers: The Legitimacy of the Chinese Communist Party in Rural Areas," in Kjeld Erik Brodsgaard and Zheng Yongnian, eds., *Bringing the Party Back In: How China Is Governed* (Singapore: Eastern Universities Press, 2004).

[13] Chalmers, "Corporatism and Comparative Politics," p. 60; see also Schmitter, "Still the Century of Corporatism?" pp. 22–25.

[14] Timothy Garton Ash, *The Uses of Adversity: Essays on the Fate of Central Europe* (New York: Vintage, 1990); Marcia A. Wiegle and Jim Butterfield, "Civil Society in Reforming Communist Regimes: The Logic of Emergence," *Comparative Politics*, vol. 25, no. 1 (October 1992), pp. 1–24; Vladimir Tismaneanu, *Reinventing Politics: Eastern Europe from Stalin to Havel* (New York: The Free Press, 1992); Henry E. Hale, "Democracy or Autocracy on the March? The Colored Revolutions as Normal Dynamics of Patronal Presidentialism," *Communist and Post-Communist Studies*, vol. 39, no. 3 (September 2006), pp. 305–329.

"salient" groups or suppresses them through coercion. A regime can shift between exclusionary and inclusionary policies over time and even practice them simultaneously. For instance, the CCP has allowed the All-China Federation of Trade Unions in recent years to advocate strongly the interests of labor in the policy and legislative process but also imprisoned those who advocate the formation of independent trade unions. Both inclusionary and exclusionary forms of state corporatism are intended to "restrict the autonomy of groups they encapsulate" and are understood as variants of authoritarianism. Even inclusive policies within state corporatism are not similar to the kind of pluralism associated with societal corporatism.[15] The notion of exclusionary and inclusionary poles also fits well with the CCP's strategy of incorporating certain individuals, groups, and interests into the political system while continuing to exclude others. It is willing to co-opt successful entrepreneurs into the party, in part to help promote the goal of economic modernization and in part to prevent these entrepreneurs from becoming a potential source of opposition outside the state. At the same time, it continues to exclude and in many cases persecute those who challenge the CCP's priorities with explicitly political goals, including bottom-up demands for new and autonomous social organizations.[16]

Official Business Associations

As the private sector began to emerge in the 1980s, the CCP established several business associations to provide institutional links with the private sector. The main ones are the catch-all associations that are organized by the scale of the enterprise rather than the industrial sector. The heads of these business associations generally serve simultaneously as party or government officials. The Self-Employed Laborers Association (SELA, *geti laodongzhe xiehui*) is aimed at small-scale operations with small numbers of workers and low sales volumes. The Private Enterprises Association (PEA, *siying qiye xiehui*) encompasses slightly larger

---

[15] Stepan, *State and Society*, pp. 73–81; quotation is on p. 74n.
[16] Teresa Wright, "Contesting State Legitimacy in the 1990s: The China Democracy Party and the China Labor Bulletin," in Peter Hays Gries and Stanley Rosen, eds., *State and Society in 21st Century China: Crisis, Contention, and Legitimation* (New York: Routledge, 2004).

enterprises and was created at the urging of private entrepreneurs who did not want to be confused with *getihu*. Over time, the stigma attached to being a *getihu* faded, and the distinction between *getihu* and other private enterprises also began to blur. For example, many *getihu* have many more than seven employees, and some entrepreneurs belong to both associations because they have more than one enterprise. As a result, the distinction between the SELA and PEA also diminished. In several counties included in the surveys, the two associations were essentially merged, with the same person managing both. The Industrial and Commercial Federation (ICF, Gongshang lian)[17] includes the largest and most prestigious enterprises and is normally thought to have the most clout. Although SELA and PEA are products of the post-Mao era, the ICF has its origins in the 1950s united front strategy of linking capitalists with the state. Its status is equivalent to one of the eight "democratic parties," holdovers of the pre-1949 period that exist to perpetuate the myth of the CCP's united front.

In a classic state corporatist arrangement, each of the business associations is headquartered in Beijing, with local branches throughout China. These associations are dependent on the state for most of their budgets and are often headed by current or retired officials. At the local level, the SELA, PEA, and ICF are under the local government's industrial and commercial bureau (*gongshang ju*) or the party's United Front Work Department and normally share office space and leaders with them. For example, in Hunan's county C, the vice chief of the United Front Work Department was also the party secretary of the ICF. But he acknowledged that a prominent businessman must be president of the ICF in order for it to be effective in promoting cooperation between the state and business; otherwise it will be seen as simply an extension of the state. In some counties, SELA and PEA were managed by the ICF, which in turn was managed by the industrial and commercial bureau.

Most of the private entrepreneurs in this study belonged to one or more business associations (see table 4.1). The distribution of membership varied significantly depending on the level of development among

[17] The national level association of the ICF is commonly known as the All-China Federation of Industry and Commerce (Zhonghua quanguo gongshangye lianhehui) and sometimes the General Chamber of Commerce.

TABLE 4.1. *Membership in Business
Associations, 1999 and 2005 (percent; columns
sum to more than 100 because some
entrepreneurs belonged to more than one
business association)*

	1999	2005
ICF	33.2	28.1
PEA	33.2	32.3
SELA	32.4	24.2
Other state-sponsored associations	4.6	4.1
None	30.3	36.0
Self-organized associations	–	17.3

the eight counties studied: ICF and PEA members were more common
in the prosperous counties, and SELA members were concentrated in
the poor ones. Membership in the SELA and PEA is supposedly mandatory for all registered *getihu* and private enterprises, respectively, but
this requirement may not be ironclad. Over 30 percent of respondents
in both the 1999 and 2005 surveys claimed they did not belong to any
of the official business associations, regardless of how their firms were
registered or which counties they lived in. Whether they had managed
to somehow evade their required membership, forgot they were members, or were so alienated from the associations that they disavowed
belonging to them, a substantial proportion of businessmen claimed
to be outside the CCP's corporatist net. Most of them were also not
party members. In contrast, membership in the ICF is voluntary and
includes both private and state-owned enterprises.

    In all counties, a key role for business associations is party building,
a traditional practice for mass organizations, which were designed to
help the party monitor its environment (a more detailed discussion of
party building in the private sector will be presented later in this chapter). When leaders of local business associations listed their responsibilities, they typically began with political and ideological work and party
building and then mentioned business services. Political work usually
entailed study meetings on special topics, such as national policy and
foreign affairs. In Shandong's city Z, ideological work consisted of
making sure entrepreneurs paid taxes, followed the law, and in other

TABLE 4.2. *Cadres' Views on the Role of Business Associations*

	1999	2005
1. The main role of business associations is to:		
Provide party leadership over the private sector	47.8	31.8
Represent the members of the associations	42.4	57.0
Other	9.8	11.2
2. Industrial and commercial associations are an effective means of party leadership over local private enterprises		
Strongly agree	35.4	22.9
Agree	41.7	55.6
Disagree	16.1	17.5
Strongly disagree	6.7	4.0

ways behaved as model citizens. Several of its members received the honorary title of "outstanding builder of socialism with Chinese characteristics." In all communities, business associations mobilized their members to participate in charitable activities, such as building and repairing schools and roads, hiring the unemployed and disabled, and providing food and gifts to the poor (charity work will be described in more detail in chapter 7). Local officials in several counties said they worked to make entrepreneurs not only rich but also ideologically advanced (*fu er si jin*).

As the CCP's support for the private sector increased, the business associations' responsibilities also shifted from party work toward business-related matters. The proportion of local officials who believed the main responsibility of these associations was to provide party leadership over the private sector dropped from 47.8 percent in 1999 to 31.8 percent in 2005, a decrease of one-third (see table 4.2). In contrast, the share who felt the main responsibility was to represent the associations' members increased from 42.4 percent to 57 percent. More importantly, local officials also expressed less confidence in the associations' ability to exercise party leadership: in 1999, 35.4 percent strongly agreed they could, but only 22.9 percent strongly agreed in 2005 (a drop of more than one-third). This skepticism is well founded: as will be shown, party building in the private sector has been more successful at promoting the firms' interests than exerting party leadership.

Another function of local business associations is to serve as "bridges" between the state and the business sector: they provide information to the state about developments in the private sector, and they provide businessmen with an opportunity to interact with the state.[18] In Hebei's county S, the head of the ICF said its overall function was to participate in the deliberation of policies. It coordinated the annual meetings of the local people's congress and people's political consultative conference and convened conferences that allowed local businessmen to discuss policies (*canzheng yizheng*) with local officials. Business associations in other counties also organized *canzheng yizheng* meetings between their members and local officials. The heads of local ICF, PEA, and SELA branches also participate in local politics themselves and often have concurrent appointments in local people's congresses and people's political consultative conferences. They also recommend other entrepreneurs to be appointed to these local bodies (see chapter 6 for more details).

After promoting party building and being a bridge between government and business, a third set of activities of business associations concerns providing services to their members. These include management services, financing, trade, quality control, legal matters, and so on. Associations can assist with obtaining licenses and trademarks, and some have lent money to local firms. All of them maintain Web sites through which they provide information, and some also produce monthly newsletters. The ICF in Shandong's city Z led several delegations to conduct investigations in Wenzhou and other cities in Zhejiang and also arranged for its members to attend trade negotiation conferences. In Shandong's county Q, the ICF led groups abroad to open new markets and gain information on new technologies. Jean Oi has described the Chinese bureaucracy as "an information grid where government officials are the primary nodes in the network that provides information to local enterprises."[19] This was particularly important in the early reform era, when markets and sources of information were

---

[18] Jonathan Unger, "'Bridges': Private Business, the Chinese Government and the Rise of New Associations," *China Quarterly*, no. 147 (September 1996), pp. 795–819; Christopher Earle Nevitt, "Private Business Associations in China: Evidence of Civil Society or Local State Power?" *China Journal*, no. 36 (July 1996), pp. 25–43.

[19] Jean C. Oi, *Rural China Takes Off: Institutional Foundations of Economic Reform* (Stanford, CA: Stanford University Press, 1999), p. 123.

not well developed and cadres were the only readily available source of information. As time went on and the entrepreneurs' personal experiences, range of contacts, and access to information widened, the government became less essential as the main source of information. Nevertheless, this remains one of the main resources business associations provide to their members. By dispensing this information through their Web sites instead of more private channels, they turn this information from a private good to a collective good.

How effective are the official business associations at meeting these diverse responsibilities? Whereas my original survey found indications that these business associations could serve as vehicles for collective action by business toward the state, in particular by influencing the local implementation of policies, research by other scholars challenged this viewpoint.[20] They found that many business associations are too tightly controlled by the state to represent effectively the interests of their members, and they do not adequately serve as links between the state and business. As a result, these scholars argue that most businessmen have little regard for these official business associations. In contrast to my original assessment, but more consistent with the findings of other scholars, the more recent survey data suggest that private entrepreneurs are less confident in the efficacy of their business associations.

As shown in table 4.3, the percentage of entrepreneurs who felt the business associations represented the government's interests rose dramatically, from 54.8 percent to 78.1 percent, while the percentage of those who felt these business associations were able to represent

---

[20] Kenneth C. Foster, "Embedded within State Agencies: Business Associations in Yantai," *China Journal*, no. 47 (January 2002), pp. 41–65; Kennedy, *Business of Lobbying in China*; Kristen Parris, "The Rise of Private Business Interests," in Merle Goldman and Roderick MacFarquhar, eds., *The Paradox of China's Post-Mao Reforms* (Cambridge, MA: Harvard University Press, 1999), pp. 275–282; Bjorn Alpermann, "'Wrapped up in Cotton Wool': Political Integration of Private Entrepreneurs in Rural China," *China Journal*, no. 56 (July 2006), pp. 33–62; Kellee S. Tsai, *Capitalism without Democracy: The Private Sector in Contemporary China* (Ithaca, NY: Cornell University Press, 2007), chapter 5; Ao Daiya, "Siying qiyezhu zhengzhi canyu yanjiu baogao" (Report on the Political Participation of Private Entrepreneurs), in Zhang Houyi et al., eds., *Zhongguo siying qiye fazhan baogao*, no. 6 (2005) (A Report on the Development of China's Private Enterprises) (Beijing: Shehui kexue wenxian chubanshe, 2006), pp. 61–83.

TABLE 4.3. *Attitudes toward Business Associations (percentage who agreed with the statements below)*

	1999	2005		1999	2005
Industrial and commercial associations represent the government's viewpoint on most issues					
All entrepreneurs[a]	54.8	78.1	Cadres	62.4	55.6
ICF	52.6	81.6			
PEA	62.4	75.2			
SELA	47.3	82.6			
Other	61.9	76.7			
Industrial and commercial associations are able to represent the interests of their members					
All entrepreneurs[a]	81.9	83.3	Cadres	77.9	83.5
ICF	85.4	91.3			
PEA	89.2	86.0			
SELA	80.2	81.4			
Other	90.5	79.1			
Industrial and commercial associations are able to influence local policy implementation					
All entrepreneurs[a]	68.3	48.7	Cadres	25.1	29.3
ICF	66.4	51.3			
PEA	65.0	52.3			
SELA	70.9	50.9			
Other	61.9	37.2			

[a] Includes those who do not belong to a business association.

their members' interests remained about the same.[21] In addition, the percentage who felt their associations could influence the local implementation of policy declined by about a third, from 68.3 percent to 48.7 percent. The biggest decline was for the poorer counties: in the 1999 survey, respondents in relatively poor counties were much more optimistic about the ability of their business associations to influence policy implementation, but in the 2005 survey, they were slightly less optimistic than those in more prosperous counties. The declining influence of business associations is also seen in the smaller percentage of their members who seek their assistance on business and related matters, from 51 percent to 30.8 percent (see table 4.4). The percentage of

[21] When private entrepreneurs belonged to more than one business association, they were asked which one they identified with most closely, and the analysis that follows is based on this distinction.

TABLE 4.4. *Helpfulness of Business Associations*
(percentages)

	1999	2005
Sought the help of their business associations:		
All entrepreneurs[a]	51.0	30.8
ICF	44.9	43.7
PEA	69.6	41.2
SELA	58.5	40.2
Other	57.9	41.9
Found the associations to be helpful or very helpful:		
All entrepreneurs[a]	87.7	90.5
ICF	92.9	91.8
PEA	88.0	92.1
SELA	87.2	91.2
Other	100	88.9
Would seek their associations' help again in the future:		
All entrepreneurs[a]	79.7	72.6
ICF	79.2	81.1
PEA	85.9	77.2
SELA	84.8	78.3
Other	88.2	67.4

[a] Includes those who do not belong to a business association.

those willing to seek their associations' help in the future also declined, but not as sharply, from 79.7 percent to 72.6 percent. However, among those who did seek assistance, satisfaction with the help they received remained high: 87.7 percent in 1999 and 90.5 percent in 2005 said their associations had been very or somewhat helpful. These recent survey data indicate that business associations are now generally seen as less effective in promoting either the collective or private interests of China's entrepreneurs.

Ironically, the trend among local cadres is just the opposite: a higher percentage believe that the official business associations represent the interests of their members and are able to influence the local implementation of policy, but a smaller percentage believe the associations represent the government's interests. Although there was some convergence between entrepreneurs and cadres, the differences between them remained large and significant on the questions of whether the business associations represent the government and are able to influence local policy implementation. Officials in general have a more charitable view of the effectiveness of business associations than do their members.

Self-Organized Business Associations

Because the state-run business associations were not seen as effective means to represent the interests of entrepreneurs, a variety of new and self-organized business associations emerged in the years after the 1999 survey. These new business associations are often industry-specific, organized from the bottom up, and active at lobbying the state and in some cases unilaterally setting industry standards and regulations.[22] This has complicated the CCP's ability to monitor the private sector. Instead of having just three main business associations to organize and control, the CCP now faces a more diverse range of business associations over which it has less control. This growing diversity of business associations is challenging the CCP's corporatist strategy. Although officially there can be only one organization in each community that represents a particular group, in practice this restriction is frequently circumvented. More importantly, these self-organized associations are not structured in a corporatist fashion: they are less dependent on the state for their budgets or their leadership and are not organized in vertical hierarchies. Instead, they exhibit some of the characteristics of a civil society. Autonomy from the state is the crucial missing element in the Chinese context, as all registered organizations must have a unit within the party or government as their sponsor and are vulnerable to being shut down at the state's discretion. But it is also widely recognized that most organizations in China, including business associations, do not want to be autonomous from the state but instead seek to be embedded in the state in order to achieve their goals. Many do not enjoy the legal protection typical of a civil society but instead rely on personal ties and networks. They do not attempt to challenge or change the status quo but to make it work for them.

At a time when the CCP is cracking down on a variety of non-governmental associations for fear they could contribute to a "color revolution" in China, why have self-organized business associations

---

[22] Kennedy, *Business of Lobbying in China*.

been able to flourish? As described in chapter 1, these business associations belong to the noncritical realm of civil society, which does not pose an inherent threat to the regime but instead contributes to the economic growth the CCP believes it needs to stay in power. These business associations have lobbied on behalf of legislation, regulatory policies, and technical standards favored by their members, which can include not only private enterprises but also SOEs and foreign firms.[23] Closing down a business association with prestigious Chinese and foreign members would have a chilling effect, creating the confrontational atmosphere between government and business that the regime has been actively trying to avoid and that would jeopardize the contingent support of China's capitalists, support the CCP has been actively courting. Equally important, these new business associations are not seen as politically threatening because they seek cooperation on specific economy-related issues and have not pursued a separate political agenda. As such, they support the CCP's basic reform and opening strategy. In the future, these self-organized business associations could provide the basis for a more extensive network of civil society organizations, but so far the CCP has been able to clearly distinguish between the political and market dynamics – the critical and noncritical realms, respectively – of civil society, monitoring and suppressing the former while cooperating with the latter.[24]

China's cities now have numerous trade and industrial associations, often with overlapping memberships. One remarkable trend has been the proliferation of chambers of commerce that represent Wenzhou merchants in other Chinese cities.[25] In this case, the associations do not represent a particular sector of the economy but the interests of businessmen with a common origin. This is reminiscent of a traditional form of organization: in the pre-1949 period, local groups organized

---

[23] Kennedy, *Business of Lobbying in China.*

[24] On the different dimensions of civil society and their relationships with the state, see Michael W. Foley and Bob Edwards, "The Paradox of Civil Society," *Journal of Democracy*, vol. 7, no. 3 (July 1996), pp. 38–52; Gordon White, Jude Howell, and Shang Xiaoyuan, *In Search of Civil Society: Market Reform and Social Change in Contemporary China* (Oxford: Oxford University Press, 1996), Yanqi Tong, "State, Society, and Political Change in China and Hungary," *Comparative Politics*, vol. 26, no. 3 (April 1994), pp. 333–353.

[25] Joseph Fewsmith, "Chambers of Commerce in Wenzhou Show Potential and Limits of 'Civil Society' in China," *China Leadership Monitor*, no. 16 (Fall 2005).

people with common origins, known as *tongxianghui*. The reemergence of these kinds of groups is significant because it represents the kind of horizontal links between organizations that the CCP has long prohibited. The Leninist nature of the Chinese political system is characterized by vertical links and communication flows, whereas horizontal ties are more characteristic of a pluralist system. The emergence of Wenzhou chambers of commerce in other cities therefore merits further attention. They are allowed to exist because they belong to the economic realm of civil society and are not perceived as posing a political threat to the CCP. In contrast, the party harshly repressed the attempt to organize local chapters of the China Democracy Party and imprisoned its leaders because they were from the political realm of civil society and posed a more obvious threat. This is similar to Stepan's distinction between inclusionary and exclusionary poles within a corporatist system: the CCP is willing to incorporate economic interests such as the Wenzhou chambers of commerce but uses coercion to suppress what it sees as political threats.

How effective are these new self-organized business associations in representing the interests of their members? Based on the responses in the 2005 survey, they appear to be better able than the official business associations to help their members and to represent their interests to the state. Over 17 percent of the respondents belonged to one or more self-organized business associations; of these, over three-quarters (77.1 percent) also belonged to at least one of the three main state-run business associations. They are roughly evenly distributed across all eight cities and counties in the sample, except for the two poorest sites, where only about one in ten entrepreneurs in the sample belong to a self-organized business association. The members of these associations are more likely to seek association help when they encounter problems: 57.4 percent reported doing so (compared with 42.7 percent of members of state-run associations), and of them 43.8 percent believed them to be more helpful than the official business associations, 36.2 percent felt they were equally effective, and only 19 percent felt they were less effective. A remarkable 90.5 percent of members of these self-organized associations felt they were better able to represent their interests than were the official business associations. However, on the question of local policy implementation, members of these self-organized associations were roughly evenly divided: just 52.8 percent said they were better able to influence policy implementation than were the official business associations. As vehicles for collective action, they may be particularly effective on business-related issues but are not seen as effective means of influencing local policy implementation.

Summary

In contrast to my original findings, the most recent survey data indicate that China's business associations are unlikely to be used as vehicles for collective action against the state, nor do they effectively monitor the private firms on behalf of the party. All of China's business associations, whether they are state-run or self-organized, limit their activities to business-related issues and have not yet shown a propensity to promote policy preferences on other social or political issues. Rather than being agents of change, they are more likely to cooperate with the state in their common goal of economic development. Under these circumstances, the growing diversity of business associations complicates the CCP's ability to monitor the private sector but does not challenge its political monopoly.

BUILDING PARTY BRANCHES IN THE PRIVATE SECTOR

One hallmark of a Leninist party is the penetration of both state and society with a network of party cells, but this is now being challenged with the explosion of new enterprises. Privately owned and foreign-funded enterprises are being created so fast that the party cannot create organizations within most of them, and many do not even have party members in them. This rapid expansion of the nonstate sectors has weakened the CCP's ability to monitor and control what goes on there. As Andrew Walder notes, monitoring capacity is one of the key elements of a communist system. As it declines, so does the stability of the political system.[26] Despite the fact that the party's traditional style of party building has not been able to keep pace with economic and social change (especially the growth of small and medium-sized enterprises and the mobility of firms, managers, and workers), it has not abandoned the practice. Rather than adopt a new approach for

---

[26] Walder, "Decline of Communist Power."

monitoring its environment, it has tried to portray its grassroots organizations as beneficial to firms, neighborhoods, and members, but with limited success.

An additional problem arising from the weak presence of the party in the nonstate sectors of the economy is that these sectors are sources of some of China's best talent. The people who are attractive to private enterprises and joint ventures as prospective managers and workers are also attractive to the party as potential future members and officials. If the party is not actively recruiting in these growing sectors of the economy, it will shut itself off from an important source of human talent.

Paternalistic Party Building

Local party-building efforts in the private sector exemplify the paternalistic attitudes of officials toward private entrepreneurs. While officials rely on the private sector to provide economic growth that creates more jobs and tax revenue, they also have a generally low regard for the business acumen and management abilities of most entrepreneurs. Local officials interviewed at the time of the survey repeatedly emphasized how success in party building was directly related to promoting economic development. After investigations of counterfeit, fake, and shoddy products in Hebei's county H, its party committee decided this problem was the fault of poor party building in the private sector. It then created a "nonpublic enterprise party building leading small group" headed by the county party secretary. Other members included the heads of the Organization Department, United Front Work Department, Communist Youth League, Federation of Trade Unions, Women's Federation, and the ICF. Only in this way did they believe they could achieve improvements in product quality: better party building, not inspections by the government's industrial and commercial bureau, was the solution to this problem.

Many local officials believe that party organizations can improve firm performance by promoting corporate culture during party meetings. This view was mentioned by officials in Zhejiang, where the private sector is most advanced, as well as Hunan, where it lags. The ICF head in Zhejiang's district H claimed to have read American books on corporate culture, in particular the encouragement to pay attention to the long-term interests of the firm and its employees, not just short-term benefits. He felt the party organizations in firms could help promote this idea in China, where it is lacking.

These paternalistic attitudes are not without merit. China's entrepreneurs often lack the accounting, investment, and management skills necessary to expand their businesses. Because of the policies of the Maoist era, young entrepreneurs did not have the opportunity to learn the family business. Even though many entrepreneurs come from families with capitalistic backgrounds, they were not able to engage in business for several decades and did not have the opportunity to learn on the job. The policy oscillations of the reform era also contributed to short time horizons for many businesses. Instead of trying to steadily expand their businesses by reinvesting profits, many entrepreneurs preferred to keep their assets as liquid as possible in order to transfer them abroad if policy again shifted away from economic reform. Many private entrepreneurs prefer to appoint only family members to key management positions, which limits how large the firm can grow and precludes bringing in more qualified personnel. Many also have short time horizons: they try to maximize short-term profits instead of expanding market share, improving product quality, or establishing brand identity. For these reasons, local officials see party building not just as a means of party leadership but more importantly as a way to put into practice the party's pledge to "support, encourage, and guide" China's private sector. The head of the Organization Department in Hebei's county H put this most succinctly when he said that in recent years, "we have adhered to the principle of 'embrace the economy and grab party building, grab party building to push development.'" The success of this approach was also evident to him: economic growth had increased by 24.7 percent over the previous year, and tax revenue increased by 22.5 percent.

Challenges of Party Building

The goal of party-building work in the private sector is quite clear: to "carry out party work wherever there is economic work, and create party organizations wherever there are party members." Any enterprise with three or more party members is expected to form its own party branch; those with less are expected to form joint party branches with other firms or with local business associations. So far, the accomplishments of party building have fallen far short of these lofty goals because of the changing economic and social environment in China.

The near absence of party organizations and recruitment in private firms has been a cause of concern for the CCP. The weakness of party building in the private sector was reportedly one of the motivations behind the CCP's efforts to promote Jiang Zemin's "Three Represents" slogan.[27] *People's Daily* reported that of the 1.2 million private firms in 1998, only 14 percent had even a single party member and only 0.9 percent had party cells.[28] In Shenzhen, the party acknowledged that party building in private enterprises was the weakest part of party building: of the more than 13,000 private enterprises in 1995, only 17 had basic-level party organizations, and less than 1 percent of workers in private enterprises were party members.[29] In Hainan, only 147 of its more than 130,000 private enterprises had "the conditions to set up a party branch" (that is, had at least three members) and only 108 had actually done so. Of the 396,420 people employed in Hainan's private sector, only 3,780 of them – less than 1 percent – were party members.[30] In 2003, there were more than 44,000 party branches and committees in approximately 3 million private enterprises nationwide.[31] Even considering that many firms share a party branch, these numbers still indicate that most firms did not have a party organization.

To camouflage these paltry numbers, the CCP occasionally puts them in the best possible light. For example, Ouyang Song, deputy head of the CCP's Central Organization Department, reported in June 2006 that the CCP had created party organizations in "85 percent

---

[27] You Dehai, "'Sange daibiao' tichu de jingguo yi fabiao de beijing" (The Process of Raising and Background of Issuing the 'Three Represents'), *Xuexi yu shijian* (Wuhan) (September 2000), pp. 18–20, 45.

[28] *Renmin ribao*, September 12, 2000, p. 11.

[29] Lu Ruifeng et al., "Shenzhen shi siying qiye dangde jianshe wenti yu duice" (Problems and Counter-measures in Party Building in Shenzhen's Private Enterprises), *Tequ lilun yu shixian* (Shenzhen) (December 1995), pp. 37–39.

[30] "CPC Grassroots Units Set Up in Private Firms in Hainan," *Xinhuanet*, April 15, 2002 (http://xinhuanet.com.english/2002–04/15/content_359006.htm), accessed November 17, 2006.

[31] "CPC Branches in Private Enterprises," *People's Daily* (online English edition), July 1, 2003.

of the 98,000 private businesses of more than 50 staff members that meet conditions of establishing CPC organizations [i.e., have more than three party members]."[32] This is a very misleading statement: China had over 4 million private enterprises by the end of 2005, so the statement applies at best to less than 3 percent of China's private firms, and then only to firms with at least three party members. Moreover, the statement applies only to firms with over 50 employees, whereas the private firms in China have an average of only 15 workers. Ouyang's statement therefore applies to only a very small and select subgroup of the private sector and ignores the broader reality: besides large-scale firms, the party's presence in the private sector remains weak. In my 2005 survey, only 28.9 percent of all firms, and only 48.1 percent of the firms with at least 50 workers, had party organizations.[33] As will be shown, challenges to party building in the private sector include structural factors, the attitudes of workers and owners, and the unsystematic management of party-building work.

Structural Factors

The small size of private enterprises in China makes for one challenge in party building. In 2004, private firms in China had an average of 15 employees. In my 2005 sample, the average is about 75, but that is skewed by some very large firms. The median firm has only 22 workers. (By comparison, firms in the 1999 survey had an average of 42 workers and a median of 15.) The typically small size of private firms means that few of them have the minimum three party members needed to form their own party branch. For example, in Zhejiang's city X (which had only one SOE at the time of the survey), less than 500 of the 57,000 nonpublic enterprises had over 50 workers and three party members; of these select few, all but two had a party organization. As

---

[32] Richard McGregor, "Firms Come to the Party in China," *Financial Times*, July 15, 2006.

[33] This is consistent with the 2006 survey of the private sector sponsored by the CCP's United Front Work Department and the ACFIC, which found that less than 30 percent of private firms had party organizations and 31.7 percent did not have a single CCP member among their workers and staff. See *2006 nian Zhongguo diqici siying qiye chouyang diaocha shuju fenxi zonghe baogao* (Comprehensive Report on the Data Analysis of China's 2006 Seventh Survey of Private Enterprises), report available at http://www.chinapec.com.cn/websites/news/newscontent.asp?id=1922, accessed September 11, 2007.

a result, the emphasis on party building in this city since 2002 switched to medium- and small-scale firms, where the party's presence was much weaker. In Shandong's city Q, only 133 of the 2,893 private enterprises had three or more party members (4.6 percent), and only 142 of them had created their own party branch or shared one with other firms (4.9 percent). In areas where the private sector is less developed, party building is even thinner. Hebei's county S had 5,343 private or *geti* enterprises with 14,313 employees but only 651 party members among them; only 30 of these enterprises had three or more party members. Hunan's city J had 193 private and 6,600 *geti* enterprises but only 247 party members among their employees. Thirteen enterprises had their own branches, and 17 others had joint branches. These examples point out the very skewed and misleading portrayal of party building by Ouyang Song noted earlier. Among all firms in both the 1999 and 2005 surveys, the likelihood that a firm will have a party organization is strongly related to the size of the firm: whether measured in terms of annual sales, fixed assets, or the number of workers, larger firms are far more likely to have party organizations within them.

In addition to the small size of enterprises, other aspects of the private sector also hampered party building. Firms frequently close down or move to a new location, making it difficult for local party officials to keep tabs on them. The proportion of private sector employees who belong to the party is typically smaller than for the population as a whole and the state-owned sector in particular. A 2001 study of the private sector in Ningbo found that less than 3 percent of its employees were party members, compared with 5.2 percent of the city population and 17.3 percent of SOE employees.[34]

Ambivalence of Workers

Even where firms have enough party members among their staff and workers to form a party branch, party building is still difficult. If such employees have taken a leave of absence from their original employer, they may not have long-term plans with their current workplace. For

---

[34] Zhang Wenyuan et al., "Cong Ningbo shi shehui jieceng bianhua kan feigong youzhi jingji zuzhi dangjian gongzuo" (Viewing Party-Building Work in Nonpublic Enterprises from Social Structural Changes in Ningbo), *Zhonggong Ningbo shiwei dangxiao xuebao* (CCP Ningbo City Party School Report), January 2002, pp. 54–59.

TABLE 4.5. *Party Building in the Private Sector, 1999 and 2005*

	1999	2005
Firms with party organizations (percent):		
All entrepreneurs	18.4	28.9
Xiahai entrepreneurs	33.1	46.3
Co-opted entrepreneurs	38.5	44.1
Want to join CCP	10.0	15.7
Do not want to join CCP	7.5	10.2
Firms whose workers have joined CCP in recent years (percent):		
All entrepreneurs	24.7	39.5
Xiahai entrepreneurs	36.3	55.7
Co-opted entrepreneurs	37.5	57.0
Want to join CCP	20.7	32.1
Do not want to join CCP	15.3	14.4
Entrepreneurs who would prefer to hire a party member over a nonparty member, all else being equal (percent):		
All entrepreneurs	54.1	62.0
Xiahai entrepreneurs	63.5	73.4
Co-opted entrepreneurs	77.3	77.1
Want to join CCP	62.9	69.0
Do not want to join CCP	31.8	30.2

others, the process of transferring their membership is simply not worth the trouble; as several local officials acknowledged, the formalities involved in transferring one's party membership are fairly cumbersome. According to the head of the Organization Department in Hunan's county C, rural party members in particular do not want to transfer their ties because they would have to pay higher dues than if their ties remained in their villages. This is such a big disincentive to transfer their ties that it is a wonder that the policy has not been modified. Many employees in private firms are even reluctant to reveal their membership, especially to their bosses, fearing they could be fired. This concern is supported by the survey data: most entrepreneurs who are not in the party and do not want to be would prefer *not* to hire a party member, all else being equal (table 4.5). As a consequence, many party members conceal their membership, do not establish ties with local party organizations, and stop attending meetings and paying party dues. Local officials refer to them as "pocket" party members because their membership is kept hidden. In Zhejiang, there were

11,000 hidden party members in 1999, equivalent to the number of new recruits over the next two years.[35]

Many CCP members have joined the "floating population" of migrant workers for the same reason as the general population: the promise of better and higher-paying jobs elsewhere. From the party's standpoint, this creates two problems. First, most migrant party members are young and middle-aged and either business-oriented or "backbone workers," precisely the kinds of people the party is trying to attract. Second, migrant party members lose touch with their original party unit and usually do not register with the party committee in their new location and thus cannot perform their responsibilities or "vanguard role." The absence of a party organization makes it easy for them to avoid party discipline, neglect paying party dues and taxes, and engage in criminal or disruptive activities, thereby setting a poor example for other vendors and workers.

The mobility of party members also contributes to the weakness of party building in the private sector. Most migrant party members come from rural areas and are unwilling to join party branches in their new workplaces or neighborhoods. They believe that if they encounter difficulties, they are more likely to get assistance from party organizations in their hometowns, where they have some degree of status and connections, than in their new and often temporary working and living arrangements.[36] Local party committees therefore have tried to organize these migrant party members and monitor their activities. Mobility certificates are given to party members who have been away from their villages for more than six months. They are supposed to register with the party committee in their new locale, take part in meetings and study sessions, and pay dues.[37] However, these new regulations seem weak and unlikely to entice migrant party members back into

[35] Tao Qing, "Feigong youzhi jingji zuzhi dangjian gongzuo de xianzhuang fenxi" (Analysis of the Current Status of Party Building in Nonpublic Enterprises), *Zhonggong Ningbo shiwei dangxiao xuebao* (CCP Ningbo City Party School Report), February 2002, pp. 56–59.

[36] Zhou Linghua and Zheng Hefu, "Siying qiye: Dangjian luohou de yuanyin ji duice" (Private Enterprises: The Causes and Policies toward Sluggish Party Building), *Dangzheng luntan* (Shanghai) (January 1995), pp. 29–30.

[37] *Ming Pao* (Hong Kong), February 3, 1995, p. A4, in FBIS, February 6, 1995, p. 24. The most recent directive is "CPC Central Committee Opinion on Intensifying and Improving Management of Mobile CPC Members," Xinhua, June 28, 2006.

party life. These migrant party members have already decided that their economic interests outweigh their obligations to the party, which interfere with getting rich because time lost in party meetings is time lost earning money. Adding new responsibilities to the migrant party members in the new locale is unlikely to return them to active party life.

Local party committees do not want party members to escape their obligations to pay dues and participate in party life, however. In Shandong's city Q, the local Organization Department investigated the private sector in 2003 and afterward required 450 workers to transfer their party ties to their current firm (this was over 12 percent of the party members working in the private sector). This technique is not foolproof, however; party members may also choose to have organizational ties where they live rather than where they work. The head of the Organization Department in Hunan's county C said that 20,000 party members in the nearby municipality transferred their ties from their enterprises to their new communities (*shequ*). In this sense, party-building efforts in the private sector conflict with the desire to make *shequ* a more important focus of party life, especially for those who previously worked for SOEs. Research on party building in *shequ*, however, has also revealed that the experiment has produced very limited results.[38]

Attitudes of Entrepreneurs

The main challenge to party building in the private sector is the entrepreneurs themselves, who frequently resist creating party organizations in their firms. Local officials complain that most entrepreneurs care only about profits and efficiency and have little regard for the party's goal of building organizations wherever there are party members. According to these officials, entrepreneurs believe the party organization should serve the interests of the enterprise and not be a separate office or organ. In the words of the head of the Organization Department in Zhejiang's city X, entrepreneurs in general have a "cold negative rejection mentality" when it comes to party building. His counterpart in Hunan's county C said that entrepreneurs do not want

---

[38] Kazuko Kojima and Ryosei Kokubun, "The '*Shequ* Construction' Programme and the Chinese Communist Party," in Brodsgaard and Zheng, *Bringing the Party Back In*.

to establish party organizations, do not want to interact with party organizations, and do not want to be managed by them. "Enterprise bosses do not care about party-building organizations," he said. "They only care about their own economic interests." Unless party organizations contribute to the economic productivity of the firm, entrepreneurs see little value in having them. Even reformed SOEs that already have a complete party organization do not want their secretaries to attend party meetings during work hours.

The main solution to these problems of party building in the private sector has been to recruit entrepreneurs into the party, as described in chapter 3. Red capitalists are far more likely than nonparty members to have party organizations in their firms and also more likely to have party members among their workforce (table 4.5). In Shandong's city Z, a former SOE general manager opened a private firm in 1996. Over the years, its workforce grew from 10 to 600, including 10 party members. But the firm did not have a party organization, and the party members working in it still had party ties with their original work unit, or *danwei*. Once the local Organization Department and the township party committee learned of this, they arranged to have the party admit the owner, who then created a party branch in the firm. Local officials subsequently began an investigation of all private enterprises to find other potential recruits. Red capitalists may also use cooperation in party building as a bargaining chip: at Shenzhen's party congress in 2005, a group of private entrepreneurs formed their own delegation for the first time. In return for their representation at the congress, they promised to help the party build organizations in private firms that had resisted the party's efforts thus far.[39]

If party membership is not enough to change the entrepreneurs' opposition to party building, local officials allow red capitalists to be the secretaries of the party organization in their own firms.[40] In many firms, family members hold the top management positions, including in the party organization. This would seem to contradict the goal of

---

[39] McGregor, "Firms Come to the Party in China."

[40] In Wenzhou in 2001, 45 percent of party secretaries in private enterprises were their owners. See Xue Fei, "Feigong youzhi qiye dangjian de teshuxing fenxi jiqi zhidu chuangxin" (The Special Nature of Party Building in Nonpublic Enterprises and Its Institutional Innovations), *Tansuo* (Exploration) [Zhejiang edition] (January 2002), pp. 36–40.

party building, which is to allow the party to monitor what goes on in the private sector. Having private entrepreneurs and their relatives also head their firms' party organization is an inherent conflict of interest and presumably benefits the entrepreneur far more than the party. But local officials support this model, seeing it as mutually beneficial, advantageous for local economic development, and fully consistent with higher-level directives to allow the rich and talented to become party members and allow party members to become rich and talented.

Just as workers in private firms are reluctant to transfer their party ties to their workplace, so are some owners. As the head of the Organization Department in Hebei's county S pointed out, some red capitalists both open factories and hold village-level posts (70 percent of village branch secretaries in this county were reportedly business owners). They do not want to transfer their ties to their firm because they want to retain influence in party and government affairs in their villages. In the villages, they have the right to vote and to run as a candidate, but they would lose these rights if they transferred their party membership to their enterprise. Not surprisingly, other officials in this county reported that entrepreneurs who want to join the party face opposition from village party secretaries, who fear the entrepreneurs will try to seize political control.

Resistance to party branches has been particularly strong in foreign-invested enterprises. In the 1990s, many foreign investors did not want to have party members as employees, much less have a party organization within their enterprise. As a result, the party had to remain "underground" in many of these ventures in deference to the foreign partner's wishes. In addition, many party members either lacked the necessary management expertise and sales techniques and were unable to find jobs in foreign-invested enterprises or joint ventures or, in a wonderful example of sour grapes, believed that "it would hurt the party's dignity to learn from foreign capitalists" and were therefore unwilling to work for them. As a result, most key posts were filled by the foreign partner's personnel.[41] Even when the party was allowed to

---

[41] *Liaowang*, June 13, 1994, pp. 24–25, in FBIS, July 15, 1994, pp. 21–24. As always, the solution to these problems is said to be more education: to bring the practical skills of party members up to speed on the one hand and to correct the erroneous views toward foreign capitalists on the other.

organize itself in these types of enterprises, party life was weak because it was subordinate to economic and business interests. Except for the annual democratic appraisal meeting, all other party activities took place in workers' spare time. As a result, party life was restricted to the circulation of documents, self-study, and one-on-one talks. A study of joint-venture firms in Shanghai found that many had no formal party branch and no full-time party officials. At best, the party leader served as chairman of the state-authorized union and tried to conduct party activities from that post. Much of the party's work seemed more in keeping with union activities than with monitoring compliance with party policies: mediation between labor and management in labor disputes and carrying out social functions within the enterprise, such as caring for sick workers. Although party members were still expected to attend study meetings, these meetings often focused on production and sales strategies or management skills rather than political education. These may be useful functions that benefit the enterprise's performance, but they turn the members of these party organizations into support staff instead of leading personnel.[42]

In recent years, the presence of party members and party organizations in joint ventures and foreign-invested enterprises has become less objectionable. The case of Wal-Mart has received the most attention, not only by the CCP but also the media. Wal-Mart has a well-deserved reputation for not allowing its workers to unionize in its U.S. stores and initially took a similar stance in China. After extensive negotiations, it finally agreed in 2004 to allow trade unions to form in its outlets in China, but it continued to resist efforts to also create branches for the party and its Communist Youth League. It was not until August 2006 that it finally relented and allowed the first CCP and CYL branches to form.[43] The CCP and the ACFTU intend to use Wal-Mart as a model

---

[42] "Zhagen hezi qiye fahui dang de zhengzhi youshi" (Establish Joint Ventures, Promote the Party's Political Superiority), *Dangzheng luntan* (Shanghai) (October 1999), pp. 21–23.

[43] "Wal-Mart Sees First Communist Branch in Local Outlet," *People's Daily* (online English edition), August 24, 2006. The prolonged struggle to establish trade unions in Wal-Mart's China operations is described in Anita Chan, "Organizing Wal-Mart: The Chinese Trade Union at a Crossroads," *Japan Focus* (http://japanfocus.org/products/topdf/2217), accessed September 26, 2006.

for other large foreign subsidiaries and joint ventures in the hopes of expanding their presence in this sector.

Despite these varied efforts, party building in the private sector remains far from complete. As table 4.5 shows, most private firms in the sample, including the majority of firms headed by red capitalists, do not have party organizations within them. But the party's presence in the private sector is growing: the proportion of firms with party organizations grew by 50 percent during the years between the two surveys. It is well to remember that these surveys targeted relatively large firms, and even within the sample, the likelihood of having a party organization increases with firm size. In the 2005 survey, only 15.2 percent of firms with less than 22 workers (the median size) had a party organization, compared with 42.3 percent for those above the median. In its party-building efforts in the private sector, the CCP has chosen to grasp the large private firms and release the small, at least at first; in communities where the CCP had been able to create party branches in most large firms, local party-building efforts then shifted to smaller firms.

In addition, entrepreneurs who want to gain access to China's formal political institutions are more willing to create party organizations in their firms to show their supportive attitudes.[44] As will be shown in chapter 6, entrepreneurs who seek to be elected or selected for political posts try to show their support for the party's activities; for example, by allowing party organizations to be created in their enterprises and actively participating in party meetings.

Management of Party Building

Despite the priority attached to party building in the private sector, there are no systematic and standardized procedures for managing party organizations. Not only is there no national model, management procedures even vary in the same locality. Echoing Jiang Zemin's earlier concern, officials in Hunan's city J said that if the CCP does

---

[44] Chen Guangjin, "1992–2004 niande siying qiyezhu jieceng: Yige xin jieceng de chengzhang" (Private Entrepreneurs between 1992 and 2004: The Emergence of a New Social Stratum), in Zhang Houyi et al., eds., *Zhongguo siying qiye fazhan baogao*, no. 6 (2005), pp. 251–257.

not improve its management of private enterprises, the situation will become very dangerous in the future.

Management of party building is a combination of vertical (*tiao*) and horizontal (*kuai*) methods.[45] The vertical dimension is provided by officially sponsored business associations, primarily PEA and SELA (which in some localities have been merged), and under the general supervision of the local ICF. Business associations are especially relevant for small and medium-sized firms that do not have enough party members for their own branch. Joint branches shared by several firms are typically managed by one of the official business associations. Because business associations have a better understanding of the specific features of private enterprises, they may be better able to administer vertical management over party building there. The horizontal component is provided by the local Organization Department, which has a more leading and direct role. A key part of its job is to convince entrepreneurs to allow party organizations in their firms in the first place. In addition, it is in charge of recruiting new members and getting "pocket" and migrant party members to transfer their membership (i.e., their organizational ties) to their current firm and compel them to participate in party life. This combination of vertical and horizontal methods results in a confusing division of labor. Local officials in charge of party building complained that there was no standardized management model: some party branches are managed by the Organization Department, some by the village and township offices, some by SELA, some by street committees, and so on. In one of the Shandong survey sites, management of party committees in private enterprises is handled by the CCP's United Front Work and Organization Departments; in the other Shandong site, it is handled mostly by the combined PEA/SELA.

A complicating factor in the management of party building is that its results are not part of cadre evaluations. In only one county (where the private sector was relatively undeveloped) was it part of the regular development plan. In other areas, officials recommended that it be

---

[45] On the general practice of *tiao* and *kuai* in China's administration, see Kenneth Lieberthal, *Governing China: From Revolution through Reform* (New York: Norton, 2004).

included in annual performance evaluations for cadres. Otherwise, the work would not be given much importance. Unless it became a "hard target" for local cadres, there would be no negative consequences if progress were not made.[46] In general, local officials in all the communities covered in the survey complained about the lack of a systematic and standardized process for the management and evaluation of party-building work.

Local officials involved in party building acknowledged that the quality of service and level of support provided by local party and government offices were directly related to the entrepreneurs' attitudes toward party-building work. It is not enough for them to tout the importance of party building; they also had to address the economic interests of the enterprises. These kinds of initiatives put party branches in the service of the firms, which is just how the entrepreneurs want it. Given the predominantly pro-business orientation of most party and government officials at all levels in China, party organizations within private enterprises support the business interests of the firms and do not burden party members in the firms with additional duties that would not be in the firms' interest. This is exactly the fear that critics of the party's relationship with the private sector have in mind: the importance of the party's traditional interest in politics and ideology is becoming increasingly diminished. The need to promote rapid economic growth is the primary factor in the party's work, which has led to the integration of wealth and power in contemporary China, especially at the local level.

Summary

Just as "grasp the large, release the small" is the CCP's strategy for SOE reform, it is likewise an appropriate metaphor for its party-building efforts in the private sector: owners of large firms are more likely to

---

[46] On the importance of hard targets in cadre performance, see Kevin J. O'Brien and Lianjiang Li, "Selective Policy Implementation in Rural China," *Comparative Politics*, vol. 31, no. 2 (January 1999), pp. 167–186; Maria Heimer, "The Cadre Responsibility System and the Changing Needs of the Party," in Kjeld Erik Brodsgaard and Zheng Yongnian, eds., *The Chinese Communist Party in Reform* (London: Routledge, 2006).

be recruited, and efforts to create party branches also concentrated on large firms. Because red capitalists are more likely to have party organizations in their firms, recruiting more entrepreneurs also allows the CCP to expand its presence in the private sector. If the survey data reported here are generalizable to other areas of China, then the CCP's party-building efforts in the private sector are yielding positive but still limited results, especially in firms owned by red capitalists. But the data also indicate that some entrepreneurs, especially those with small and medium-sized firms, prefer to remain outside the party's embrace.

CONCLUSION

The party has maintained its traditional practices of building institutional bridges to the main social groups and organizing party branches wherever its members live and work, even though economic and social changes that have accompanied the party's reform agenda have complicated its party-building efforts. Party building in the private sector also reveals the paternalistic aspect of crony communism in China. Local party and government officials do not hold the management and entrepreneurial skills of local businessmen in high regard, and they view party building as a means of improving the quality of individual firms and the private sector as a whole. The party is determined not just to support the private sector but to guide it as well.

Party building has fallen short of these lofty goals, however. The formal business associations are seen by the businessmen as representing the state's interests more than their own, and fewer businesses rely on them to solve their problems. The need for more effective institutions to promote collective interests has led to an explosion of self-organized business and trade groups, which are generally seen as more effective than the official business associations. As a result, the CCP's corporatist strategy of using formal institutions as bridges to the private sector has had limited success. However, even the self-organized business associations limit their activities to business matters and do not get involved in broader political and social issues. The CCP is willing to allow these numerous business groups to exist and operate because they belong to the economic realm of civil society and share the CCP's interest in promoting economic development. Party organizations within private firms similarly are primarily used to promote economic interests rather than overtly political goals. Although these bridges and branches have not proven to be effective at providing party leadership over the private sector, they have indirectly contributed to meeting a key goal of the party's survival strategy – preventing the emergence of an organized opposition.

5

Views on the Economic, Political, and Social Environments

The emergence of a private sector in China has given rise to speculation that it will eventually lead to pressures for political change. Advocates of modernization theory see the social changes that accompany economic growth in China to be precursors of political change.[1] The growing number of private entrepreneurs, the even larger middle class, and their greater integration into the political system give hope to some that their influence will ultimately push China in the direction of greater democracy.[2] Expectations that China's private entrepreneurs will be agents of political change are based on two assumptions. First is that the Chinese Communist Party is a passive actor in this process.

---

[1] Robert M. Glassman, *China in Transition: Communism, Capitalism, and Democracy* (New York: Praeger, 1991); Henry S. Rowen, "The Short March: China's Road to Democracy," *The National Interest*, no. 45 (Fall 1996), pp. 61–70; Henry S. Rowen, "The Growth of Freedoms in China," APARC Working Paper, Stanford University, 2001; Shaohua Hu, *Explaining Chinese Democratization* (Westport, CT: Praeger, 2000); Ronald Inglehart and Christopher Welzel, *Modernization, Cultural Change, and Democracy: The Human Development Sequence* (Cambridge: Cambridge University Press, 2005).

[2] Gordon White, Jude Howell, and Shang Xiaoyuan, *In Search of Civil Society: Market Reform and Social Change in Contemporary China* (Oxford: Oxford University Press, 1996); Thomas Gold, "Bases for Civil Society in Reform China," in Kjeld Erik Brodsgaard and David Strand, eds., *Reconstructing Twentieth-Century China: State Control, Civil Society, and National Identity* (Oxford: Oxford University Press, 1998); Kristen Parris, "The Rise of Private Business Interests," in Merle Goldman and Roderick MacFarquhar, eds., *The Paradox of China's Post-Mao Reforms* (Cambridge, MA: Harvard University Press, 1999).

As previous chapters have emphasized, however, the CCP has actively promoted the expansion of the private sector, proactively recruited large numbers of entrepreneurs into the party (even though the majority of "red capitalists" were in the party before going into business), and strived with limited success to build corporatist-style institutional links and extend party organizations into private firms. The second assumption is that entrepreneurs hold policy preferences, values, and interests that are fundamentally different from those of incumbent officials in the party and government. In order to be agents of change, entrepreneurs would need to have both the motive and the opportunity to wield their influence in ways that will lead to change. Given the CCP's growing support for the private sector and the entrepreneurs' growing presence in the party, they clearly have the opportunity, but are their views on economic, political, and social matters so different from those of local officials that they will be motivated to change the system in which they have prospered?

This chapter will compare the views of local officials and private entrepreneurs in order to assess areas of common interest and potential discord between political and economic elites at the local level. The analysis will begin with broad questions about the policy environment and then turn to more specific issues. In particular, the focus will be on the views of officials and entrepreneurs on a number of key issues: the pace, process, and extent of economic and political reforms; the consequences of economic growth for social stability; the severity of business problems; and overall satisfaction with living standards and social status. If private entrepreneurs are to serve as agents of political change, they should have views distinctly different from those of incumbent officials. Their involvement in the political process would allow them to assert new policy preferences and pressure the government to accommodate them. On the other hand, if the views of entrepreneurs and local officials are basically similar, then their views will mutually reinforce one another rather than lead to changes in policy, much less fundamental political change. Under these circumstances, the growing number of private entrepreneurs and their greater integration into the political system will be more likely to support the status quo than challenge it and thereby perpetuate the crony communist system in China.

THE PACE, PROCESS, AND EXTENT OF REFORMS

Survey data from eight counties spread across four provinces at two points in time provide the basis for comparing the views of local party and government officials with those of private entrepreneurs in their communities. The survey data indicate growing satisfaction with the pace of economic and political reform (see table 5.1). The overwhelming majority of both entrepreneurs and officials are satisfied with the pace of economic reform, with clear increases in the percentage of those who feel it is "about right" and even larger decreases in the percentage of those who feel it is too slow. Entrepreneurs' relationships with the party influenced responses to this question, with red capitalists more likely to feel the pace of economic reform was too fast and less likely to feel it was just right. The level of development also had an impact: in the poorest counties in the 2005 survey, 26.5 percent of the entrepreneurs believed that the pace of reform was too slow compared with 18.5 percent in the moderately prosperous counties and 10.6 percent in the richest counties. In the areas that have not yet prospered under the reforms, support for a faster pace of change is understandably highest. Among officials, in contrast, there is no difference associated with the level of development. What does matter in their case is bureaucratic rank: in the 2005 survey, more county-level officials than township/village officials believed economic reform was too slow (28 percent vs. 18.3 percent); conversely, twice as many township/village officials believed it was too fast (12 percent vs. 5.9 percent). Nevertheless, the vast majority of officials at both levels believed the pace was about right.

On the issue of the pace of political reform, there is a similar but smaller central tendency among entrepreneurs, with decreases in the percentages who believe it is either too fast or too slow and a consequent increase in the percentage who believe it is "about right."[3] Satisfaction with the pace of reform does not depend on party membership: similar percentages of both those who are closest to the party (the *xiahai* red capitalists) and those who are most removed from it (who do not want to join the CCP) thought that the pace of political reform was

---

[3] The question was mistakenly left off the cadre questionnaire in the 2005 survey, so comparisons with entrepreneurs are not possible.

TABLE 5.1. *The Pace of Reform in China*
(percentages)

	Entrepreneurs		Cadres	
	1999	2005	1999	2005
Pace of economic reform				
Too fast	9.7	12.5	8.9	9.4
About right	58.9	70.3	60.6	68.2
Too slow	31.4	17.2	30.5	22.4
Pace of political reform				
Too fast	5.7	4.4	5.6	$-^a$
About right	55.1	59.8	37.5	$-^a$
Too slow	39.1	35.8	56.9	$-^a$

[a] This question was not asked of cadres in the 2005 survey.

too slow, and in both cases the percentages were smaller in 2005 than in 1999. The large and increased percentage who expressed satisfaction with the pace of political reform indicates general support for the party's economic and political reform agenda. However, it is also true that the percentage of entrepreneurs who believe the pace of political reform is too slow is twice as large as those who believe the pace of economic reform is too slow. The level of development again has a significant impact on entrepreneurs' views, but in the opposite direction from that concerning the pace of economic reform: entrepreneurs living in the more prosperous counties are more likely to feel that the pace of political reform is too slow. Geography also plays a role: the two Hunan counties have the highest percentages of those who feel the pace of political reform is too slow (53.4 percent and 43.7 percent), and Hebei has the two lowest (28.3 percent and 27.4 percent), despite their differences in level of development (Hebei's county S is the poorest in the sample, whereas its county H and the two Hunan counties are in the moderately prosperous category). What types of political reforms entrepreneurs might be inclined to support are not apparent from the survey data, but at a minimum we can infer from these data that most entrepreneurs would not support a slowdown in political reform.

What role should society play in the reform process? That is one of the fundamental questions facing the party and proponents of political change in China. Upholding the party's ability to control the reform agenda has been a hallmark of the post-Mao era, beginning with Deng Xiaoping's "Four Cardinal Principles," which set parameters around political activity. These principles, announced in the context of the 1978–1979 "Democracy Wall" movement, were upholding the socialist road; the people's democratic dictatorship; the leading role of the CCP; and Marxism–Leninism–Mao Zedong Thought. Although the meaning and importance of three of the principles changed in later years, the core principle – the leadership of the CCP – has never wavered. Political protests in 1986–1987 and 1989 were in large part motivated by the conflict between political activists who wanted to join the policy debate and party leaders who insisted on the primacy of party leadership. The extent to which entrepreneurs support party leadership in initiating further economic and political reform is therefore one indicator of their support for the status quo, which is based on party supremacy. In a larger sense, support for party leadership in initiating reform is also a measure of whether one holds traditional values of deference to the state as opposed to more modern values that assert an active role for nonstate actors.

Depending on whether the issue is economic or political reform, the views of entrepreneurs are quite different.[4] In both the 1999 and 2005 surveys, entrepreneurs were nearly unanimous: over 95 percent of entrepreneurs supported party leadership in economic reform (see table 5.2).[5] In the potentially more controversial area of political reform, there was more diversity in responses and remarkably less support for party leadership. Roughly half of both entrepreneurs and cadres supported party leadership in the 1999 survey, but that support dropped in 2005, when over 60 percent favored some societal role. Among entrepreneurs, however, there were notable differences. Over half of the red capitalists supported party leadership in 1999, whereas most non-CCP entrepreneurs did not. In 2005, in contrast,

---

[4] On the questions for whether the party should initiate further economic and political reform without societal involvement, respondents could strongly agree, agree, disagree, or strongly disagree.

[5] The wording on the cadre questionnaire was slightly different, making comparisons with entrepreneurs difficult. In both 1999 and 2005, roughly 95 percent of cadres agreed that further economic reform was not only the responsibility of the party and government but that private entrepreneurs should also be involved.

TABLE 5.2. *Support for State Leadership in Initiating Economic and Political Reform (percentage who agree)*

	1999	2005
1. Measures to further deepen economic reform should be initiated by party and government leaders, not by society		
Entrepreneurs	96.5	96.0
Xiahai entrepreneurs	96.0	95.5
Co-opted entrepreneurs	98.5	98.2
Want to join CCP	97.2	98.1
Don't want to join CCP	95.6	93.1
2. Measures to further deepen political reform should be initiated by party and government leaders, not by society		
Entrepreneurs	50.1	37.7
Xiahai entrepreneurs	60.3	43.0
Co-opted entrepreneurs	55.4	28.7
Want to join CCP	40.1	37.0
Don't want to join CCP	46.9	36.7
Cadres	48.0	38.1
County	43.2	31.4
Township/village	54.6	43.1

majorities of both types of entrepreneurs supported a societal role. Not surprisingly, *xiahai* entrepreneurs were most likely to still support party leadership; after all, they are already embedded in the party. Even among them, however, the majority favored societal involvement, and the difference between them and other entrepreneurs was not significant when other variables were held constant. Younger and better-educated entrepreneurs were more likely than others to support a societal role, as were those in the most prosperous counties. A comparison of the views of cadres and entrepreneurs finds no significant difference between them. There were significant differences among cadres in both surveys, however: township and village cadres were more likely to prefer party leadership. Although the percentages of both county and township/village officials that supported party leadership in initiating political reform dropped by similar amounts, the absolute difference between them remained the same. Other key variables – age, education, and level of development – were not significant, only rank was. Despite these various differences, a more basic trend requires highlighting: support for party leadership in political reform fell for all groups in these surveys, and in 2005 substantial majorities favored societal involvement. This was true of both cadres and entrepreneurs alike.

Apart from the convergence of views regarding the pace of reform and the potential role of society in the reform process, how well do local officials and entrepreneurs agree on whether reforms have been implemented in their communities? According to the survey data, not very well. As shown in table 5.3, there are sharp differences between and within the two groups. On every item, a higher percentage of cadres reported that political reforms have been carried out locally, and on most items the difference is tremendous, up to twice as much.[6] On most items, more county-level cadres than township/village officials reported that reforms had taken place. This is the case for every item in the 1999 survey and five out of seven in 2005. To some degree, these differences make sense. Cadres are responsible for implementing and documenting local political reforms and may be aware of changes even if they are not as readily perceptible to others, such as private entrepreneurs. Moreover, county officials have a broader scope of knowledge: these reforms may have been carried out somewhere in the county but not necessarily in the townships where the surveys were conducted with township and village cadres. Some reforms may have been carried out primarily at the county level, so higher-level officials would naturally have more knowledge of them than would township and village officials. Political reforms are unevenly implemented in China, not only horizontally, with some provinces, cities, and counties more successful than others, but also vertically, with reforms at higher levels not extending down to the grass roots. Among the eight counties in the survey, no county is either a notable trailblazer or a notable laggard. Zhejiang's urban district H, the most prosperous site in the survey, comes closest to being a trailblazer: it is always above average, and ranks first or second on most questions, but not by wide margins.

---

[6] This is not an objective measure of political reform or a test of political knowledge. I did not collect information on which of these reforms were being implemented to be able to compare responses to what was actually occurring in the different communities. The questions concern only the perceptions of respondents about what kinds of reforms were being implemented locally.

TABLE 5.3. *The Extent of Local Political Reforms, 1999—2005*
(percentage who agree)

	1999	2005
Raise Cadre Knowledge of the Legal System		
Entrepreneurs	69.3	72.0
Xiahai entrepreneurs	71.7	76.7
Co-opted entrepreneurs	84.9	78.4
Want to join CCP	68.9	68.6
Don't want to join CCP	61.9	64.6
Cadres	91.7	92.1
County	95.5	94.5
Township/village	86.6	90.0
Strengthen Laws and Regulations		
Entrepreneurs	74.7	69.8
Xiahai entrepreneurs	79.5	71.1
Co-opted entrepreneurs	80.3	70.7
Want to join CCP	71.9	76.5
Don't want to join CCP	70.6	60.6
Cadres	79.0	74.2
County	81.8	68.9
Township/village	75.3	78.1
Lower Ages of Cadres		
Entrepreneurs	61.8	57.4
Xiahai entrepreneurs	72.4	57.3
Co-opted entrepreneurs	68.2	65.3
Want to join CCP	60.0	58.4
Don't want to join CCP	52.5	51.2
Cadres	79.0	76.7
County	81.8	75.6
Township/village	75.3	77.5
Village Elections		
Entrepreneurs	51.6	46.6
Xiahai entrepreneurs	63.8	50.0
Co-opted entrepreneurs	53.0	57.5
Want to join CCP	46.7	46.7
Don't want to join CCP	48.1	34.7
Cadres	72.9	73.5
County	77.3	74.0
Township/village	67.0	73.1

(continued)

TABLE 5.3 *(continued)*

	1999	2005
Strengthen Party's Leading Role in the Economic Transition Process		
Entrepreneurs	**41.4**	**41.8**
Xiahai entrepreneurs	45.7	47.2
Co-opted entrepreneurs	54.5	55.7
Want to join CCP	44.4	37.3
Don't want to join CCP	31.3	29.5
Cadres	**67.7**	**69.2**
County	71.2	71.4
Township/village	62.9	67.5
Strengthen People's Congresses at All Levels		
Entrepreneurs	**38.8**	**35.5**
Xiahai entrepreneurs	55.1	37.1
Co-opted entrepreneurs	37.9	43.7
Want to join CCP	31.1	35.7
Don't want to join CCP	35.0	27.6
Cadres	**67.7**	**65.6**
County	74.2	68.9
Township/village	58.8	63.1
Open Policymaking Process to Democratic Parties and Nonparty People		
Entrepreneurs	**25.2**	**25.3**
Xiahai entrepreneurs	28.4	27.5
Co-opted entrepreneurs	27.7	28.1
Want to join CCP	24.4	24.7
Don't want to join CCP	23.3	20.9
Cadres	**55.5**	**58.4**
County	63.6	59.7
Township/village	44.3	57.5

Even though Shandong's county Q had been designated by Beijing as a "national model county in the practice of self-rule by villagers," it did not get high marks among either cadres or entrepreneurs for actually implementing village elections: the percentages of both groups who recognized the implementation of village elections in this county was only average.

There are also huge differences between red capitalists and non-CCP entrepreneurs regarding their awareness of local political reforms. On every item in the 1999 survey and five of seven in 2005, red capitalists are more likely to report that political reforms have been carried out than non-CCP entrepreneurs. This results in part from the fact that as party members they have access to better information. It is also because of the red capitalists' higher level of participation in China's formal political institutions (which will be discussed in more detail in the next chapter). Those who have been local people's congress delegates are more likely than other entrepreneurs to recognize political reforms, with higher percentages on all seven items in both the 1999 and 2005 surveys. Similarly, those who have been candidates in village elections had higher scores on all items in 1999 and six of seven in 2005. Red capitalists are far more likely to participate in both these forms of political participation than are non-CCP entrepreneurs. As a result, their awareness of political reforms is higher across the board.

The group that is least aware of political reforms is the one that is farthest removed from the CCP's reach: on all items in 2005 and most in 1999, entrepreneurs who are not in the CCP and do not want to be are least likely to acknowledge any type of political reform. This may be because they are disaffected and cynical and not impressed by the nature or extent of political reforms or because they are simply not interested in politics and therefore not aware of what is occurring. But these differences among entrepreneurs pale in comparison to the contrast between entrepreneurs and cadres.

The other key finding is that the recognition of political reforms did not increase between 1999 and 2005: on every item, the percentage of respondents who recognized the implementation of a given reform either remained essentially unchanged or declined. This stagnation in the extent of political reform did not create dissatisfaction, however: as noted, the overall percentage of entrepreneurs who said the pace of political reform was too slow dropped between 1999 and 2005. Moreover, the level of satisfaction with the *pace* of reform was not related to recognition of actual *implementation* of political reforms. In fact, on several items, those who said the pace of reform was too slow were most likely to recognize that reforms were being implemented. Even among the entrepreneurs who did not want to join the CCP, who were least likely to recognize local reforms, the percentage who believed the pace of political reform was too slow dropped from 44.1 percent to 38.5 percent. In other words, even though entrepreneurs may not report that reforms are being implemented locally even if they are, this has not led to increased support for a faster pace of political reform.

CONSEQUENCES OF GROWTH

One of the most salient differences in development strategy is the trade-off between economic growth and political stability. The need to preserve stability amid rapid economic development is a primary justification for maintaining authoritarian rule in China as well as many other countries.[7] The goals of growth and stability are often seen as complementary in China. One of the most common slogans to describe the goals of economic policies is *fazhan yu wending*, literally development and stability as two sides of the same coin. In practice, however, they receive different emphases. For example, the CCP promoted the goal of creating a "relatively well-off society" to justify the pursuit of rapid growth during the Jiang Zemin era but shifted toward an emphasis on building a "harmonious society" under the leadership of Hu Jintao and Wen Jiabao once the negative social consequences of rapid growth and the threat to political and social stability in particular had become too apparent to ignore. Moreover, survey respondents were able to distinguish priorities between these goals. They are not mutually exclusive but are given different priorities at different points in time and by different groups of people.

This trade-off became particularly salient in China as the number of local protests increased sharply in recent years. The number of public protests more than doubled during the period between the two surveys, from 32,000 in 1999 to 87,000 in 2005.[8] Many of these protests have been the consequence of the strategy of rapid growth, such as the conversion of agricultural land for industrial development, environmental degradation, and official corruption (see chapter 7 for more details). This growing threat to stability, and the attention given to it by Beijing, should have helped change the views of local officials, leading them to attenuate their support for growth at the expense of stability.

---

[7] Samuel P. Huntington, "The Goals of Development," in Myron Weiner and Samuel P. Huntington, eds., *Understanding Political Development: An Analytic Study* (Boston: Little, Brown, 1987).
[8] Richard McGregor, "Data Show Social Unrest on the Rise in China," *Financial Times*, January 19, 2006.

TABLE 5.4. *Preference for Growth over*
Stability among Cadres and Entrepreneurs
(percentages of those who prefer growth
over stability as top goal)

	1999	2005
All entrepreneurs	41.7	44.6
Xiahai entrepreneurs	39.1	42.9
Co-opted entrepreneurs	29.9	47.3
Want to join CCP	42.1	42.1
Don't want to join CCP	47.9	47.5
All cadres	60.6	49.1
County cadres	76.2	59.3
Township/village cadres	39.6	41.6

Survey data allow us to see how this trade-off between growth and stability is perceived at the local level both between levels of the state and between political and economic elites. Both cadres and entrepreneurs were asked whether their top priority was promoting growth or maintaining stability. One of the most remarkable findings in the first survey was the apparent cleavage between cadres and entrepreneurs on this trade-off, one of the few where the two groups were "diametrically opposed."[9] However, disaggregating cadres reveals a more interesting story: the difference is not between cadres and entrepreneurs but between county cadres and the rest of the respondents (see table 5.4). In 1999, county cadres were most in favor of promoting growth as their top priority: 76.2 percent favored growth over stability, almost double the percentage of township/village cadres and entrepreneurs. The difference between township/village cadres and entrepreneurs was not significant. These results are not surprising: the first survey was conducted at the high point of the growth-first strategy of the Jiang Zemin era, and county cadres had a strong incentive to support growth over stability. Economic growth was a "hard target" that they had to meet in order to get favorable annual reviews and increase their prospects for promotion.[10] Why did this priority on

[9] Bruce J. Dickson, *Red Capitalists in China: The Party, Private Entrepreneurs, and Prospects for Political Change* (Cambridge: Cambridge University Press, 2003), pp. 132–134.

[10] Kevin J. O'Brien and Lianjiang Li, "Selective Policy Implementation in Rural China," *Comparative Politics*, vol. 31, no. 2 (January 1999), pp. 167–186; Maria Heimer,

economic growth not influence the priorities of township and village cadres to the same extent? We would need to know more about the specific targets assigned to local cadres and how they vary by bureaucratic level to know for sure, but it is clear that township and village officials are at the front line of defense against popular protest and political instability. Although they also need to promote economic growth, the responsibility for stability falls on them. But the change in priority from the elitism of the Jiang era to the populism of the Hu/Wen era is only partially reflected in the perceptions of local leaders. In 2005, a clear majority of county officials remained in favor of growth over stability, even though the percentage dropped relative to 1999. The numbers for township/village officials and entrepreneurs, however, showed a slight increase in those who favored growth, but the majority of these groups still had maintaining stability as their top priority. Differences among entrepreneurs and between entrepreneurs and township/village cadres were not statistically significant in 2005, but the difference between both groups and county cadres was ($p[t] < .001$).

The level of economic development has a limited impact on these results. In 1999, the differences among cadres and between county cadres and entrepreneurs were significant in all eight counties ($p[t] < .001$), regardless of their level of development. Similarly, the difference between township/village cadres and entrepreneurs was not significant in any county. In 2005, the differences between county cadres and the other groups narrowed, and in the four least-developed counties the differences were no longer statistically significant. In a multivariate analysis (not shown here), those living in the most prosperous counties, where long-term growth and expansion of the private sector were fastest, were more likely to prefer stability to growth, all else being equal.

These results show the significant differences between levels of the state, political and economic elites, and levels of development on the goals of development. From other questions in the survey, it is possible to get a more specific look at what respondents saw as potential threats to stability. All respondents were asked whether social changes

"The Cadre Responsibility System and the Changing Needs of the Party," in Kjeld Erik Brodsgaard and Zheng Yongnian, eds., *The Chinese Communist Party in Reform* (London: Routledge, 2006).

resulting at least in part from ongoing modernization were threats to stability. The specific questions were:[11]

- Competition between firms and individuals is harmful to social stability.
- If a country has multiple parties, it can lead to political chaos.
- If everybody does not share the same thinking, society can be chaotic.
- Locally, if there are many groups with different opinions, that can influence local stability.

People who agree with these statements have a more traditional, Confucian orientation toward preserving harmony and stability through unity. Those who disagree do not see diversity and pluralism as an inherent threat to stability, a more modern viewpoint. The responses from my two surveys are shown in table 5.5, and several trends are worth highlighting. First, on every question in both the 1999 and 2005 surveys, county-level cadres had the lowest scores, indicating that on average they were less concerned with threats to stability arising from economic competition and social pluralism than were township and village officials and all groups of entrepreneurs. In contrast, the views of township/village officials were largely similar to those of entrepreneurs. Second, on the three questions concerning increasing pluralism or diversification, all groups of entrepreneurs saw less of a threat to stability in 2005 than in 1999. In a few cases, the decline was slight, but in most it was greater than five percentage points. Changes among cadres were not as systematic. Third, the biggest difference is on the first question, regarding competition: in

---

[11] These questions were originally used in Taiwan to measure the shift from traditional to modern political values, and the latter three were later included in the Asian Barometer Survey. See, for example, William L. Parish and Charles Chi-Hsiang Chang, "Political Values in Taiwan: Sources of Change and Constancy," in Hung-mao Tien, ed., *Taiwan's Electoral Politics and Democratic Transition: Riding the Third Wave* (Armonk, NY: M. E. Sharpe, 1996), pp. 27–41; Yu-tzung Chang, Yun-han Chu, and Frank Tsai, "Confucianism and Democratic Values in Three Chinese Societies," *Issues and Studies*, vol. 41, no. 4 (December 2005), pp. 1–33; Andrew J. Nathan and Tse-Hsin Chen, "Traditional Social Values, Democratic Values, and Political Participation," *Asian Barometer Working Paper Series*, no. 23 (2004); Chung-min Park and Doh Chull Shin, "Do Asian Values Deter Popular Support for Democracy? The Case of South Korea," *Asian Barometer Working Paper Series*, no. 26 (2004).

TABLE 5.5. *Perceived Threats to Stability among Private Entrepreneurs and Local Cadres (percentage who agree)*

	1999	2005		1999	2005
1. Competition between firms and individuals is harmful to social stability					
All entrepreneurs	24.5	26.4	All cadres	11.9	12.2
Xiahai entrepreneurs	18.7	22.5	County cadres	9.9	10.1
Co-opted entrepreneurs	22.7	27.7	Township/village cadres	14.7	13.8
Want to join CCP	25.2	27.8			
Don't want to join CCP	29.2	29.4			
2. If a country has multiple parties, it can lead to political chaos					
All entrepreneurs	48.0	45.7	All cadres	40.5	40.4
Xiahai entrepreneurs	50.8	49.9	County cadres	36.9	33.9
Co-opted entrepreneurs	47.7	47.3	Township/village cadres	45.3	45.3
Want to join CCP	49.3	44.8			
Don't want to join CCP	42.9	39.8			
3. If everybody does not share the same thinking, society can be chaotic					
All entrepreneurs	37.6	30.7	All cadres	22.0	21.6
Xiahai entrepreneurs	33.9	33.1	County cadres	16.7	18.7
Co-opted entrepreneurs	43.1	26.1	Township/village cadres	29.5	23.8
Want to join CCP	43.6	31.5			
Don't want to join CCP	33.8	29.7			
4. Locally, if there are many groups with different opinions, that can influence local stability					
All entrepreneurs	43.3	34.8	All cadres	33.8	28.8
Xiahai entrepreneurs	40.0	30.5	County cadres	32.3	16.9
Co-opted entrepreneurs	46.5	31.3	Township/village cadres	35.8	37.5
Want to join CCP	41.3	38.9			
Don't want to join CCP	44.7	38.6			

both years, all groups of entrepreneurs were much more concerned about this threat to stability than were officials, and that concern grew between 1999 and 2005 both in absolute terms and relative to officials.[12] Although concerns about social diversity declined for all groups of entrepreneurs, concerns about economic competition rose

---

[12] In Dickson, *Red Capitalists in China*, the percentage of entrepreneurs who agreed that economic competition was a threat to stability in the 1999 survey was misreported due to a coding error (pp. 130–131).

for all of them. This is ironic because entrepreneurs were less concerned about the business environment than were officials, as will be shown; in particular, they saw local, national, and foreign competition as both less prevalent and less severe in 2005 than in 1999. But their concern that this competition could spill over into social instability was much more pronounced than it was for cadres, who were more likely to observe competitive pressures but much less likely to be worried about their effects on society. Finally, both entrepreneurs and cadres saw economic competition as less of a threat to stability than political and social diversity. In both surveys, entrepreneurs and officials agreed on the rank ordering of threats to stability: economic competition was lowest, competition between parties was highest, and competition among individuals and groups fell in between. Although the absolute levels varied over time and among subgroups, the rank ordering was the same. This similarity highlights the shared views of private entrepreneurs and local officials, especially regarding the consequences of social diversification.

Responses to these questions were highly correlated in the 2005 survey, allowing them to be combined into an index to show how other variables help explain attitudes about the effects of competition and diversity.[13] The responses to each question were coded 0–3, ranging from "strongly agree" to "strongly disagree," yielding an index that ranges from 0 to 12. In the 2005 survey, this index had a mean of 7.01 and a standard deviation of 2.42. Just as county cadres were the most likely to give growth priority over stability, they were also the least likely to be concerned about threats to stability, whether arising from economic competition or social and political diversity (see table 5.6). In a multivariate analysis, the negative coefficients for *township/village cadres* and *entrepreneurs* indicate that these groups have more traditional concerns that economic competition and social pluralism can harm stability. The other variables have effects consistent with other research explaining value orientations: those who are better educated and live in more prosperous communities are more likely to hold

---

[13] Pairwise correlations between the four questions ranged from .17 to .46, all significant beyond the .001 level. Among entrepreneurs, the four questions were only weakly correlated in 1999, mostly because of the question on economic competition. Among cadres, in contrast, these four questions were moderately correlated in the 1999 survey. To simplify the discussion here, I will focus only on the 2005 data.

TABLE 5.6. *Traditional and Modern Value
Orientations among Cadres and Entrepreneurs
(OLS regression coefficients with robust standard
errors in parentheses)*

Township/village cadres[a]	−.668*
	(.261)
Entrepreneurs[a]	−.581*
	(.239)
Age	−.017
	(.011)
Gender	−.239
	(.190)
Level of education	.595**
	(.096)
Years in county	−.001
	(.007)
Level of development	.037*
	(.016)
Rate of growth, 1999–2003	−.008
	(.004)
Size of private sector	.469
	(.274)
Constant	6.191**
	(.739)
N	1,276
Adjusted R^2	.067

[a] Reference group is county cadres.
*$p < .05$; **$p < .001$.

modern values (tests for curvilinear relationships for age and education were negative). Even when holding constant the respondents' status as cadres or entrepreneurs, these other socioeconomic characteristics remain significant. Among entrepreneurs, there is no statistically significant difference between red capitalists and other entrepreneurs or between entrepreneurs and township/village cadres.

These findings are consistent with those regarding the trade-offs on the goals of development and reinforce the point that entrepreneurs have more in common with township/village officials, with whom they have greater proximity and therefore more opportunities to interact, than they do with county officials. County cadres stand out as being less concerned about stability, whether derived from growth, competition, or increased pluralism.

THE BUSINESS ENVIRONMENT

In this section, the views of private entrepreneurs and local party and government officials on the severity of problems in the business environment will be compared. In both the 1999 and 2005 surveys, entrepreneurs and officials were asked to assess the severity of several problems related to business, either for the community as a whole (for cadres) or for their individual enterprises (for entrepreneurs). The same list of problems was used in both surveys in order to compare responses. Respondents were asked whether each issue was not a problem, something of a problem, a severe problem, or a very severe problem, and their answers were coded 0–3 accordingly. This lets us examine both the prevalence of a problem and its severity.[14] On none of the items is there a significant difference between county and township/village cadres, so they will be combined in the analysis that follows. Significant differences between red capitalists and other entrepreneurs were only present on some items: transportation and enterprise management in 1999 and finding qualified workers, local competition, dealings with officials, and local government support in both the 1999 and 2005 surveys. To simplify matters, I will first concentrate on differences between cadres and entrepreneurs and then consider differences among entrepreneurs in a multivariate analysis.

Table 5.7 presents the responses from the two surveys. Several trends are apparent and merit highlighting. First, cadres had a more pessimistic view of the business environment facing the private sector than did the private entrepreneurs themselves. On all but one issue, cadres saw each of the problems as both more prevalent and more severe than did the entrepreneurs. The exception is for local government support of the private economy, which cadres saw as less of a problem than did entrepreneurs. However, entrepreneurs saw this as becoming more prevalent between 1999 and 2005, despite the changes in central policy and perceptions of local cadres. Whereas chapter 2 showed the CCP's growing support for the private sector, in both rhetoric and practice, not all entrepreneurs perceived this support for

---

[14] Several obvious business issues, such as taxes and corruption, were not included in the questionnaire at the suggestion of local officials, who deemed them too sensitive. "Dealings with local officials" may implicitly include those kinds of issues but is not a direct indicator of them.

TABLE 5.7. *Perceived Prevalence of Severity of Local Business Problems, 1999 and 2005*

	% Who see problem		Severity of problem (0–3)		Difference of means (severity of problem)
	Cadres	Entrepreneurs	Cadres	Entrepreneurs	
1999					
Transportation	47.5	29.7	0.63	0.40	0.23**
Local government support	64.2	65.0	0.92	1.13	−0.21*
Dealings with officials	79.3	68.9	1.25	1.16	0.09
Qualified workers	84.5	66.2	1.52	1.12	0.40**
Opening markets	90.7	84.7	1.90	1.56	0.34**
Local competition	91.2	81.7	1.66	1.42	0.24**
Enterprise management	93.0	68.7	1.88	1.09	0.79**
National competition	95.5	84.5	1.93	1.64	0.30**
Finding lenders/investors	97.8	88.3	2.32	1.99	0.33**
Foreign competition	97.8	89.9	2.58	2.26	0.32**
2005					
Transportation	56.9	47.9	0.70	0.62	0.08
Local government support	63.9	70.7	0.87	1.13	−0.26**
Dealings with officials	78.1	70.7	1.11	1.08	0.03
Qualified workers	94.6	81.3	1.74	1.43	0.31**
Opening markets	96.0	85.1	1.91	1.55	0.37**
Local competition	92.8	84.1	1.58	1.38	0.20**
Enterprise management	94.6	77.5	1.83	1.25	0.58**
National competition	95.7	82.6	1.82	1.52	0.30**
Finding lenders/investors	99.6	89.2	2.20	1.81	0.39**
Foreign competition	98.2	85.0	2.46	1.96	0.50**

$*p < .01; **p < .001.$

themselves. The generally more pessimistic view of the business environment among local officials most likely is because they are responsible for the entire community and firms of all types and sizes. In contrast, the survey targeted large-scale enterprises, which might be slightly less susceptible to these kinds of business pressures. These findings suggest that entrepreneurs would be likely to find a sympathetic ear from local officials if they faced business difficulties.

Second, perceptions of the prevalence and severity of the problems moved in opposite directions: on most of the issues, a larger percentage of cadres and entrepreneurs perceived a problem, but the severity of most problems declined. For example, cadres and entrepreneurs agreed that one of the most severe problems in both 1999 and 2005 was finding new investors and lenders. Both groups saw it as more prevalent but also less severe. The difference of means on the severity of the issue remained significant and actually grew, even though both groups saw it as less severe, because the decrease for entrepreneurs was larger than for cadres. This reinforces the earlier point that entrepreneurs do not have to convince local cadres that problems exist because cadres are consistently more pessimistic about the business environment.

Third, and related to the first two points, although the perceived prevalence and severity of these problems varies, cadres and entrepreneurs were in close agreement on the rank ordering of the problems (see table 5.8). With the exception of enterprise management, which cadres saw as more prevalent and more severe than did the entrepreneurs in the samples,[15] the two groups generally agreed on which problems were the worst. Moreover, the most severe problems were ranked consistently across the two surveys. This reinforces the observation that entrepreneurs are likely to find that local officials are aware of the existence of these problems and agree with them on which ones are of greatest concern. This would diminish their need to pressure local officials to gain their attention and get them to respond, and therefore also reduce their inclination to be agents of change.

[15] Interviews with local officials, conducted at the time of the surveys, reinforced this concern about the management abilities of local entrepreneurs. Local governments in several of the counties included in this survey held regular training sessions on business practices, firm management, and even corporate culture. The Central Party School and provincial party schools (in Zhejiang, Guangdong, and elsewhere) have also offered classes to improve the business acumen of private entrepreneurs.

TABLE 5.8. *Rank Order of Business Problems, 1999 and 2005*
(from least to most severe)

Cadres	Entrepreneurs
Rank Order 1999	
Transportation	Transportation
Local government support	Enterprise management
Dealings with officials	Qualified workers
Qualified workers	Local government support
Local competition	Dealings with officials
Enterprise management	Local competition
Opening markets	Opening markets
National competition	National competition
Finding lenders/investors	Finding lenders/investors
Foreign competition	Foreign competition
Rank Order 2005	
Transportation	Transportation
Local government support	Dealings with officials
Dealings with officials	Local government support
Local competition	Enterprise management
Qualified workers	Local competition
National competition	Qualified workers
Enterprise management	National competition
Opening markets	Opening markets
Finding lenders/investors	Finding lenders/investors
Foreign competition	Foreign competition

Multivariate analysis allows us to see how other factors besides occupation shape perceptions of the business environment. Rather than trying to explain views on individual problems, I created an index of five business problems: finding qualified workers, enterprise management, finding lenders and investors, opening markets, and transportation.[16] Each of these individual variables is coded 0–3, so putting all five in an index creates a variable with values ranging from 0 to 15.[17] The other business environment items in the questionnaires were

---

[16] The five individual variables had pairwise correlations between .15 and .40, all statistically significant at the .001 level.

[17] This index has a bell-shaped distribution with a mean value of 6.79 and standard deviation of 2.78 in 1999 and a mean of 7.03 and standard deviation of 2.65 in 2005.

left out of the index for different reasons. Dealings with local officials and the level of local government support for the private sector prove to be important independent variables in the analysis. Questions about local, national, and foreign competition are left out of the index because too many entrepreneurs did not answer these questions. On this index, the difference between county and township/village cadres in their assessment of the local business environment is not significant. To simplify the presentation, I again combine them in the analysis. On the other hand, there is a substantial difference between red capitalists and other entrepreneurs, so I include dummy variables for those who were in the party before going into business (whom I refer to as *xiahai entrepreneurs*) and those who were recruited into the party after being in business (*co-opted entrepreneurs*).

Even in the multivariate analysis, the difference between cadres and entrepreneurs still stands out as a key explanatory variable (see table 5.9). The coefficient for *cadre* is large, positive, and statistically significant at the .001 level, indicating that local officials are more pessimistic about the business environment than are entrepreneurs, even when other variables are held constant. This is most likely because they are concerned with problems that affect their whole community, not simply an individual firm. The negative signs for *xiahai entrepreneurs* and *co-opted entrepreneurs* indicate that they have a less severe view of the business environment than do non-CCP entrepreneurs, which is to be expected, but only *co-opted entrepreneurs* is statistically significant, and then only in 1999. One of the main motivations for entrepreneurs to join the CCP is to gain advantages in business, including help in avoiding or solving problems. According to these survey data, party membership has a larger impact on perceptions of the business environment for co-opted entrepreneurs than for those who were already in the party before going into business.

However, when *dealing with officials* and *local government support* are added to the mix, the picture changes. The coefficients for both *xiahai* and *co-opted entrepreneurs* decrease and lose their statistical significance, suggesting that even red capitalists are not immune from enduring poor relations with local leaders and therefore facing a variety of business-related problems. In contrast, the coefficient for cadres remains statistically significant. In addition, including these two

TABLE 5.9. *Explaining Perceptions of the Business Environment, 1999 and 2005 (OLS regression coefficients with robust standard errors in parentheses)*

	1999		2005	
Cadres[a]	1.928***	1.866***	1.528***	1.736***
	(.300)	(.272)	(.209)	(.200)
Xiahai entrepreneurs[a]	−.470	−.251	−.295	−.111
	(.314)	(.296)	(.205)	(.194)
Co-opted entrepreneurs[a]	−.864*	−.527	−.406	−.126
	(.391)	(.359)	(.245)	(.220)
Age	−.005	−.003	.004	−.000
	(.015)	(.013)	(.011)	(.011)
Level of education	−.088	−.007	.104	.093
	(.095)	(.088)	(.105)	(.095)
Years in county	−.008	−.006	−.025***	−.014*
	(.008)	(.008)	(.006)	(.006)
Level of development	.028	.059	.077***	.065***
	(.038)	(.036)	(.018)	(.017)
Rate of economic growth	.006**	.004*	−.013***	−.014***
	(.002)	(.002)	(.004)	(.004)
Size of private sector	–	–	−.389	.115
			(.306)	(.291)
Dealing with officials	–	.791***	–	.823***
		(.133)		(.101)
Local government support	–	.312*	–	.435***
		(.132)		(.100)
Constant	6.061***	4.314***	6.978***	5.202***
	(.869)	(.832)	(.608)	(.596)
Observations	613	594	1243	1226
Adjusted R^2	.151	.264	.108	.237

[a] Reference group is non-CCP entrepreneurs.
*$p < .05$; ** $p < .01$; *** $p < .001$.

variables in the model greatly improves the explained variance, indicating that relations between local officials and private entrepreneurs are a key explanation for which entrepreneurs face other kinds of business problems.[18] These results are consistent in both the 1999 and 2005

---

[18] In a separate analysis of cadres alone, not shown here, the variables *dealing with officials* and *local government support* had a similar impact on the amount of explained variance. Local officials who recognized that relations between entrepreneurs and officials and local support for the private sector were problems were also more likely to perceive other business problems as more severe, all else being equal.

surveys, showing the durability of the issue. These data give greater depth to an observation of a businessman in Xiamen, who told David Wank, "If your connections (*guanxi*) with officialdom are good, then your business can develop, but if they are bad then officialdom squeezes you and you can't get anywhere."[19] This is directly related to the contingent support that China's capitalists have for the status quo: if even cronies find that dealing with officials is difficult and that local support for the private sector is not adequate, they would be more inclined to withdraw their support. They may not necessarily favor a more democratic system that would benefit other social groups, but they may desire more responsive and accountable government to advance their own economic interests.[20]

Conversely, the local context had inconsistent effects. The more prosperous the community, all else being equal, the more likely respondents were to see business problems, but the correlation between level of development and business problems was only significant in the 2005 survey. In the 1999 survey, respondents living in communities with high rates of growth were less likely to be concerned about business problems, but in the 2005 survey, they were more likely to be concerned. In addition, the longer the respondents had lived in their communities, the less likely they were to perceive business problems, but here again, the relationship is only significant in the 2005 survey.

In sum, the emphasis on economic development has made local officials closely attuned to the business environment. After all, officials must maintain high rates of growth for their own career advancement. Compared with the economic elites in their communities, officials have a more pessimistic view of the problems facing local business, so entrepreneurs do not have to bring these problems to the attention of local officials. Moreover, the local political and economic elites analyzed here generally agree on which problems are most prevalent and severe. These factors suggest that entrepreneurs will find sympathetic ears among local officials. This encourages cooperation and reduces the need for entrepreneurs to press for political or economic change.

---

[19] David L. Wank, *Commodifying Communism: Business, Trust, and Politics in a Chinese City* (Cambridge: Cambridge University Press, 1999), p. 4.
[20] The role of capitalists as "contingent democrats" is analyzed in Eva Bellin, "Contingent Democrats: Industrialists, Labor, and Democratization in Late-Developing Countries," *World Politics*, vol. 52, no. 2 (January 2000), pp. 175–205.

OVERALL LIFE SATISFACTION

Material life is good for China's private entrepreneurs. The vast majority of respondents in both surveys felt their standard of living was
improving (see table 5.10). There is some difference between subgroups of entrepreneurs in the intensity of their agreement: the majority of those who were in the CCP or wanted to be strongly agreed that
their standard of living was improving, whereas only about a third of
those who did not want to join strongly agreed and the rest simply
agreed. But the more significant point is how prevalent improvements
in living standards were. What is particularly striking is the consistency
of responses: for all four subgroups, the percentages who agreed that
their material life was improving were nearly identical across the two
surveys.

Questions about social status elicited more varied responses, but
again the vast majority of entrepreneurs felt their social status was
improving, although not as many as believed their standards of living were increasing. In the aggregate, there is remarkable consistency
in responses regarding improvements in social status, but among the
subgroups of entrepreneurs they are not as stable as responses about
living standards. As had been the case for improvements in living standards, entrepreneurs who did not want to join the CCP had the lowest
percentage who agreed, as well as the lowest percentage who strongly
agreed. Even among this subgroup, however, the vast majority agreed
their social status was rising. In contrast, co-opted entrepreneurs were
most likely to agree that their material lives and social status were
rising.

By these measures, the vast majority believe their lives are improving. This is important for their potential to be agents of change. As
research by Ronald Inglehart has shown, satisfaction with one's quality
of life is a good predictor of support for the incumbent regime. Those
who are satisfied with their lives are more likely to see the regime
as legitimate. Inglehart's argument is specifically tied to democracies:
"Satisfaction with one's life as a *whole* is a stronger predictor of stable
democracy than is satisfaction with the political system" (emphasis in
original). But the same logic may well apply to nondemocratic regimes
as well:

Precisely because overall life satisfaction is deeply rooted and diffuse, it provides a more stable basis of support for a given regime than does political

TABLE 5.10. *Level of Life Satisfaction among Entrepreneurs and Local Cadres, 1999 and 2005 (percentage who agree)*

	1999	2005
Standard of living improved in past year		
All entrepreneurs	93.4	93.7
Xiahai entrepreneurs	95.2	95.6
Co-opted entrepreneurs	97.0	97.0
Want to join CCP	96.6	94.6
Don't want to join CCP	87.8	88.3
All cadres	82.5	88.1
County	78.9	89.0
Township/village	87.5	87.5
Social status improved in past year		
All entrepreneurs	80.3	80.6
Xiahai entrepreneurs	80.3	82.1
Co-opted entrepreneurs	95.4	88.6
Want to join CCP	80.0	84.3
Don't want to join CCP	74.5	70.0
Social status of cadres has risen in past decade		
All cadres	41.9	53.8
County	36.4	55.5
Township/village	49.5	52.5
Social status of private entrepreneurs has risen in past decade		
All cadres	99.1	97.8
County	98.5	98.3
Township/village	100	97.5

satisfaction. The latter is a narrower orientation that taps support for specific incumbents at least as much as support for the regime.... Political satisfaction taps support for the current incumbents; life satisfaction taps support for the type of political system, or regime.[21]

Based on the responses of entrepreneurs, it seems clear that they are highly satisfied with their lives and that their level of satisfaction has

[21] Ronald Inglehart, *Modernization and Postmodernization: Cultural, Economic, and Political Change in 43 Societies* (Princeton, NJ: Princeton University Press, 1997), pp. 176–177. Inglehart also mentions in passing that "the same cultural factors that stabilize and sustain democracy can also stabilize authoritarian regimes" (p. 166), but he does not explore this insight in any detail.

been as stable in China as Inglehart suggested it is elsewhere. By that standard, it would seem that most entrepreneurs are likely to support the status quo rather than seek changes to it.[22]

Cadres appear to be less satisfied with their lives. Compared with entrepreneurs, a slightly lower percentage of cadres reported improvements in their standards of living; nevertheless, the overwhelming majority believed their standard of living was improving.[23] Perceptions of social status reveal a much starker contrast: almost all cadres believed the social status of entrepreneurs has been rising, but only about half believed cadres themselves are enjoying an improved social status. It is important to note that the responses of entrepreneurs and cadres cannot be directly compared: entrepreneurs were asked about their personal status, whereas cadres were asked about the status of entrepreneurs and cadres as a group. Undoubtedly, many who feel the status of cadres as a whole is improving also believe that their own status is rising, and vice versa, but we cannot simply equate the two. This is the only topic where cadres were directly asked to compare themselves with entrepreneurs, and the differences in both surveys are striking.

Another trend is also present: more county-level cadres believe their standard of living and social status have been improving in the most recent survey. This is particularly the case for social status, where the increase is over 50 percent. But that is still well below the percentage that believe entrepreneurs have it good. Township and village cadres

---

[22] In contrast, life satisfaction among the general population was considerably less sanguine. Public opinion surveys by Horizon Research showed declining satisfaction among urban residents: in 1997, 80 percent were satisfied, but in 2001, only 63 percent; cited in Minxin Pei, *China's Trapped Transition: The Limits of Developmental Autocracy* (Cambridge, MA: Harvard University Press, 2006), p. 197. According to the 2006 *Blue Book of Chinese Society* (p. 53), between 2003 and 2005, those who were "very satisfied" with their overall life situation declined from 68.2 percent to 56.1 percent; see Zhang Hui and Yuan Yue, "2005 nian Zhongguo jumin shenghuo zhiliang diaocha baogao" (Survey Report on the Quality of Life of Chinese Residents in 2005), in Ru Xin, et al., eds., *2006 nian: Zhongguo shehui xingshi fenxi yu yuce* (Blue Book of China's Society 2006: Analysis and Forecast on China's Social Development) (Beijing: Shehui kexue wenxian chubanshe, 2006), p. 53.

[23] The wording of the questions was slightly different: entrepreneurs were asked about their material standard of living (*Wuzhi shenghuo shuiping*); cadres were asked about their standard of living (*shenghuo shuiping*). The practical difference, however, is slight.

express little change in their quality of life and their perceptions of the social status of cadres. In light of Inglehart's argument, it would be a stretch to argue that cadres are more likely to be agents of change because they have lower levels of overall life satisfaction and therefore less support for the regime. After all, they *are* the regime and should be expected to defend the rights and privileges that come with their status, even if they do not believe their social status is keeping pace with that of entrepreneurs.

CONCLUSION

In this study comparing the views of local officials and private entrepreneurs, several themes have been highlighted. First, local officials have become more in favor of the private sector and more in synch with how entrepreneurs view their business environment. In fact, local officials have a more pessimistic view of the business environment than do entrepreneurs, perhaps because they have the whole community in mind, not just a single firm (as do the entrepreneurs in the samples). But although they are acutely aware of threats to local business, especially those arising from economic competition, they are much less likely to see economic competition as a threat to social stability more generally.

County cadres stand out as the distinctive group. They are most likely to favor growth over stability, even in a political environment that attempts to balance the trade-off, and least likely to be concerned with the consequences of growth, both in the form of competition between firms and individuals and in the form of social pluralism. In contrast, the views of township and village cadres and private entrepreneurs are closer to each other than either group is to those of county cadres. In part, this may result from career strategies, especially if the hard target of economic growth is based on the county level and the pressure to maintain stability is passed down to lower levels. But more research is needed to confirm why the preference for growth is not shared by cadres at all levels. Also it may result in part from shared interests with entrepreneurs, produced by closer proximity and more regular interaction, and undoubtedly even familial ties in some cases. As Melanie Manion and Lily Tsai showed in rather different contexts, the closer the ties between local cadres and society, the more alike their viewpoints will be and the more likely that the local government will deliver the goods expected by the local society.[24] Lacking valid indicators on electoral quality and local social institutions (the key variables for Manion and Tsai, respectively), I cannot directly test their theories on electoral connections and social capital. But the results presented here suggest that the vertical dimension may also help explain the degree of affinity between local officials and the rest of society, especially economic elites. This is also consistent with findings of Kent Jennings and others that the notion of the state needs to be disaggregated in order to be most useful, in this case by dividing local cadres according to their bureaucratic level.[25] In my previous study, I made much of the difference between entrepreneurs and cadres on the trade-off between promoting growth and maintaining stability. By adding the question of bureaucratic level, a more interesting and nuanced picture emerges.

On most of the questions examined here, the views of entrepreneurs cohere fairly well. Whereas Kellee Tsai finds the lack of a uniform viewpoint as indicating China's entrepreneurs do not constitute a class,[26] the data from my two surveys show they are nevertheless distinctive when compared with those of local officials. Entrepreneurs may not have a singular voice, as indeed most groups do not, but their views are similar on a range of issues. Entrepreneurs are more likely to favor stability over growth, more likely to see the potential social consequences of economic competition, and more likely to see the risks of emerging pluralism. More importantly, the views of *xiahai*, co-opted, and non-CCP entrepreneurs have become more similar over time. If entrepreneurs emerge as agents of change, it is hard to see them

---

[24] Melanie Manion, "The Electoral Connection in the Chinese Countryside," *American Political Science Review*, vol. 90, no. 4 (December 1996), pp. 736–748; Lily Lee Tsai, "Cadres, Temple and Lineage Institutions, and Governance in Rural China," *China Journal*, no. 48 (July 2002), pp. 1–28.

[25] Kent Jennings, "Local Problem Agendas in the Chinese Countryside as Viewed by Cadres and Villagers," *Acta Politica*, vol. 38 (2003), pp. 313–332.

[26] This is the main theme of Kellee S. Tsai, "Capitalists without a Class: Political Diversity among Private Entrepreneurs in China," *Comparative Political Studies*, vol. 38, no. 9 (November 2005), pp. 1130–1158; see also Kellee S. Tsai, *Capitalism without Democracy: The Private Sector in Contemporary China* (Ithaca, NY: Cornell University Press, 2007). Apart from our differing interpretations on this point, our findings are remarkably similar, a nice example of replication in research.

advocating either economic or political liberalization. This similarity of views is particularly salient in the causes of business problems: dealing with officials and the level of local government support are causes of business problems for all groups of entrepreneurs, including the red capitalists, who are part of the crony communist system. Simply being a crony is no guarantee of harmonious relations with local officials. These attitudes alone may not lead China's capitalists to withdraw their support for the status quo in favor of democracy, but if they persist and are wide-spread, they may motivate private entrepreneurs, and red capitalists in particular, to seek a more responsive (for instance, less corrupt) government.

The changing views of co-opted entrepreneurs merit highlighting. This group has the greatest potential for being an agent of change if it were to bring new policy preferences into the party, but the survey data presented indicate it is becoming increasingly satisfied with the current state of affairs. In the 1999 survey, it was the most concerned group among the entrepreneurs about growth threatening stability, but in 2005 it was the least concerned. Similarly, the percentage of co-opted entrepreneurs who felt pluralism was a threat to stability fell by a larger amount than those of either *xiahai* entrepreneurs or entrepreneurs who did not belong to the party. Although the percentage who felt the pace of political reform was about right declined slightly, from 61 percent to 59 percent, the percentage who felt the pace of economic reform was about right increased from 62 percent to 72 percent. Among all subgroups of entrepreneurs, they were most likely to agree their living standards and social status – and by implication their overall life satisfaction – were rising. These findings do not indicate any significant degree of discontent that would lead the co-opted entrepreneurs to press for political change. Instead, the growing levels of satisfaction on these related indicators suggest that co-opted entrepreneurs, and most entrepreneurs for that matter, are not likely to pose a political challenge under the current circumstances. Rather than being potential agents of change working from within the party, they may prove to be a key source of support for the party's agenda. Given the high standards for admitting entrepreneurs into the party (as detailed in chapter 3), it is likely that those who are most supportive of the party's policies are also most likely to be co-opted. Under those conditions, co-opted entrepreneurs are not likely to be agents of political change but instead are more inclined to perpetuate the crony communist system once they have become part of it.

This chapter showed that there is little substantive difference between entrepreneurs and local officials on most issues. These findings call into question one of the key assumptions about private entrepreneurs serving as agents of political change in China: that they hold views on economic, political, and social issues that are fundamentally different from those of incumbent officials. Absent such a difference, their involvement in China's political system may instead serve to support the status quo rather than bring pressure for change into it. The next chapter will explore this question in more detail: which entrepreneurs participate in China's formal political institutions, and why?

6

Private Entrepreneurs in Public Service

Participation in China's Formal Political Institutions

Throughout the reform era, the CCP has focused on economic development as its main task. Since the 1990s, it has increasingly relied on the private sector to provide the economic growth that the party's leaders believe is necessary to maintain the legitimacy it needs to keep itself in power. In order to promote cooperation between the party and the private sector, the CCP has gradually integrated entrepreneurs into the Chinese political system. As noted in chapter 3, large numbers of private entrepreneurs have become members of the political elite by joining the CCP. In addition to being members of the party, many entrepreneurs also belong to other prominent political bodies, further integrating them into the political system.

Previous research into the political participation of China's entrepreneurs has generally focused on the motives of the entrepreneurs themselves.[1] This assumes that entrepreneurs who enter the political arena are primarily self-selected, but in fact that is only one part of the equation. Because the CCP plays an influential role in deciding who may participate in China's formal political institutions, it is also necessary to inquire into its strategy for deciding which entrepreneurs

---

[1] See, for example, Hongbin Li, Lingsheng Meng, and Junsen Zhang, "Why Do Entrepreneurs Enter Politics? Evidence from China," *Economic Inquiry*, vol. 44, no. 3 (July 2006), pp. 559–578; Gilles Guiheux, "The Political 'Participation' of Entrepreneurs: Challenge or Opportunity for the Chinese Communist Party?" *Social Research*, vol. 73, no. 1 (Spring 2006), pp. 219–244.

will be allowed to participate. As will be shown throughout this chapter, many of the same characteristics that explain which entrepreneurs are co-opted into the party also help explain which ones are active in the political process. Both the entrepreneurs' interest in joining the political world and the willingness of local officials to grant them access must be examined to properly understand political participation by China's entrepreneurs.

This chapter will begin by describing the increased involvement of private entrepreneurs in formal political roles and the processes by which they are elected or selected for these roles, and then inquire into the characteristics of the entrepreneurs who are most active in politics. It will show that capitalists who participate in China's formal political institutions are very much a part of the crony communist system and more likely to support the status quo than to favor political change. This is precisely the goal behind the CCP's co-optation strategy: to integrate China's capitalists into the political system in order to encourage their continued support and cooperation.

THE GROWING PROMINENCE OF ENTREPRENEURS IN POLITICS IN CHINA

With the emphasis on economic development in China, private entrepreneurs and business associations have begun to play an increasingly prominent political role. At the National People's Congress (NPC) in spring 2003, 55 entrepreneurs were selected as deputies. Among the delegates to the 10th Chinese People's Political Consultative Conference (CPPCC), also held in 2003, were 65 entrepreneurs from private and nonstate firms.[2] Although these numbers signify the full integration of the private sector into the political system, they still represent a small percentage of the members of those bodies: 1.9 percent of the NPC and 2.9 percent of the CPPCC. Nationwide, over 9,000 entrepreneurs have been elected to people's congresses (PCs) at the county level and above and 30,000 to people's political consultative conferences (PPCCs).[3]

---

[2] "More Private Entrepreneurs Enter China's Top Advisory Body," *People's Daily Online*, March 2, 2003.

[3] Zhang Houyi, "Jinru xin shiqi de Zhongguo siying qiyezhu jieceng" (Chinese Private Entrepreneurs Enter a New Era), in Ru Xin, et al., eds., *2004 nian: Zhongguo shehui xingshi fenxi yu yuce* (Blue Book of China's Society 2004: Analysis and Forecast

The Chinese media have given much attention to entrepreneurs who serve in PCs and PPCCs at various levels.[4] Some of China's most prominent – and most wealthy – entrepreneurs have been elected or selected for high-ranking posts:

- **Yin Mingshan** (b. 1938, number 268 on the 2006 *Forbes* list of the richest people in China) is chairman of the Lifan Group in Chongqing, a leader in China's motorcycle industry. A victim of the 1957 Anti-Rightist Campaign, he spent more than 20 years in labor camps. After 1978, he taught English at the Chongqing Television University, and in 1985 he founded the Chongqing Education Publishing House. In 1992, he left the education and publishing worlds and established the Lifan Group to produce and service motorcycles. In 2002, he was elected president of the Chongqing Municipal Industrial and Commercial Federation. In 2003, he became the first private entrepreneur to join the provincial-level leadership of the CPPCC when he was elected vice chairman of the Chongqing Municipal PPCC (since 1997, Chongqing municipality has held provincial-level status, as do Beijing, Tianjin, and Shanghai). Yin has been a member of the national CPPCC since 1998. Unlike most other entrepreneurs who have been appointed to high-level positions, Yin is not a CCP member.[5]
- **Xu Guanyu** (b. 1961) is chairman of the board of the Zhejiang Chuanhua Group in Hangzhou, which produces chemical and high-tech agricultural products. In 1995, the Chuanhua Group was the first private firm in Zhejiang to establish its own party committee. In January 2003, soon after Yin Mingshan's election in Chongqing, Xu was elected to the post of vice chairman of the provincial PPCC in Zhejiang. He is a CCP member and has served in leadership positions of the PPCC and ICF at the district, municipal, and provincial levels in Zhejiang.

on China's Social Development) (Beijing: Shehui kexue wenxian chubanshe, 2004), p. 318.
[4] "Private Firm Bosses Take to Politics," *China Daily*, July 2, 2003; "Private Entrepreneurs Sparkle on Political Stage," *China Daily*, December 3, 2003; "Yin Mingshan: First Private Entrepreneur to Enter Municipal Leadership" (http://www.china.org.cn/english/NM-e/54414.htm).
[5] According to Yin, he has applied to become a party member several times but has been told he can benefit the party more by working on its behalf from the outside. See Peter Harmsen, "Capitalism is on the Rise in China – But Not in the CCP," Agence France-Presse, June 18, 2005, reprinted in *Taipei Times*, June 18, 2005.

- **Rong Hai** (b. 1957, number 109 on the *Forbes* list) is president and CEO of the Sea Star Group in Xi'an. After several years as professor of computer engineering at Xi'an University, Rong invested his life savings in Sea Star, originally a one-room operation that quickly grew into a sprawling industrial complex specializing in computer systems and information technology. In 1991, Sea Star became Compaq's general agent in northwest China. By the mid-1990s, Sea Star had branched out into real estate and general merchandise retail trade. Rong joined the CCP in 1974 as a "sent down youth," has been a delegate to the National People's Congress since 1998, and is also a member of the ACFIC.
- **Zhang Guoxi** (b. 1952, number 204 on the *Forbes* list) went from being an apprentice wood carver to becoming one of China's first millionaires, with a reputation for enjoying the good life. He made his fortune with his first company, which opened in 1976 and specialized in wood carving. By the late 1980s, he realized that he needed to diversify, and his Guoxi Group expanded into chemicals, hotels, tourism, and auto parts manufacturing. Zhang has won over 200 national and provincial-level awards, including model worker and outstanding entrepreneur. He is a CCP member and first became a delegate to the CPPCC in 1992.
- **Qiu Jibao** (b. 1962, number 313 on the *Forbes* list) is chairman of Zhejiang's Feiyue Group, China's largest producer and exporter of sewing machines. He is a member of the Zhejiang provincial PPCC, vice chairman of the All-China Youth Federation, and was a delegate to the 16th Party Congress. After being selected as a delegate to the party congress, a reporter asked him about his relationship with the party secretary in his firm. Qiu responded, "Regarding political matters, I follow the secretary's instructions; regarding production, he follows my instructions."
- **Xia Shilin** (b. 1952) is chairman of the Shenghua Group in Zhejiang, which produces biological pesticides. He is a CCP member and also secretary of his firm's party branch. In 2000, the State Council named him a "national model worker" even though he was chairman of his company. As an NPC delegate, he has shown a particular interest in fighting business fraud and revising the tax law so that private entrepreneurs will not be subject to both the enterprise income tax and the personal income tax when they receive a share of the firm's profits.

- **Zhang Wenzhong** (b. 1962, number 183 on the *Forbes* list) is chairman of the Wu-Mart Group, the first private Chinese enterprise whose stock was traded overseas. Originally trained as a mathematician concentrating in systems engineering, he established the Wu-Mart group in 1994, opening the first supermarket in Beijing and expanding into a larger retail chain. By 2005, Wu-Mart had over 600 outlets and 10,000 employees worldwide. In 2003, the Xinhua News Agency named Zhang the most influential commercial figure in China. He is a member of the CCP and a delegate to both the NPC and the CPPCC.
- **Lin Shengxiong** (b. 1966) is chairman of Shengxiong Group in Zhejiang, which specializes in infrastructure construction. He is perhaps best known as one of China's leading philanthropists for his support of poor students and contributions to "Project Hope." He began his career in the SOE sector in positions that included director of a printing factory, deputy general manager of a mine works company, and deputy general manager of a hydropower company, and eventually he became chairman of the Shengxiong Group, a privatized SOE. At the age of 36 in 2002, he received the "Most Outstanding Youth" award. Lin became an NPC delegate in 2003.

The correlation between wealth and political influence is particularly noteworthy at the national level. Those who have responded to the CCP's call to "take the lead in getting rich" (*daitou zhifu*) have been rewarded with high-profile political posts. On the list of China's 100 wealthiest people, one-third belong to either the NPC or CPPCC and 25 percent are CCP members. Rupert Hoogewerf, who has compiled annual lists of wealthy Chinese, said that private entrepreneurs have "gone from being the greatest threat to the party and have now become its greatest supporters."[6]

Local officials in several survey sites mentioned that entrepreneurs were more interested in being PC or PPCC delegates than being delegates to the local party congress. According to these officials, being a delegate to the party congress is seen as having only momentary value. The main purpose of the party congress is electing local party leaders. Once that is done, the party congress does not convene again for

---

[6] Tim Lee Master, "Rich Start Earning from New Found Status," *The Standard* (Hong Kong), June 10, 2004.

another five years. Being a delegate to a party congress may be prestigious and a sign of an individual's influence and stature, but by itself it is seen as less important than being a PC or PPCC delegate. Belonging to the PC or PPCC, on the other hand, gives delegates regular and recurring access to decision makers and the opportunity to influence laws and regulations. People's Congress delegates formally approve the CCP's nominees for government posts and in a few high-profile cases have rejected those nominees. They also approve annual work reports from the government, giving them some degree of influence and oversight. Although PCs and PPCCs meet only once per year for about a week, delegates may conduct investigations, liaison with citizens, and meet with officials all year round. The ability to participate in the deliberation of policy (*canzheng yizheng*) is a tangible benefit of PC and PPCC membership.

This ready access to decision makers provides obvious benefits for entrepreneurs and their firms. It gives them protection from government seizures of their land and properties; provides preferential access to loans and licenses; fosters discretionary treatment in the implementation of policies; and in general helps them further cultivate personal relationships with leaders who are in a position to influence their business operations. These are tangible benefits available to members of the crony communist system and help maintain support for the CCP among China's capitalists. To some degree, bribery can achieve the same purpose, but some entrepreneurs are also motivated to operate aboveboard or at least to add another option to their repertoire of interactions with the state. Yin Mingshan, an NPC and CPPCC delegate since 1998 and the first entrepreneur to be chosen for a provincial-level leadership post, said, "I love to voice my opinions on state affairs so that the policies will be better implemented."[7] In addition, being a PC or PPCC delegate gives one the opportunity to promote the collective interests of the private sector, such as property rights, tax policy, infrastructure development, and competitiveness. Xia Shilin, an NPC delegate and chairman of the Shenghua Group in Zhejiang, acknowledged in 2003 that, "Private entrepreneurs are now urging the government to put forward regulations or laws to officially guarantee

---

[7] "Private Businessmen Have Big Say in State Affairs," *Xinhuanet*, March 1, 2001.

their properties."[8] At the first session of the 10th National People's Congress in March 2003, *China Daily* reported 10 motions on fighting fraud, shoddy goods, and tax evasion.[9] Business associations also lobby on behalf of collective interests. Shanghai's ICF was involved in the drafting of that city's labor law, ensuring that it would be favorable to business.[10] Political posts could also put a veneer of respectability on businessmen whose wealth was obtained through less than honest means. For example, Lai Changxing was selected as a member of the Fujian People's Political Consultative Conference.[11]

But joining the political arena is not simply the choice of individuals in China. The CCP plays a determining role in who is allowed to participate and who is not. For this reason, an understanding of its co-optation strategy is essential for analyzing the political participation of China's capitalists. Even in positions that are decided by public elections, the CCP nominates some candidates and screens the rest to be sure that only politically reliable individuals gain access to positions of influence. Concerning private entrepreneurs in particular, they are not given an equal opportunity to participate in PCs and PPCCs but are selected by local officials. Following Jiang Zemin's July 1, 2001, speech, which authorized admitting entrepreneurs into the party and more generally integrating them into China's political system, local united front and industrial and commercial offices were directed to make arrangements to bring entrepreneurs into PCs and PPCCs.[12] In the sections that follow, I will show how both individual motives and

---

[8] Tang Fuchun, "Deputy Profile: Xia Shilin," China.org, March 16, 2003 (http://www.china.org.cn/english/features/58434.htm), accessed October 25, 2006.

[9] Xu Binglan, "Deputies Promote Good Faith in Business," *China Daily*, March 19, 2003.

[10] Young Nam Cho, "The Politics of Lawmaking in Chinese Local People's Congresses," *China Quarterly*, no. 187 (September 2006), pp. 602–606.

[11] Shawn Shieh, "The Rise of Collective Corruption in China: The Xiamen Smuggling Case," *Journal of Contemporary China*, vol. 14, no. 42 (February 2005), p. 82.

[12] Ao Daiya, "Siying qiyezhu zhengzhi canyu yanjiu baogao" (Report on the Political Participation of Private Entrepreneurs), in Zhang Houyi et al., eds., *Zhongguo siying qiye fazhan baogao*, no. 6 (2005) (A Report on the Development of China's Private Enterprises) (Beijing: Shehui kexue wenxian chubanshe, 2006), pp. 61–83. This report on the political participation of China's private entrepreneurs criticized this tendency to arrange their participation because the limited opportunities available for them to participate in China's formal political institutions could not meet the growing demand for increased participation (see pp. 69–70).

the party's preferences influence which entrepreneurs enter the political arena.

ELECTION AND SELECTION PROCESSES

There are different means by which individuals become PC delegates, PPCC delegates, and candidates in village elections. These are also different types of institutions, which also has some bearing on who participates in them.

People's Congress delegates are directly elected by voters at the township and county levels; above that, they are indirectly elected by delegates at the lower level (e. g., county delegates elect municipal or prefecture-level delegates, who in turn elect provincial delegates). Some candidates are nominated from village small groups and other local constituencies; according to articles 29 and 31 of the 1995 electoral law for people's congresses, groups of at least 10 voters in electoral districts may nominate candidates. In other cases, nominations come from political parties and mass organizations.[13] For example, in Shandong's city Z (one of the most prosperous in the sample), the county ICF recommended 52 entrepreneurs to the PC, including one to the provincial PC. Election committees, normally dominated by the CCP, decide on the final slate of candidates, which must exceed the number of delegates to be elected. This process for nominating and selecting candidates is designed to promote the party's affirmative action goals (a certain number of candidates should be women or ethnic minorities, for example) as well as to ensure the party's interest in getting loyal party members elected.[14] Roderick MacFarquhar found that provincial PC delegates were not chosen for their expertise "but rather as a reward for achievements in their own métier or as representatives of certain groups in society."[15] A similar strategy undoubtedly informs

---

[13] "1995 Electoral Law of the National People's Congress and Local People's Congresses of the People's Republic of China," at www.chinaelections.org.

[14] Kevin J. O'Brien, "Agents and Remonstrators: Role Accumulation by Chinese People's Congress Deputies," *China Quarterly*, no. 138 (June 1994), pp. 363–365; Melanie Manion, "Chinese Democratization in Perspective: Electorates and Selectorates at the Township Level," *China Quarterly*, no. 163 (September 2000), pp. 767–772.

[15] Roderick MacFarquhar, "Provincial People's Congresses," *China Quarterly*, no. 155 (September 1988), p. 665.

lower-level nominations as well. Although part of the responsibilities of local PCs concern lawmaking, their primary role seems to be government oversight, both in the approval of the CCP's nominees for government posts and in the monitoring of the government's work through annual reports.[16] Candidates get screened and approved by local officials before they are presented to voters for election. There is little competition in these elections, and because citizens do not fully understand what these delegates do or how it matters to them, they do not put much credence in them.[17]

Delegates to the PPCC, in contrast, are not elected at all but are chosen through a series of recommendations and consultations. At all levels, the PPCCs are intended to be a forum for CCP members, members of the democratic parties,[18] and nonparty individuals representing sectors such as business, science, and education. Each of these groups is assigned a certain number of delegates. In Shandong's city Z, the ICF also recommended 86 entrepreneurs to the county PPCC, including one to the provincial PPCC. In Hebei's county H, vice chairmen of the officially sponsored business associations, including the local ICF, have concurrent posts in the PC or PPCC. After negotiations among the CCP, democratic parties, and nongovernmental sectoral and professional groups, the outgoing PPCC agrees on and selects the incoming group of delegates.[19] The PPCCs discuss policy issues and make recommendations to the party and government but have no decision-making authority. They meet simultaneously with the annual

---

[16] Dali L. Yang, *Remaking the Chinese Leviathan: Market Transition and the Politics of Governance in China* (Stanford, CA: Stanford University Press, 2004), pp. 259–278; Minxin Pei, *China's Trapped Transition: The Limits of Developmental Autocracy* (Cambridge, MA: Harvard University Press, 2006), pp. 57–65.

[17] Manion, "Chinese Democratization in Perspective," p. 768; O'Brien, "Agents and Remonstrators," pp. 359–360. In their exposé of cadre misconduct in rural Anhui, Chen Guidi and Wu Chuntao refer to the president of a local PC and vice president of a county PPCC as "honorary positions"; see Chen Guidi and Wu Chuntao, *Will the Boat Sink the Water? The Life of China's Peasants* (New York: Public Affairs, 2006), pp. 83–84, 113.

[18] Although China is normally regarded as a one-party state, there are in fact eight so-called fraternal or democratic parties; see James D. Seymour, *China's Satellite Parties* (Armonk, NY: M. E. Sharpe, 1987); Gerry Groot, *Managing Transitions: The Chinese Communist Party, United Front Work, Corporatism, and Hegemony* (New York: Routledge, 2004).

[19] Shen Shiguang, "Members of CPPCC Selection Needs Reform," *People's Daily*, July 4, 2003, from www.chinaelections.org.

meeting of the PC at the same level, and together they are referred to as the "two meetings." The top posts in the PPCC are usually held by incumbent and former party leaders. Although the PPCC lacks direct influence, being a delegate is nevertheless prestigious because it signifies membership in the local elite.

The means by which entrepreneurs become candidates in village elections are rather different from what was described earlier. Village elections can make a real difference in people's lives because the elected officials can influence matters of economic development and public goods provision.[20] Nominations for candidates are usually generated from within the village; according to the election law, higher-level officials are not allowed to intervene in the process either by rejecting candidates nominated by villagers or selecting candidates of their own. According to various reports, however, this provision is often violated. Nevertheless, in principle and for the most part in practice, entrepreneurs who have been candidates in village elections have chosen to do so. They are a more self-selected group than PC and PPCC delegates.

Because of these differences in selecting PC and PPCC delegates and candidates for village elections, the characteristics of these groups of people might also be expected to be quite different. These differences will be examined in the sections that follow.

EXPLAINING POLITICAL PARTICIPATION
BY CHINA'S ENTREPRENEURS

The survey data collected in 1999 and 2005 allow us to see broad trends in participation by entrepreneurs in local PCs, PPCCs, and village elections. In addition, they allow us to analyze the characteristics

---

[20] Lily Lee Tsai, "Cadres, Temple and Lineage Institutions, and Governance in Rural China," *China Journal*, no. 48 (July 2002), pp. 1–28; Lianjiang Li and Kevin J. O'Brien, "The Struggle over Village Elections," in Merle Goldman and Roderick MacFarquhar, eds., *The Paradox of China's Post-Mao Reforms* (Cambridge, MA: Harvard University Press, 1999), pp. 129–144; Tianjian Shi, "Economic Development and Village Elections in Rural China," *Journal of Contemporary China*, vol. 8, no. 22 (1999), pp. 425–442; Jean C. Oi, "Economic Development, Stability and Democratic Village Self-Governance," in Maurice Brosseau, Suzanne Pepper, and Shu-ki Tsang, eds., *China Review 1996* (Hong Kong: Chinese University Press, 1996), pp. 125–144; Kevin J. O'Brien, "Implementing Political Reform in China's Villages," *Australian Journal of Chinese Affairs*, no. 32 (July 1994), pp. 33–60.

that explain which entrepreneurs are most likely to participate in these formal institutions. These include political characteristics, individual and firm attributes, cultural factors, and contextual factors. I will begin by briefly describing the different types of variables and then show their impact on the political participation of private entrepreneurs in China.

Political Characteristics

The most important factors explaining formal political participation in China are the individual's political characteristics, primarily membership in the CCP. Because the party wants to guarantee that all political institutions are under its control, most officials, bureaucrats, and PC and PPCC delegates at all levels are party members. Among entrepreneurs, we need to distinguish between two types of party members: *xiahai entrepreneurs*, who were party members before going into business; and *co-opted entrepreneurs*, who joined the party after going into business. Local officials in several of the survey sites believed that some entrepreneurs wanted to join the CCP in order to gain access to political posts. The entrepreneurs themselves were less forthcoming about this: when asked why they joined the CCP or wanted to, most said they joined to benefit themselves or their firms, because they supported the party and its policies, or because they wanted to "serve the people." But some did admit to their interest in politics: 10.4 percent of co-opted entrepreneurs and 8.8 percent of those who wanted to join the CCP listed their desire to participate in politics as a main reason for joining.[21] All else being equal, members of the CCP should be more likely to participate in the formal political institutions than nonparty members.

In addition to party membership, membership in business associations is another important attribute. The Industrial and Commercial Federation is the local chapter of the All-China Federation of Industry and Commerce (often referred to as the General Chamber of Commerce), an officially sponsored organization headquartered in Beijing and with chapters throughout the country. Its members include owners and managers of both private and state-owned enterprises. Unlike the

---

[21] This was an open-ended question; respondents could give any reason they wanted. Their responses were then coded into broad categories, as indicated here.

Self-Employed Laborers Association and the Private Enterprises Association, in which membership is mandatory for licensed entrepreneurs, membership in the ICF is voluntary. Members of the ICF are typically owners and managers of large-scale enterprises (including SOEs) and therefore symbolize the economic elites of the community. In the 2005 survey, 28.1 percent of entrepreneurs were members of the ICF. *ICF members* should be more likely to participate in formal political institutions than nonmembers because they represent the political and economic elites of their communities.[22] At the 10th session of the national-level CPPCC, which opened in 2003, 57 of the 65 private entrepreneurs who were delegates also held leading positions in provincial and municipal-level ICFs.[23]

In contrast, 36 percent of entrepreneurs in the 2005 survey reported that they did not belong to any business association. These people are mostly outside the crony communist system: 44.7 percent of those who are not in the CCP and do not want to join are also not in a business association. They also operate firms that are much smaller compared with those entrepreneurs who belong to any of the official business associations: their sales volume, fixed assets, and number of workers are on average less than half that of other entrepreneurs. Entrepreneurs who belong to *no business association* should therefore be less likely to participate in all three types of institutions. Because they are not in any of the organizations that integrate the party with the private sector, they are less likely to be trusted by local officials and less likely to be selected as candidates. Their disengagement from both the party and official business associations might also suggest that they are unwilling to play by the party's rules and are therefore willing to change the rules. Their responses to other questions, however, indicate that they are largely apolitical. In explaining why they did not want to join

---

[22] In this analysis, all who belong to the ICF are included, unlike the analysis of the role of business associations in chapter 2, where those who belonged to other business associations and identified more with one of them were recoded so that each individual was describing only one association. On this question, it is less important how the entrepreneurs feel about the ICF than how the CCP feels about ICF members. It should also be noted here that membership in PEA or SELA was not correlated with being a PC or PPCC delegate or a candidate in village elections.

[23] "Zhengxie shijie yici huiyi zhong de 'laoban' weiyuan (mingdan)" (The Namelist of 'Bosses' at the First Plenary Session of the 10th CPPCC), *Renmin wang* (http://www.people. com.cn/GB/jinji/31/179/20030304), accessed July 25, 2005.

the CCP, 17.6 percent said they were too busy to consider joining the party, and another 8.8 percent reported being more interested in business than politics at present. That being the case, they should also be less likely to run in village elections. By extension, counties with large numbers of entrepreneurs who claim not to belong to any of the official business associations should also have small numbers of entrepreneurs in public posts. In fact, the two counties with the highest percentages of entrepreneurs who claim not to belong to any of the official business associations also had below average percentages participating in PCs and PPCCs, and one of them (Shandong's city Z) had the absolute lowest for both. This further suggests that acceptance into the local political and economic elite is contingent on membership in the government-sponsored business associations.

Individual and Firm Characteristics

Age, gender, and *education* have consistent and well-established effects on the extent of political participation: older people are more likely to participate than younger, men more than women, and better educated more than less well educated. These individual characteristics should have similar effects for China's entrepreneurs. It is also possible that the effect of age and education is curvilinear, with the oldest or best-educated entrepreneurs slightly less likely to participate than those who are middle-aged or have high school or lower degrees.[24] In addition, the larger the firm (measured by the natural log of its *sales revenue*)[25] and the longer an entrepreneur has been in business (*years in business*), the more likely he or she will participate. For PC and PPCC delegates, who are screened by the party, the larger the firm and the longer they have been in business, the more important they are

---

[24] For example, Tianjian Shi found a curvilinear relationship between education and participation, with the level of participation much lower for people with more than 18 years of schooling (i.e., those with at least some graduate schooling); see Tianjian Shi, *Political Participation in Beijing* (Cambridge, MA: Harvard University Press, 1997), pp. 145–148. It should be noted that Shi used a broader definition of participation than the narrow one used here.

[25] Alternative ways to measure firm size, such as the number of workers or amount of fixed capital, are highly correlated with sales revenue (above .73 in 1999 and above .80 in 2005); all of them produce nearly identical statistical results. Sales revenue is chosen because of its intuitive meaning.

likely to be in the local community and the more familiar local officials will be with them. For candidates in village elections, these attributes signify their stake in the local economy and their desire to protect their interests.

Cultural Factors

In addition to the objective measures just described, political participation may also be affected by the individuals' values. I include two cultural variables in the analysis. First is satisfaction with their economic and social status, which was analyzed in chapter 4. Two questions concerning improvements in the living standards and social status of the entrepreneurs were combined into a *life satisfaction* index.[26] This is meant to approximate the "overall life satisfaction" orientation described by Inglehart: "Satisfaction with one's life as a whole is one of the best available indicators of subjective well-being.... If a society has a high level of subjective well-being, its citizens feel that their entire way of life is fundamentally good. Their political institutions gain legitimacy by association."[27] Inglehart views overall life satisfaction and subjective well-being as essential elements of a stable democracy, but by extension it also implies that it will legitimize and stabilize an authoritarian regime as well. An authoritarian regime does not need to be legitimate to survive, and indeed many survive without legitimacy, regardless of how it is defined.[28] But if a regime is deemed legitimate, there will be more support for it. In short, those who are satisfied with their life overall are less likely to seek to change their political institutions under any type of regime.

---

[26] Respondents were asked if their living standards and social status had improved in the past year. The responses to each question were coded 0–3, ranging from "strongly disagree" to "strongly agree." Responses to the two questions were highly correlated ($r = .59$, $p < .0001$). Values in the index range from 0 to 6, with higher scores indicating more satisfaction. The mean score was 4.51, with a standard deviation of 1.16.

[27] Ronald Inglehart, *Modernization and Postmodernization: Cultural, Economic, and Political Change in 43 Societies* (Princeton, NJ: Princeton University Press, 1997), pp. 176–178.

[28] Adam Przeworski, "Some Problems in the Transition to Democracy," in Guillermo O'Donnell, Philippe C. Schmitter, and Laurence Whitehead, eds., *Transitions from Authoritarian Rule*, vol. 3: *Comparative Perspectives* (Baltimore: Johns Hopkins University Press, 1986).

The second cultural variable is orientation toward politics. All respondents were asked a series of questions to measure whether they believed increased economic and social diversity were threats to stability (see chapter 5 for more discussion of these questions). The specific questions were:

- Competition between firms and individuals is harmful to social stability.
- If a country has multiple parties, it can lead to political chaos.
- If everybody does not share the same thinking, society can be chaotic.
- Locally, if there are many groups with different opinions, that can influence local stability.

These questions were combined to create an index of *modern values.*[29] Low scores on this index indicate that the respondent has the traditional concern with maintaining stability as the primary goal, whereas high scores indicate a more "modern" view that growing competition and pluralism are not inherent threats to stability.[30]

If China's private entrepreneurs are to serve as agents of change, then we should look for those who have low levels of life satisfaction and high levels of modern values; these are the ones who would be most likely to desire change in the existing political institutions. For that same reason, we should expect that the CCP should limit their participation in formal political institutions in favor of those who are

[29] Pairwise correlations between the four questions were moderate, ranging from .17 to .47; all were significant at the .0001 level. The responses to each question were coded 0–3, ranging from "strongly disagree" to "strongly agree," yielding an index that ranges from 0 to 12, with higher scores meaning more modern and less traditional values. The index has a mean of 7.01 and a standard deviation of 2.42.

[30] These questions were originally used in Taiwan to measure the shift from traditional to modern political values, and three were later included in the Asian Barometer Survey. See, for example, William L. Parish and Charles Chi-Hsiang Chang, "Political Values in Taiwan: Sources of Change and Constancy," in Hung-mao Tien, ed., *Taiwan's Electoral Politics and Democratic Transition: Riding the Third Wave* (Armonk, NY: M. E. Sharpe, 1996), pp. 27–41; Yu-tzung Chang, Yun-han Chu, and Frank Tsai, "Confucianism and Democratic Values in Three Chinese Societies," *Issues and Studies,* vol. 41, no. 4 (December 2005), pp.1–33; Andrew J. Nathan and Tse-Hsin Chen, "Traditional Social Values, Democratic Values, and Political Participation," *Asian Barometer Working Paper Series,* no. 23 (2004); Chung-min Park and Doh Chull Shin, "Do Asian Values Deter Popular Support for Democracy? The Case of South Korea," *Asian Barometer Working Paper Series,* no. 26 (2004).

more likely to be supportive (i.e., those who are satisfied with their lives and whose political values emphasize the importance of social harmony and stability over diversity and pluralism).

Contextual Factors

All of the variables described concern the individual entrepreneurs or their firms. In order to control for variation in local context, I consider each county's *level of development* (based on per capita GDP); the economic growth rate over the five years prior to the survey (*GDP change*); and the importance of the private sector to the local economy, measured by the percentage of firms that are privately owned (*private sector share*). If there is a systematic strategy for selecting which entrepreneurs will be allowed to participate in China's formal political institutions, then the level of development, rate of growth, and size of the private sector should not be related to the probability of being a PC or PPCC delegate. What should matter is *who* gets selected, regardless of the economic conditions. Because candidates in village elections are more self-selected, their numbers should be higher in the more prosperous areas and where the private sector is relatively large.

THE RESULTS

In the analysis below, I will show how the political, individual, cultural, and contextual variables described influence which private entrepreneurs participate in China's formal political institutions.[31]

People's Congresses

As shown in table 6.1, nearly the same percentage of respondents served in PCs in 2005 as in 1999.[32] Being a PC delegate was not only

---

[31] The same sets of questions were asked in the 1999 survey, but the cumulative number of nonresponses on the many variables makes the results suspect. Although responses were good for most individual questions, in the combined model of 15 variables, over one-third of the respondents did not provide answers to at least one of the questions. In the 2005 survey, the cumulative response rate on the combined model was over 90 percent. For these reasons, only the 2005 data are analyzed here.

[32] Li, Meng, and Zhang use survey data in which 17 percent of respondents were PC members; see Li, Meng, and Zhang, "Why Do Entrepreneurs Enter Politics?" My

TABLE 6.1. *Percentage of Private Entrepreneurs in Political Posts*

	1999	2005
People's Congress		
All entrepreneurs	11.3	10.5
Xiahai entrepreneurs	19.1	18.0
Co-opted entrepreneurs	24.6	15.5
Want to join CCP	5.1	3.0
Don't want to join CCP	5.6	4.5
People's Political Consultative Conference		
All entrepreneurs	4.9	5.3
Xiahai entrepreneurs	6.1	4.2
Co-opted entrepreneurs	6.5	8.9
Want to join CCP	4.4	6.5
Don't want to join CCP	3.8	3.4
Village Chief or Representative Council		
All entrepreneurs	16.1	13.7
Xiahai entrepreneurs	22.8	20.2
Co-opted entrepreneurs	40.6	21.4
Want to join CCP	10.7	10.3
Don't want to join CCP	6.2	3.4

fairly common but also widely distributed: there was at least one in each of the 24 townships in the sample. As expected, red capitalists are more likely to be selected for membership on local PCs than are non-CCP entrepreneurs: 82 percent of PC delegates in the sample were party members. This is par for the course: 60–80 percent of PC delegates at all levels are typically CCP members.[33] The CCP likes to keep a monopoly on political participation, and therefore it uses party membership as an important criterion for appointments to PCs. The distribution of the kinds of entrepreneurs who served, however, changed dramatically. Comparing the 1999 and 2005 surveys, the probability that a co-opted entrepreneur was a PC delegate dropped by about one-third.

surveys found a much lower level, consistent with a study of entrepreneurs' political participation in Wenzhou and Guangzhou; see Ao, "Siying qiyezhu zhengzhi canyu yanjiu baogao," p. 69.

[33] O'Brien, "Agents and Remonstrators," p. 364; Pei, *China's Trapped Transition*, pp. 63–64.

The probability for *xiahai* entrepreneurs remained similar, but because this group's share of the respondents grew so dramatically between 1999 and 2005 (from 25.1 percent to 34.1 percent), the percentage of *xiahai* entrepreneurs among PC delegates grew from 40.7 percent to 58.6 percent.

In addition, membership in the ICF was also an important credential: 59.5 percent of the delegates were ICF members in the 2005 sample. Similarly, those who do not belong to any business associations are less likely to serve in PCs than those who belong to any of the official business associations. For those who serve in PCs, membership in the CCP and ICF both pay high dividends, as does active participation in them: PC delegates report that they attend party and federation meetings more frequently than do other entrepreneurs.

The results for the individual characteristics are mostly as expected (see table 6.2). Older entrepreneurs are more likely to have served as PC delegates (a test for curvilinearity was negative, meaning that the likelihood of participation did not drop for the oldest entrepreneurs in the sample). The effect of education, in contrast, is curvilinear: those with college or graduate degrees are slightly less likely to have been PC delegates than those who only hold high school degrees.[34] The larger the firm, the more likely that the entrepreneur has been a delegate. These are economic elites, and size matters. However, gender by itself does not matter. The vast majority of both entrepreneurs and delegates are men, but there is no significant difference in the probability that male and female entrepreneurs have been delegates, all else being equal.

The relationship between cultural variables and PC membership is consistent with the party's strategy of co-optation: those who are less likely to challenge the status quo are more likely to be PC delegates. Respondents who said their living standards and social status were rising were more likely to be delegates. In other words, overall life

---

[34] In their study of political participation by China's entrepreneurs, Li, Meng, and Zhang found that education was not a statistically significant predictor of PC membership, but they used years of education as their measure. Using years of education in my model yields insignificant results. Looking for a curvilinear relationship based on the highest degree, rather than total years, produces better results and is more consistent with selection criteria used by the CCP: it is the degree that matters, not how many years were spent in school. See Li, Meng, and Zhang, "Why Do Entrepreneurs Enter Politics?"

satisfaction is strongly and positively correlated with being a PC delegate. In addition, those with more traditional political orientations – who see economic competition, group diversity, multiple viewpoints, and a multiparty system as threats to stability – are more likely to be delegates. In fact, PC delegates are not only more conservative than other entrepreneurs but also express much more conservative views than local officials. In short, entrepreneurs who are more likely to support the status quo – the ones with high levels of life satisfaction and more traditional political values – are more likely to be PC delegates. Given that most survey respondents who are PC delegates are also red capitalists, this suggests a conscious selection strategy: only the most conservative red capitalists are chosen.

As was expected, contextual factors have less of an impact than the political, individual, and cultural variables. The level of development, GDP change, and private sector share in the eight counties in the survey are not statistically significant when other explanatory variables are held constant.[35]

People's Political Consultative Conferences

The most notable features in PPCC membership are low frequency and uneven distribution. Approximately 5 percent of respondents were PPCC delegates in both the 1999 and 2005 surveys, much lower than the 35 percent reported in the ACFIC's 2002 survey of private entrepreneurs but similar to Kellee Tsai's 2002 survey, in which 6.5 percent of respondents belonged to local PPCCs, and a study of political participation by entrepreneurs in Wenzhou and Guangzhou, where only 4.35 percent were PPCC members.[36] The ACFIC survey included a larger share of large private firms than even my surveys: firms in that sample had an average of 169.4 workers, compared with the national

---

[35] It is also worth pointing out here that both counties in Shandong (one the poorest in the sample, the other among the most prosperous) have the lowest levels of membership of entrepreneurs in PCs. Whether this is just a coincidence, a reflection of official attitudes, or the apolitical nature of entrepreneurs in Shandong is not clear.

[36] Kellee S. Tsai, *Capitalism without Democracy: The Private Sector in Contemporary China* (Ithaca, NY: Cornell University Press, 2007), p. 125; Ao, "Siying qiyezhu zhengzhi canyu yanjiu baogao." Data from the 2002 and earlier ACFIC surveys are available from the Universities Service Centre of The Chinese University of Hong Kong. Li, Meng, and Zhang use the ACFIC survey data.

average of 11.4 and the average in my 2005 survey of 74.4. The analysis below will show a positive and significant relationship between firm size and PPCC membership, which may partially explain why the ACFIC survey and mine have such different results.[37] This discrepancy is all the more perplexing because of the distribution of PPCC delegates: almost half in the 2005 survey came from the two counties in Hunan, and outside of Hunan there were no PPCC delegates in 7 of the 18 townships in the sample. This is largely consistent with the 1999 survey, where over one-third of PPCC delegates also came from Hunan, a smaller but still disproportionate share. Despite these factors, the results of my survey are generally consistent with the ACFIC data and unless noted are similar when the Hunan counties are omitted. In other words, the relationship between the variables remains the same even though the frequency of PPCC membership is quite different.

In contrast to PCs, the impact of political characteristics on PPCC membership is quite different. First of all, the coefficients for *xiahai* and co-opted entrepreneurs are not significant (see table 6.2). The reason is quite clear: in the 2005 survey, only a slight majority of the PPCC delegates were red capitalists (53.4 percent). This may seem like a curious finding because the PPCC system is supposedly designed to allow local officials to consult with others in their community on a range of policy issues. If half of its members are also CCP members – i.e., members of the political elite – then the range of views expressed at PPCC meetings is likely to be narrower than if it brought together people who were not already "in the system." On the other hand, if the purpose of appointing PPCC delegates is to select people who are politically reliable, who are likely to endorse the policy decisions of local leaders, but who also will be able to lend an air of legitimacy to the consultations, then selecting party members who hold positions outside the party and government makes good sense.

Membership in business associations, on the other hand, has a similar effect for PPCCs as for PCs, and presumably for similar reasons. Because membership in the PPCCs is more prestigious than powerful, local officials are more likely to select people who are already part

---

[37] Li, Meng, and Zhang also found a large and statistically significant effect for firm size on PPCC membership using the ACFIC data; see Li, Meng, and Zhang, "Why Do Entrepreneurs Enter Politics?"

TABLE 6.2. *Determinants of Private Entrepreneurs' Participation in China's Formal Political Institutions (probit regression coefficients with robust standard errors in parentheses)*

	PC	PPCC	Village Candidates
Political Factors			
Xiahai entrepreneurs	.620***	−.311	.816***
	(.164)	(.237)	(.153)
Co-opted entrepreneurs	.704***	.129	.757***
	(.196)	(.217)	(.164)
ICF member	.302*	.685***	−.101
	(.147)	(.181)	(.144)
No business association	-.361*	−.883*	−.099
	(.179)	(.380)	(.135)
Individual and Firm Characteristics			
Age	.033**	.018	−.009
	(.011)	(.013)	(.011)
Gender	−.030	−.267	−.203
	(.247)	(.350)	(.195)
Level of education	1.281**	1.123	.713
	(.509)	(.640)	(.450)
Level of education^2	−.211*	−.199	−.156*
	(.088)	(.108)	(.077)
Sales revenue (log)	.147***	.173**	−.039
	(.049)	(.060)	(.039)
Years in business	.018	.027	.023
	(.013)	(.016)	(.012)
Years in county	.003	−.013*	.014
	(.007)	(.006)	(.009)
Cultural Factors			
Life satisfaction	.135*	.001	.133**
	(.068)	(.065)	(.050)
Modern values	−.090***	.070*	−.054*
	(.026)	(.031)	(.023)
Contextual Factors			
Level of development (per capita GDP)	.008	−.083**	−.031
	(.019)	(.023)	(.018)
Rate of growth, 1999–2003	−.002	−.007	.002
	(.004)	(.005)	(.004)
Size of private sector	−.523	−.124	−.082
	(.276)	(.317)	(.237)
Constant	−5.707***	−3.961**	−1.957**
	(1.109)	(1.293)	(.804)
N	962	962	962
Chi^2	114.38***	80.96	96.09
Pseudo R^2	.252	.277	.152

*$p < .05$; ** $p < .01$; *** $p < .001$.

of the establishment. The ICF symbolizes the local economic establishment, and therefore its members are more likely to be chosen for PPCC membership than others: 75 percent of PPCC delegates in the survey were also ICF members. On the other hand, those who do not belong to any of the official business associations are not part of the establishment and are less likely candidates for these posts, as seen by the large, negative, and significant coefficient. Because business associations nominate PPCC delegates, they are most likely to nominate their own members. To put it more explicitly, only one of the PPCC delegates in the sample did not belong to any business association. In the model presented in table 6.2, most of the explanatory power comes from just two variables: those who belong to the ICF and those who belong to no business association. These two variables account for 64.3 percent of the explained variance. Because they indicate who does and does not belong to the local economic elite, they are the most important criteria for who is selected to be a PPCC delegate.

Also unlike the findings for PC delegates, the age and level of education of entrepreneurs remarkably do not have a significant impact on which ones are chosen as PPCC delegates; tests for both linear and curvilinear relationships were negative.[38] But business issues do matter: the larger the firm, the more likely its owner was a PPCC delegate. This reinforces the notion that PPCC delegates are drawn from among local elites and do not represent the local community more generally. This finding is reinforced by the negative relationship between the number of years entrepreneurs have lived in the county and the probability they were chosen to be PPCC delegates. It is apparently not necessary to have deep roots in the community to be chosen to consult with party and government leaders on policy matters.

Cultural values have starkly different effects on the probability of being a PPCC delegate compared with being a PC delegate. Satisfaction with living standards and social status is not related to being a PPCC delegate: the small and statistically insignificant coefficient for life satisfaction indicates that PPCC delegates and nondelegates are

---

[38] This is one area where the ACFIC data are different: Li, Meng, and Zhang report a positive relationship for age and a curvilinear relationship for education, both statistically significant. Even using years of education as they do does not change the results from my data.

about equally likely to believe their living standards and social status are improving. Whereas PC delegates on average had more traditional values than other entrepreneurs, having traditional values makes PPCC membership *less* likely. Perhaps local officials select entrepreneurs with more progressive/liberal values for PPCCs, because it is less risky to have them in a body that is prestigious but does not have direct influence over local government. This finding is mostly due to the PPCC delegates in Hunan, who ironically report much more modern views than do nondelegates. PPCC delegates in other counties also have a higher score on the index of modern values than do PC delegates, but the differences are not significant because of the small number of PPCC delegates outside of Hunan. The difference between entrepreneurs who have been PC and PPCC delegates and the difference between those groups and other entrepreneurs suggest that political orientation may be part of the screening process for selecting PC and PPCC delegates. More research will be needed to determine the precise criteria used to choose delegates.

As was the case for PCs, most contextual factors are weakly related to PPCC membership. The important exception is level of development, which is negative and statistically significant, suggesting that PPCC membership may be less common in more prosperous areas. The explanation for this is straightforward: there is likely a rough quota on how many entrepreneurs can be chosen to be PPCC delegates, and in more developed areas there may be more entrepreneurs from which to choose, and so the odds of any given entrepreneur being chosen are smaller than in poorer communities. However, this same logic should also apply to PC delegates, but at least according to these data it does not. Again, given the small number of observations, this result is not conclusive. Neither the rate of growth (GDP change) nor the private sector share is statistically significant for the whole sample or for the non-Hunan counties considered separately.

Village Elections

Being a candidate in village elections is another common form of political participation for entrepreneurs. The expanding role of entrepreneurs in local politics results from a combination of both individual initiative and local necessity. A key motivation is to turn their wealth into power. Successful entrepreneurs often want greater influence over local policy, and when they cannot do so indirectly through lobbying and persuasion (or bribery), they have the option of running for office. The reverse is also true: some entrepreneurs see involvement in politics as good for business: it allows them to develop further social capital, which in turn improves their business prospects. Participation by entrepreneurs in village politics in many cases is also driven by local economic necessity. Because many local governments are under tremendous financial pressure, they cannot afford to pay their officials. Having officials with independent sources of income – i.e., entrepreneurs – is therefore a practical necessity for many communities. Personal wealth also fulfills another requirement for local politicians: as vote buying becomes more prevalent in village elections, entrepreneurs are best able to buy the votes necessary to become elected.[39]

In 23 of the 24 townships in the sample, at least one of the entrepreneurs had been a candidate for village chief or the representative council. Overall, 13.7 percent of the respondents in the 2005 survey had been candidates in elections for either village chiefs or representative councils. This is a slight decline from the 1999 survey, where 16.1 percent of the entrepreneurs had been candidates (see table 6.1).[40] As noted, candidates for village elections are more self-selected, and therefore their characteristics do not suggest a given CCP strategy as clearly as those of entrepreneurs selected to be PC and PPCC delegates. The vast majority of those who have been village candidates in both surveys (72.5 percent in 1999 and 75.2 percent in 2005) were party members, reflecting the party's desire to keep all political participation under its control. But here again the types of entrepreneurs who had been candidates changed. The majority of the village-level candidates in the 2005 survey, 50.3 percent, were *xiahai* entrepreneurs. This does not reflect increased participation by this group (the percentage

---

[39] Richard Levy, "Village Elections, Transparency, and Anti-Corruption: Henan and Guangdong Provinces," in Elizabeth J. Perry and Merle Goldman, eds., *Grassroots Political Reform in Contemporary China* (Cambridge, MA: Harvard University Press, 2007).

[40] In Tsai's 2002 survey of Chinese entrepreneurs, an even smaller percentage (10.3 percent) had been candidates in village elections, and about half (5.2 percent) had won their elections; see Tsai, *Capitalism without Democracy*, p. 127.

of *xiahai* entrepreneurs that had been candidates in village elections declined from 22.8 percent in 1999 to 20.2 percent in 2005); rather, it reflects their growing share of the total number of entrepreneurs. It also indicates that a different dynamic may be at work at the local level. Previously, co-opted entrepreneurs were most likely to run as candidates, suggesting they were more interested than other entrepreneurs in acquiring political power to match their economic influence. In 1999, 40.6 percent of the co-opted entrepreneurs had been candidates, but this figure dropped to only 21.4 percent in 2005. More research is needed to find out why, but it may be because co-opted entrepreneurs encountered too much interference from higher levels, found that the pressures of political office were detrimental to their business interests, or determined that the political climate had shifted in favor of the private sector, making it less necessary for them to acquire political office.[41]

Being a red capitalist (either one who *xiahai*'d into the private sector or was co-opted into the party after being in business) is the most important factor in determining which entrepreneurs have been village candidates. Local officials are famously wary of popular voting for village positions because it gives the winners a popular mandate that officials, who have been appointed by higher levels of the state, often lack. At least among entrepreneurs in the sample, one way of reducing the uncertainty that comes from village elections is to encourage, or at least allow, party members to run. Moreover, the red capitalists who have run in village elections are also active party members: 72.5 percent report that they attend every party meeting, as opposed to only 45.2 percent of those who have not been candidates. This suggests that the party rewards not only its own members but also those who are most involved in party life.

This apparent support for red capitalists as candidates in village elections is reinforced by responses to another question in the survey: should entrepreneurs who win village elections join the CCP if they are not already members? By large margins, officials and red capitalists believe that they should, and entrepreneurs who want to join

---

[41] According to a survey of private entrepreneurs in Guangzhou and Wenzhou, limited time and energy were the main obstacles to increased political participation; see Ao, "Siying qiyezhu zhengzhi canyu yanjiu baogao," p. 80.

TABLE 6.3. *Should Winners of Village Elections Join CCP If Not Already Members? (percent)*

	1999			2005		
	Yes	Does not matter	No	Yes	Does not matter	No
All entrepreneurs	67.9	28.4	3.7	65.0	33.3	1.7
Xiahai entrepreneurs	74.4	24.8	0.8	73.3	24.0	2.8
Co-opted entrepreneurs	72.7	18.2	9.1	75.0	25.0	0.0
Want to join CCP	75.4	21.1	3.5	67.2	32.1	0.8
Don't want to join CCP	55.1	41.3	3.6	45.3	52.5	2.3
All cadres	59.0	27.5	13.5	77.6	18.0	4.4
County	44.5	35.9	19.5	75.4	20.2	4.4
Township/village	78.7	16.0	5.3	79.1	16.5	4.4

the CCP are almost equally supportive (see table 6.3). Support among county-level officials increased sharply from 44.5 percent in 1999 to 75.4 percent in 2005. In sharp contrast, most of those who do not want to join the CCP believe it does not matter, over twice the proportion for red capitalists and local officials. In both the 1999 and 2005 surveys, those who are not in the CCP and do not want to be are the least enthusiastic about entrepreneurs participating in village elections (see table 6.4). Even on this question, the ambivalence of this group indicates their desire to remain outside of the political arena and the crony communist system, which is also indicated by other data.

Local officials are less enthusiastic about entrepreneurs being village candidates than are red capitalists: only 28.7 percent feel they should be encouraged to run, compared with 38.5 percent of red capitalists. If local officials are more ambivalent than entrepreneurs on this question, at least their ambivalence has decreased over time: in the 1999 survey, 48.3 percent of officials were *opposed* to having entrepreneurs run in village elections, and another 26.1 percent felt they should only be encouraged to run if they were qualified. In the 2005 survey, those who were outright opposed declined dramatically, those who felt entrepreneurs needed to meet certain qualifications increased by a similar amount, and those who encouraged entrepreneurs' participation remained about the same.

Membership in business associations is a weaker predictor of which entrepreneurs have been candidates in village elections (see table 6.2).

TABLE 6.4. *Propriety of Private Entrepreneurs Running in Village Elections (percent)*

	1999			2005		
	Encourage participation	Only if qualified	Restrict participation	Encourage participation	Only if qualified	Restrict participation
All entrepreneurs	37.3	58.9	3.8	33.2	63.0	3.8
Xiabai entrepreneurs	40.2	52.8	7.1	39.3	57.9	2.8
Co-opted entrepreneurs	31.8	65.2	3.0	36.8	60.2	3.0
Want to join CCP	46.2	51.1	2.8	31.4	63.6	5.0
Don't want to join CCP	29.7	67.9	2.4	24.2	71.2	5.6
All cadres	25.7	26.1	48.3	28.7	68.8	2.5
County	21.8	27.1	51.1	26.1	71.4	2.5
Township/village	30.9	24.7	44.3	30.6	66.9	2.5

Whereas ICF membership was an important factor for PC and PPCC delegates, it is not for village elections. One reason for this is that PC and PPCC delegates are more fully screened and selected by the CCP for those posts; their membership in the ICF certifies their position as members of the local economic elite. That is apparently less important for village elections, where candidates rely on their personal acquaintance with others in the community and not on their reputation among higher-level officials.[42]

Finally, party members are not only more likely to run in village elections but more likely to win. Of the red capitalists who ran in village elections, 80.2 percent reported they won; of the non-CCP entrepreneurs, only 24.3 percent won. Being a party member may signal to voters that a candidate will be acceptable to higher-level officials and will not have his or her victory nullified. In addition, candidates' party membership may also signify that they have the skills and connections necessary to be a successful leader. The same attributes that make entrepreneurs attractive to the party may also enhance their appeal to voters.

Most individual-level characteristics (age, gender, firm sales, and years in business) are not significant variables in predicting which entrepreneurs have been village candidates. Only education is a significant variable, and it has a curvilinear relationship with candidacy: those with college or graduate degrees were less likely to have been candidates than those with high school or lower degrees.

Entrepreneurs who have been village candidates have cultural values similar to those who have been PC delegates. Like PC delegates, but in contrast to PPCC delegates, entrepreneurs who have run in village elections are more likely to report that their standard of living and social status are improving, the criteria used for the life satisfaction index. As village officials, they would be in a better position to preserve and perpetuate their standards of living and prestige. They also hold more traditional political views than other entrepreneurs: they

---

[42] What does matter is being a member of SELA: among members of the different business associations in the 2005 survey, SELA members had most frequently been village candidates (almost 20 percent). However, when all other variables are held constant, SELA membership falls just short of statistical significance ($p = .065$).

are more concerned about economic and social diversity influencing stability than those who have not been candidates. In contrast to PC delegates, however, village candidates are more self-selected. People's Congress delegates are screened and approved by CCP-dominated election committees and selected in part perhaps because of their political views. In contrast, entrepreneurs who have chosen to run in village elections may be motivated to do so because of their political beliefs. If these entrepreneurs are to be agents of change, it would not likely be in the direction of increased liberalization. Instead, their conservative values may lead them to try to limit the social impact of rapid growth in order to maintain stability.

Entrepreneurs who have been candidates in village elections are most likely to be from poorer counties. In the two poorest counties in the survey (one each in Hebei and Shandong, the latter of which was designated as a "national model county in the practice of self-rule by villagers"), 22.6 percent of entrepreneurs have been candidates;[43] in the three middle-level counties (in Hebei and Hunan), 13.9 percent were candidates; and in the richest (in Shandong and Zhejiang), only 8.15 percent. This makes perfect sense, as the richest counties are very urbanized (in fact, one was converted into a district of a large municipality). Even so, each of them had entrepreneurs who had been candidates in village elections. When other variables are held constant, however, none of the variables for the local economic context is significant.

Multiple Posts

Many of the entrepreneurs who have held political posts have held more than one. In the 2005 survey, about one in five of those who served in PCs also served in PPCCs, and about one in four had run for village office. There was less overlap between PPCC delegates and village candidates: only four of the respondents in the 2005 survey had

---

[43] Interviews with local officials in these two poor counties indicate that it is a common practice to have entrepreneurs hold village positions, including party positions. From their perspective, it was acceptable both to county-level officials and society at large. In the six other survey sites, local officials did not volunteer similar information.

done both. Not surprisingly, most of those with multiple posts were red capitalists: about two-thirds (14 of 22) of those who had been in both the PC and PPCC, almost all (31 of 33) of those who had been both PC and village candidates, and all four of those who had been PPCC and village candidates were red capitalists. Three hit the trifecta: they had served as delegates in a PC and a PPCC and had been a candidate in a village election. All three were red capitalists.

Summary

In all three types of political posts analyzed in this chapter, two related and recurring themes stand out: red capitalists have held a growing share of these posts, and *xiahai* entrepreneurs in particular were increasingly prominent. Not only is the CCP relying on former officials and SOE managers to help it monitor the private sector, it is also giving them preferential treatment in granting them access to political posts, whether directly elected or selected with the approval of local officials. This is consistent with the party's overall strategy for survival: it prefers that political participation be under its control and prefers that those who are active in politics be trusted party members unlikely to challenge the status quo. Accordingly, the entrepreneurs who have been PC delegates or village candidates have cultural values that are more likely to make them support the status quo and not pose a challenge to it: they also have higher levels of overall life satisfaction than other entrepreneurs, and they have more traditional values. In addition, active party life is rewarded with political power: the red capitalists selected for political posts and/or allowed to run for village office were most active in party life. All of the red capitalists who served in PCs or PPCCs identified themselves as active party members, as did 107 of the 109 who ran for village office. More specifically, the red capitalists who claimed they attend every party meeting (compared with those who said they attend frequently) were two-and-a-half times more likely to have run for village office, 50 percent more likely to have served in a PC, but slightly less likely to have served in a PPCC. Similarly, those who reported active participation in the ICF were also more likely to have been PC and PPCC delegates and even village candidates. Political activity is not limited to one type of organization:

those who are in political posts are also active in the party and/or the ICF.

CONCLUSION

Properly understanding the political participation of private entrepreneurs in China involves attention not just to their interests but also to the CCP's strategy for screening and selecting which entrepreneurs are allowed to participate in China's formal political institutions. Local cadres in several counties reported that entrepreneurs were only interested in joining the CCP if they were interested in public posts, and the survey data indicate why. Party membership is an important credential that makes participation in China's political institutions more likely: most PC and PPCC delegates and candidates in village elections in the survey were red capitalists. The desire to get involved in politics was indeed a main motivation to join the CCP, at least for some entrepreneurs.

The evidence above does not provide support for the view that entrepreneurs who participate in China's formal political institutions are inclined to be agents of change. In fact, just the opposite is true: entrepreneurs who have been PC delegates and candidates in village elections report more life satisfaction and more traditional values than other entrepreneurs. Based on the findings of previous research, people with these kinds of viewpoints are more likely to support the status quo and less likely to promote democratizing reforms. PPCC delegates have slightly more modern values than do other entrepreneurs, but they belong to an institution of little political consequence. In fact, it may be that they are chosen for that body precisely because of their political views: putting more liberal entrepreneurs into a body with some prestige but little influence is the quintessential co-optation tactic. In this way, potential "troublemakers" are brought into the political arena but kept outside the decision-making core.

Although the CCP's control of the economy and society may have diminished as a consequence of the reforms that it has sponsored, the Leninist nature of the political system remains intact. The CCP limits access to the political arena by selecting and approving only those it deems most trustworthy, and in large part that means those who are already party members. The majority of entrepreneurs who have gained access to formal political institutions are red capitalists, in particular *xiahai* entrepreneurs, who joined the party before joining the private sector. Limiting who has access to the political arena is crucial to the perpetuation of crony communism in China and remains a core element of the party's strategy for survival.

7

The Ripple Effects of Privatization

Corruption, Inequality, and Charity

The CCP's economic reform strategy, and in particular its reliance on the private sector as the engine of growth, has generated rapid, sustained growth. One of the CCP's sources of legitimacy is its ability to make the economy grow, and it has succeeded in this quest. One by-product has been its growing role in the global economy and the international system more generally. This in turn has helped fuel growing national pride, another source of the CCP's legitimacy. At the same time, its strategy of embracing the private sector has also had a variety of more negative consequences, some intended (such as regional disparities in economic development), others unintended but predictable – environmental degradation, corruption, massive loss of industrial jobs, rising income inequalities, and the resulting social and political problems that these other issues have brought about. These ripple effects threaten to undermine a third source of the party's legitimacy: its ability to maintain social order and political stability.

This chapter will focus on two of these ripple effects – corruption and inequality – which are arguably the most politically salient. These problems are in large part the consequence of its reform strategy and its reliance on the private sector as the primary engine of growth. The corrupt ties between communist and capitalist cronies have drawn attention to the inherently unequal and unfair practices that govern the market in China. Similarly, the CCP's *daitou zhifu* doctrine ("take the lead in getting rich") has justified the formation of a nouveau riche and acknowledges that the opportunity to get rich is unevenly distributed. But because so many of the nouveaux riches come from privileged backgrounds – red capitalists, friends and families of high-ranking officials, and other cronies – popular resentment against China's new economic elites has been widespread and intense. The disparity between China's remarkable aggregate growth rates and the often corrupt means by which that growth was generated, and the unequal and unfair distribution of that newly generated wealth, reveal a vulnerability in the CCP's reform strategy.

This chapter will also look at how the CCP is trying to cope with the challenges posed by these ripple effects. It is adopting populist policies to alleviate economic inequality and is encouraging charitable giving among the beneficiaries of reform, especially the red capitalists. As described in chapter 1, the very success of the CCP's crony communist strategy has led to resentment against its inherently corrupt and unequal nature, threatening its survival and continued success. Populist policies and charitable donations are intended to address some of those popular concerns in order to improve social harmony and in the process create the level of social order and political stability needed to enhance the party's legitimacy. Whether the CCP's reform strategy, and its embrace of the private sector in particular, will continue to enjoy public support will in large part be determined by how well it can manage corruption, inequality, and other ripple effects.

THE SPREAD OF CORRUPTION

Without question, corruption resulting from economic reform has been the most politically charged ripple effect of the CCP's economic strategy. Virtually every public opinion poll, whether conducted by government agencies or private firms such as Horizon Research, reveals that corruption tops the list of popular concerns. This perception is shared by most outside observers as well. According to Transparency International's list of countries ranked from least to most corrupt, China ranked 72nd out of 179 countries in 2007; it was tied with seven other countries, including Brazil, India, and Mexico. On a ten-point scale, China scored only 3.5 points, compared with 9.4 for Denmark,

Finland, and New Zealand, which tied for first, and 1.4 for Myanmar and Somalia, which tied for last.[1]

The spread of corruption was not an intended consequence of economic reform, but it was nevertheless predictable. The transition from a planned to a market economy created numerous opportunities to engage in rent-seeking and outright corruption.[2] Corruption also existed in the Maoist era, although it was of a different degree and kind. The scale of corruption was lower because of recurring political campaigns: the fear of being exposed and punished for corrupt behavior deterred many but certainly not all cadres' conduct. In addition, the limited availability of cash and luxury goods meant that bribes were more about allocating favors and bartering scarce goods and services rather than straight cash transactions. (This does not include the abuse of authority by local officials, which has been a recurring problem in post-1949 China and the target of repeated campaigns.) But in the post-Mao period, the growing economy and rising prosperity created new opportunities and incentives for corruption on a larger scale. According to a World Bank study, "The correlation between rising corruption and the expansion of the market economy [in the late 1980s] led most to see a causal link between the two." More accurately, it resulted from "the continuation of widespread discretionary bureaucratic controls over the economy" and the weakening of official prohibitions against acquiring luxury goods.[3]

Corruption was a response not just to increased opportunities and incentives but also to lower costs of detection and punishment. Although the CCP has made a sustained and sincere effort to investigate and punish corruption, the institutions it has created for

---

[1] Transparency International, *Corruption Perceptions Index 2007*, available at http://www.transparency.org/policy_research/surveys_indices/cpi/2007, accessed October 2, 2007. Transparency International uses a variety of polls to assess the perception of corruption in a country; strictly speaking it is a measure of perceptions, not a measure of actual corruption. The organization has a separate poll on the actual extent of corruption in a country, but China is not included in that sample.

[2] Andrew H. Wedeman, *From Mao to Market: Rent Seeking, Local Protectionism, and Marketization in China* (Cambridge: Cambridge University Press, 2003).

[3] Shahid Yusuf, Kaoru Nabeshima, and Dwight Perkins, *Under New Ownership: Privatizing China's State-Owned Enterprises* (Palo Alto, CA, and Washington, DC: Stanford University Press and World Bank, 2006), p. 66.

monitoring the behavior of officials and party members are noto-
riously weak. Local "discipline inspection commissions," which are
tasked with investigating corruption among party members, fall under
the leadership of the party committees at that level, allowing party
leaders to interfere with and obstruct their work. This has allowed corruption to be pervasive, and even routine, because powerful officials
can protect themselves and their underlings. Indeed, where widespread
corruption exists, the costs shift to those who are not corrupt. Officials
who refuse to take bribes can be threatened by bribe-givers, pressured
by other officials on the take, and if necessary transferred to new posts
if they insist on staying clean.

In 2004, a local official named Huang Jingao gained brief notoriety
after posting a letter on the *People's Daily* Web site describing the
"underlying rules" of Chinese politics, in which corrupt officials were
protected by higher-level authorities. Upon becoming party secretary
in Fujian's Lianjiang County, he learned that his predecessor reportedly colluded with real estate developers to force citizens from their
homes and sell their homes at below market value. But as he began
his investigation, he claimed he was repeatedly stymied by intervention
from above, as though a "large invisible net was trying to cover up this
corruption case." He eventually dropped the case, but then posted his
letter. In his previous post in Fuzhou City, he encountered similar resistance, and even wore a bullet-proof vest and hired bodyguards after
receiving death threats. His letter circulated widely on the Internet,
verifying what many Chinese already believed to be true. Soon after
his letter was posted, Fuzhou party officials harshly criticized him for
breaching party discipline. Huang was arrested soon after and charged
with corruption; he was convicted and received a sentence of life in
prison. Given the prevalence of corruption in China, and the opaque
nature of its political and legal systems, it is not clear if his letter was
a desperate effort by a corrupt official trying to deflect attention away
from his own wrongdoing or a noble but ultimately futile cry for justice that was punished by vindictive higher-level officials determined
to avoid public scrutiny of their "underlying rules."[4]

---

[4] Huang's letter entitled "Why I Have Been Wearing a Bullet-proof Vest for Six Years"
was published on *Renmin wang*, *People's Daily*'s Web site, on August 11, 2004, but
was later removed. An English translation is available on *World News Connection*.

Eradicating corruption is difficult when it has become accepted as part of the normal order of things. The credibility given to Huang's letter suggests that is how corruption is viewed in China. According to Melanie Manion, "Many [Chinese] believe the vast majority of officials are thoroughly corrupt, a view that is surely exaggerated and also part of the folklore" of corruption that affects routine interactions between officials and citizens. When you expect officials to be corrupt, you are more likely to act corruptly, for instance by giving a bribe, even for routine transactions such as obtaining a business license.[5] According to a local prosecutor in Shenzhen, "tolerable levels of corruption are no longer serious obstacles to cadre survival or promotion, as long as job performance is satisfactory."[6] Many Chinese and foreign firms doing business in China reportedly allocate a regular portion of a project's budget to bribes, gifts, and entertainment, all with the intention of gaining and maintaining the good will of corrupt officials.

As a consequence of these factors, since 1992 corruption has increased in scope, in the monetary value of specific cases, and in the level of officials involved.[7] In the early reform period before 1992, the most common forms of cadre corruption entailed official profiteering, the practice of buying goods at the low price set by the economic plan and reselling them at the higher price set by the market, and bureaucratic commerce, in which government agencies ran sideline business operations. But in the post-1992 period, when economic growth and privatization were at their peak, illegal asset stripping of state-owned enterprises undergoing restructuring, illegal land grabs, and bribery became the most severe forms of corruption. Economist Hu Angang estimated that corruption cost the Chinese economy between 987 and

---

See also Edward Cody, "A Plea for Honesty Transfixes China: Lowly Party Cadre Decries Official Corruption in Open Letter," *Washington Post*, August 14, 2004; "Chinese Anti-Corruption Hero Accused of Taking Bribes," *South China Morning Post*, February 7, 2005.

[5] Melanie Manion, *Corruption by Design: Building Clean Government in Mainland China and Hong Kong* (Cambridge, MA: Harvard University Press, 2004), p. 26.

[6] Quoted in Yan Sun, *Corruption and Market in Contemporary China* (Ithaca, NY: Cornell University Press, 2004), p. 22.

[7] Sun, *Corruption and Market in Contemporary China*; Andrew Wedeman, "The Intensification of Corruption in China," *China Quarterly*, no. 180 (December 2004), pp. 895–921; "Ten Characteristics of Chinese Corruption," http://www.china.org.cn/english/2003/Jun/66715.htm.

1,257 billion yuan (US$123–157 billion) annually, which amounted to 13–17 percent of the country's GDP in 2003.[8]

In addressing the problem of corruption, the Chinese government tends to focus primarily on cases that produce large revenue losses to the state. In contrast, Manion observed that "the forms of corruption that are the most visible, repugnant, and directly costly to ordinary citizens" are defined as mere irregularities or even "policy solutions to problems of revenue shortfalls for governments and public agencies."[9] As a result, many of the CCP's efforts at investigating and punishing corruption do not change the incentives of local officials or the perceptions of the general public. The scope of corruption and the party's denunciations of it grow in tandem. In order to seriously curtail corruption, the party would have to create a watchdog agency independent of the party officials it would investigate. Throughout its history, the CCP has refused to allow this kind of autonomous actor, insisting it has the ability to detect and correct its own problems. With the explosion of corruption that has accompanied economic reform, the CCP's monitoring mechanism has clearly met its match.

The following discussion will describe some of the main types of corruption, giving particular attention to examples involving the private sector.

Official Profiteering and Bureaucratic Commerce

In the 1980s, the CCP created a dual-price system for allocating goods in order to encourage greater productivity. Once SOEs met their quota mandated by the central economic plan, they could sell additional products at the higher price set by the market. The profits earned from these higher-priced sales could then be passed on to workers and staff in the form of higher bonuses or reinvested in the firm. But the dual-price system also created opportunities for officials and SOE managers to engage in a lucrative and illicit, but not technically illegal, form of arbitrage: they could buy low and sell high, even if they did not produce the goods themselves. Because they were taking advantage of their official positions to obtain private material benefits, this form of arbitrage was clearly corrupt behavior, but because it was

---

[8] http://www.china.org.cn/english/2004/Jan/85268.htm.
[9] Manion, *Corruption by Design*, pp. 85, 117.

beneficial to reform and economic development, the party was not particularly active in investigating and punishing those involved. This practice provided incentives to local officials to support reform because they personally benefited from it. In addition, the goods traded this way often went to TVEs and private enterprises that were not covered under the plan but were key to the success of reform and development.[10]

During the 1980s, official policy encouraged government, party, and even military organs to generate their own revenue through business activities, and the response was often enthusiastic. By 1992, almost one million businesses had been created by different bureaucratic agencies, including manufacturers, wholesalers, retail outlets, hotels, and real estate developers. These businesses could be extremely profitable because their parent agencies could buy goods at low, plan-set prices and sell them at market prices. Officials also could draw a salary from the business while remaining on the state payroll, providing individual incentives to engage in profiteering. After 1992, cadres more commonly left their official posts to "jump into the sea" of private enterprise but maintained close personal and financial ties with their former agencies, giving them distinct advantages in business.[11] This was also part of the party's strategy of encouraging its members to "take the lead in getting rich" (*daitou zhifu*), but as business operations began to interfere with core bureaucratic missions, the party curtailed business activities of party and government organs and ordered the military to divest itself of all commercial interests.[12]

Official profiteering was a major source of popular resentment. It was a primary cause of the 1989 demonstrations: specific demands to curtail corruption more than vague calls for political change caused the protests to spread to wide portions of the population, including many bureaucrats. In fact, bureaucrats who worked in agencies and sectors that were excluded from the opportunity to engage in profiteering were most likely to join the protests.[13] Although it clamped

[10] This is a main theme of Sun's *Corruption and Market in Contemporary China*.

[11] Ting Gong, "Jumping into the Sea: Cadre Entrepreneurs in China," *Problems of Post-Communism*, vol. 43, no. 4 (July–August 1996), pp. 26–34.

[12] James Mulvenon, *Soldiers of Fortune: The Rise and Fall of the Chinese Military–Business Complex, 1978–1998* (Armonk, NY: M. E. Sharpe, 2001).

[13] Yan Sun, "The Chinese Protests of 1989: The Issue of Corruption," *Asian Survey*, vol. 31, no. 8 (August 1991), pp. 762–782; see also Clemens Stubbe Ostergaard and Christina Pearson, "Official Profiteering and the Tiananmen Square Demonstrations in China," *Corruption and Reform*, vol. 6, no. 2 (1991), pp. 87–107.

down on demands for political change, the party did tacitly respond to the popular outrage against official profiteering by launching an extensive campaign against corruption during 1989–1990.[14] Given the pronounced antireform environment among central leaders at that time, the anticorruption campaign was also used as a pretext to shut down private enterprises, regardless of whether they had engaged in corrupt activities or not.

Asset Stripping and Insider Buyouts

The economic restructuring that began in the 1990s provided other opportunities for enterprise managers and local officials to enrich themselves. As described in chapter 2, managers stripped the capital, labor, equipment, and technology of SOEs under their control and transferred them without remuneration to private firms owned by their family, friends, or the managers themselves. X. L. Ding reported that illicit asset stripping from SOEs amounted to $6–12 billion in the early 1990s, and undoubtedly was higher in the years thereafter as SOE privatization began on a massive scale in 1997. The privatization of SOEs also provided another opportunity for corrupt ties between firm managers and local officials. Insider buyouts are legal but often entail huge losses to the state as SOE assets are grossly undervalued and free or discounted shares in the restructured firm are given to local officials.[15] Managers may also dip into the enterprise's own resources to buy shares for themselves, allowing them to become wealthy (at least on paper) without having to invest their own capital. These practices reinforce existing inequalities and demonstrate the inherently corrupt nature of crony communism in China: instant wealth is made available to the well connected and well positioned.[16]

[14] Manion, *Corruption by Design*, pp. 179–189; Ting Gong, *The Politics of Corruption in Contemporary China: An Analysis of Policy Outcomes* (Westport, CT: Praeger, 1994), pp. 135–147; Murray Scot Tanner with Michael J. Feder, "Family Politics, Elite Recruitment, and Succession in Post-Mao China," *Australian Journal of Chinese Affairs*, no. 30 (July 1993), pp. 89–119.

[15] X. L. Ding, "Who Gets What, How? When Chinese State-Owned Enterprises Become Shareholding Companies," *Problems of Post-Communism*, vol. 46, no. 3 (May–June 1999), pp. 32–41.

[16] For the similarly inherent corrupt nature of crony capitalism, see David C. Kang, *Crony Capitalism: Corruption and Development in South Korea and the Philippines* (Cambridge: Cambridge University Press, 2002).

Corruption in the form of asset stripping and illicit SOE privatization is possibly inevitable in China's transition economy. As also described in chapter 2, China lacks the institutional means necessary to adequately value state assets, such as standard accounting rules and third-party assessment of property values. Instead, local officials in charge of SOE privatization often rely on the judgments of firm managers, who have a vested interest in underestimating the true value of assets. What economists call "asymmetric information" easily translates into corrupt behavior.

Land Grabs

The form of corruption most likely to lead to violent conflicts between the state and society involves land-use rights. In China, the state owns all land, but in the reform era it began to lease the rights to use the land. This was initially done in the countryside, where farmers signed long-term leases of up to 15 years for the land they farmed. This was needed to give them incentives to make wise use of the land, for instance by investing in irrigation systems and improving the soil quality. But as local officials find more lucrative uses for the land, they often confiscate it from the farmers and transfer it to others, often real estate developers. The government may offer compensation to the farmers, but the amounts are often far less than the true value of the land and the improvements made to it. In turn, local officials then resell the land rights to developers for many times the amount they paid to the farmers, and profits made on the deal go into the public coffers and often indirectly into the pockets of the officials. There were over 1 million illegal land grabs between 1998 and 2005, and a survey by the Ministry of Land and Resources found that 22 percent of all land acquisitions had been done illegally, with the highest concentrations in central and western China.[17]

This forced expulsion from the land threatens the livelihood of its former occupants. After they have been forced off their land, Chinese farmers often have few means of livelihood. He Qinglian, a prominent scholar and critic of the CCP's pro-business policies, equates these

---

[17] Mark Magnier, "Farmers in China Face Great Wall," *Los Angeles Times*, April 19, 2006; "Over 20% of Land Acquisitions are Illegal," Xinhua, September 27, 2007, available at http://www.china.org.cn/english/China/225994.htm.

corrupt land grabs with England's enclosure movement of the 18th century, which devastated the peasantry.[18] In recent years, land grabs have triggered violent confrontations between farmers and local governments. In the city of Dongyang in Zhejiang, 30,000 villagers set up roadblocks and fought off more than 1,000 riot police to protest the confiscation of their land, which was given to 13 private and state-owned chemical factories. On the outskirts of Guangzhou, hundreds of villagers in Taishi protested the seizure of their land; although they were promised compensation for the land, they received only partial payments. Plans to build a power plant and reclaim a bay with landfill resulted in a prolonged and deadly confrontation between villagers and police in Dongzhou in Guangdong in December 2005. Villagers claimed they had not been compensated for their land, and pollution from the plant and the filled-in bay would ruin their fishing industry. The official report on the incident said three people were killed in the conflict, but villagers said up to 20 people had been killed, and at least 40 more were missing. In the city of Dingzhou in Hebei, hundreds of hired thugs forced villagers to evacuate their homes because the government wanted to build a factory. When the residents refused, six were killed and over 50 were hurt. The party secretary of Dingzhou was sentenced to life imprisonment for hiring the thugs who beat up the villagers. The punishment was also seen as a signal to other local officials that collusion with local mafias was not acceptable.[19] Elsewhere in Hebei, officials in the village of Shengyou in Baoding were forced to abandon their plans to requisition land for a power plant and waste disposal facility after clashes between villagers and several busloads of hired thugs resulted in six deaths and 51 wounded. The criminal investigation that followed led to the arrest or detention of 162 people, including village party officials and construction company leaders.[20]

---

[18] Cited in Sun, *Corruption and Market in Contemporary China*, p. 62. On England's enclosure movement, see Karl Polanyi, *The Great Transformation* (New York: Farrar and Rinehart, 1944); and Barrington Moore, *Social Origins of Dictatorship and Democracy: Lord and Peasant in the Making of the Modern World* (Boston: Beacon Press, 1966).

[19] For a discussion of "local mafia states" resulting from collusion between local officials and organized crime, see Minxin Pei, *China's Trapped Transition: The Limits of Developmental Autocracy* (Cambridge, MA: Harvard University Press, 2006), esp. pp. 159–165 and 219–222.

[20] Edward Cody, "For Chinese, Peasant Revolt Is Rare Victory: Farmers Beat Back Policy in Battle over Pollution," *Washington Post*, June 13, 2005; Chris Buckley, "Protests

These clashes brought condemnation from central leaders. In December 2005, Wen Jiabao warned local governments not to raise public funds by confiscating farmland and giving it to developers. He denounced the occupation of farmland without adequate compensation as both reckless and illegal, and cited them as a main cause for protests around the country.[21] Guangdong's party secretary, Zhang Dejiang, reiterated the point in January 2006, warning that local officials would lose their jobs if they proceeded with construction projects without the approval of local residents and without adequate compensation payments. Guangdong was the site of some of the most violent and deadly protests, but Zhang's warning had little effect. Soon after his warning, another clash over land occurred in Panlong village, leaving a 13-year-old girl dead and up to 60 others wounded.[22]

Local officials in some communities did learn from these violent conflicts. For instance, in the township of Zeguo in Zhejiang, the local leaders experimented with citizen deliberation to determine which development projects would be undertaken, an idea suggested by China scholar Baogang He and Stanford professor James Fishkin.[23] But many others did not get the message: according to the Ministry of Land and Resources, there were 131,000 illegal land grabs in 2006, an increase of 17.3 percent over the previous year. Zhang Xinbao, the head of law enforcement and supervision for the ministry, said, "Despite repeated crackdowns, the continued violations in land management are mainly supported by local governments."[24]

Grow, Even in China's Rich South," *International Herald Tribune*, August 24, 2005; Irene Wang, "City Chiefs Sacked over Deadly Attack on Farmers," *South China Morning Post*, June 15, 2005; Wang Xiangwei, "Mainland Official Hails Bloody Riots as a Sign of Democracy: Vice Minister Says Protests Inevitable as Country Undergoes Huge Changes," *South China Morning Post*, July 4, 2005; "Villagers Triumph in Deadly Land Grab," *South China Morning Post*, July 21, 2005.

[21] "Wen Jiabao Airs Views on China's Rural Issues," Xinhua, January 20, 2006, in *World News Connection*.

[22] "Guangdong Party Secretary Warns Officials of Dismissal over Land Disputes," Agence France-Presse, January 21, 2006, in *World News Connection*.

[23] Baogang He, "Authoritarian Deliberation: Deliberative Turn in Chinese Political Development," paper presented at the annual meeting of the Association for Asian Studies, April 6–9, 2006; Susan Jakes, "Dabbling in Democracy," *Time*, April 16, 2005; Howard French, "New Signs of Democracy in China," *New York Times*, June 2, 2005; Joel McCormick, "It's Their Call," *Stanford Magazine* (January/February 2006).

[24] Jasmine Wong, "Number of Illegal Land Grabs Soars," *South China Morning Post*, March 22, 2007.

Although most violent protests occur in the countryside, land grabs also occur in China's cities, as local officials decide to redevelop established but often dilapidated residential, industrial, and commercial areas into newer and more modern zones.[25] In Chongqing, one couple refused the government's offer to buy their house because they said it was well below its true value. They remained in their house (dubbed the "nail house" because the couple was hard as nails, *dingzihu* in Chinese) while construction crews dug a pit around them to build a large commercial development. After three years' standoff, they finally agreed to an undisclosed settlement in early 2007, which included housing of similar size elsewhere in the city.[26]

Land grabs not only cause resentment and occasional violence but also contribute to rising real estate prices and lead to losses of state revenue. Local officials in three unnamed cities gave away land for free to developers, costing the state 6.6 billion yuan. A well-connected developer received permission to build a golf course in the middle of the path of a national highway then under construction. The diversion of the highway around the golf course cost 48.5 million yuan, plus another 8.3 million yuan in compensation to the companies building the road.[27]

The case of Zhou Zhengyi (also known as Chau Ching-ngai) shows the complicated and illicit relations between real estate developers, local officials, and bankers. Born in 1961, Zhou started from lowly beginnings to become the richest man in Shanghai. At 17, he worked in a noodle shop, and later he sold clothes on the street. For a time, he worked in Japan and Hong Kong before returning to Shanghai in 1989. He made his fortune by buying stock shares given to SOE workers before their firms were listed on the stock market, paying a few yuan for the stocks and then reselling them for many times more than what he paid for them. He and his wife invested their profits in Shanghai

---

[25] Ian Johnson, *Wild Grass: Three Stories of Change in Modern China* (New York: Viking, 2005); David Barboza, "In China, Wholesale Urban Flight," *New York Times*, November 25, 2005.

[26] Richard McGregor and Yu Sun, "China's 'Nail House' Floors Developers," *Financial Times*, March 27, 2007; Zhang Pinghui, "A Lesson in Government as City Settles Demolition Row," *South China Morning Post*, April 4, 2007.

[27] Both examples are from Lawrence Brahm, "Exposing the Corruption Mountain," *South China Morning Post*, August 4, 2003.

real estate ventures through their Nongkai Group company, amassing a fortune estimated at US$320 million in 2002, when he ranked 11th on the *Forbes* list of the most wealthy Chinese. In 2003, Zhou was arrested for a complicated bank loan scheme in which he received a HK$2.1 billion loan from the Bank of China branch in Hong Kong to finance his purchase of a controlling interest in Shanghai Land Holdings. He was charged with misrepresenting the total registered capital of his companies, making it seem as though he had more collateral than he really did, and then manipulating the stock price of New Nongkai when it began to fall. He received a relatively short prison sentence of three years, compared with the maximum eight years he could have been given; the light sentence was apparently the result of intervention by Shanghai's leaders. Zhou was released from jail in 2006 after receiving credit for time served before his sentencing, but investigations into his past business deals continued. Zhou was taken back into custody in October 2006 and charged with bribing local officials to obtain property in Shanghai's Jingan district without compensating the 10,000 people who were displaced and for forging invoices for the value-added tax in order to receive tax credits. He was also implicated in the investigations surrounding Chen Liangyu's ouster as Shanghai party secretary, which concerned diverting money from the Shanghai pension fund to real estate developers. Chen's brother allegedly worked for one of Zhou's companies, and the two worked together on several real estate development projects. Investigators were looking into signs that Chen or those close to him intervened in Zhou's original case and sentencing.[28]

Bribes

Since 1992, bribery has become an increasingly prominent form of corruption in China. Some bribes are predatory in nature and require entrepreneurs and other citizens to pay for routine services, such as licenses and permits. Some entrepreneurs are willing to pay "speed

[28] Mark O'Neill, "Dead End Looms for Shanghai's Wealthiest Man," *South China Morning Post*, June 2, 2003; Wu Zhong, "Deal Hint as Chau Gets Only Three Years in Jail," *The Standard*, June 2, 2004; Bill Savadove, "Tycoon Charged with Bribery, Faking Tax Invoices," *South China Morning Post*, January 22, 2007.

money" simply to get their paperwork processed in a timely fashion. Other entrepreneurs have to pay fees and taxes to numerous government offices in order to remain in business and avoid hefty fines. Barry Naughton notes a study in Hunan where TVEs were subject to over 100 different types of fees assessed by more than 60 different offices.[29] Manion found that businesses could be required to obtain as many as 200 permits from different government departments before submitting applications for a license.[30] The numerous offices with jurisdiction over industry and commerce create multiple opportunities for rent-seeking by their officials. These are extreme examples but not uncommon ones. Zhu Rongji railed against the numerous offices required to approve a business license, vowing to establish a "one-chop shop" to encourage more commercial activity, but with little success. Some officials tack extra fees onto bank loans. According to a report by the People's Bank of China, bribes in the form of administrative fees attached to official bank loans amounted to 8.8 percent of the loan, almost equal to the "curb rate" for unofficial loans, a tacit acknowledgment of the "market" value of capital.[31] Although onerous, these forms of corruption are nevertheless growth promoting: officials take their cut but allow business to proceed. Most businessmen accept such fees as a regular part of doing business, and the state rarely punishes this kind of rent-seeking behavior. Nevertheless, they are of grave concern to businessmen, especially those who run small-scale operations with low profit margins and weak ties to political leaders – in other words, those least likely to be part of the crony communist system. This is particularly risky for the CCP because resentment against official corruption is one of the primary reasons that capitalists abandon their support for the incumbent regime.[32] Without that support, the CCP's survival would be in jeopardy.

---

[29] Barry Naughton, *The Chinese Economy: Transitions and Growth* (Cambridge, MA: MIT Press, 2007), p. 439.

[30] Melanie Manion, "Corruption by Design: Bribery in Chinese Enterprise Licensing," *Journal of Law, Economics, and Organization*, vol. 12, no. 1 (April 1996), p. 171. She notes that many of these requirements were waived after 1992.

[31] Pei, *China's Trapped Transition*, p. 119.

[32] Stephan Haggard and Robert Kaufman, *The Political Economy of Democratic Transitions* (Princeton, NJ: Princeton University Press, 1995); Eva Bellin, "Contingent Democrats: Industrialists, Labor, and Democratization in Late-Developing Countries," *World Politics*, vol. 52, no. 2 (January 2000), pp. 175–205.

As Yan Sun and others have described, economic reform decentralized decision making in China, turning many people into *yibashous*, individuals with the authority to approve projects or contracts and therefore in a position to profit from their positions. Businessmen routinely wine and dine local officials, provide lucrative jobs to their friends and family members, pay for their children's schooling, and shower them with other types of gifts and cash. This is designed to cultivate goodwill and lead to an exchange of favors between the bribe-givers and the party or government officials who receive the bribe. Some firms reportedly allocate 5–10 percent of their budgets to bribes and gifts (politely termed "activity fees," *huodong jingfei*), turning them into a regular cost of doing business.[33] One entrepreneur kept a list of bribes based on the rank of the official: 5,000 yuan for *ke* level, 10,000–20,000 yuan for *chu* level, and 30,000–50,000 yuan for *ju* level. When the official was young and inexperienced, the entrepreneur would coach him on the art of the bribe, reminding him not to deposit the money right away because it might tip off the local discipline inspection commission, the party organ in charge of investigating corruption involving party members.[34]

The sums of money in these transactions can be staggering. Wang Baosen, vice mayor of Beijing, received a total of 100 million yuan and $25 million in bribes, gifts, and other favors, including 13 million yuan for private mansions; he committed suicide in 1995 when his involvement in a financial pyramid scheme was about to be revealed. The resulting investigation implicated Chen Xitong, who at that time was Beijing's party secretary and also a Politburo member. Chen reportedly received 550,000 yuan to protect Wang and was sentenced to 16 years in prison, although he was released on medical parole in 2006. However, most observers believe his real offense was opposition to Jiang Zemin, who at that time was consolidating his power as general secretary and saw Chen as a rival. The highest-ranking official executed for corruption was Cheng Kejie, who was a vice chairman of the National People's Congress when he was arrested in 1999. While governor and vice party secretary of Guangxi during the 1990s, he and his

---

[33] Sun, *Corruption and Market in Contemporary China*, p. 61.
[34] He Dawei, Zhou Qiaochun, and Zhu Wei, "Quanneiren: Zi jie shangye huilu neimu" (Inner Circle: Uncovering Behind-the-Scenes Bribery in Business), *Jingji cankao bao*, July 3, 2006.

mistress amassed over 40 million yuan in bribes and kickbacks from real estate developers and office seekers. Liu Zhihua was one of nine deputy mayors in Beijing before he was arrested in 2006. His portfolio included construction and real estate development, which he allegedly used to attract 10 million yuan in bribes from developers and in turn approved construction projects totaling $40 billion. At the heart of the Shanghai corruption scandal, which led to Chen Liangyu's ouster as party secretary and Politburo member, was an illicit investment of 3.2 billion yuan ($400 million) in Fuxi Investment by the Shanghai pension fund. Fuxi Investment was a private firm whose chief executive, Zhang Rongkun, was 16th on *Forbes* 2005 list of wealthy Chinese and had amassed a fortune of over $600 million by the time he was 32. In April 2008, Chen was convicted for taking bribes and abusing power and sentenced to 18 years in prison. Zhang was sentenced to 19 years in prison for his role in the scandal.

The largest corruption scandal so far occurred in Xiamen, a special economic zone in Fujian. In the late 1990s, Lai Changxing developed a smuggling ring that involved hundreds of party and government officials, military and police officers, public and private firms, and banks. He spent tens of millions every year showering officials of all ranks with generous gifts to protect his smuggling operation. In return, he was able to smuggle into China goods worth an estimated 53 billion yuan, costing the government 30 billion yuan in lost tariff duties. His control over the government was so thorough that he was able to demand customs duties from other smugglers and up to 70 percent of their profits. What makes his case so unusual was that he never asked for specific favors in return for his gifts but gave generously to top officials as well as their chauffeurs and aides. He gave 1 million yuan to the mayor's wife to help her start a business and wired $500,000 to his daughter, who was attending school in the United States. He gave a vice mayor 1.4 million yuan to pay for his son's education in Australia. He gave out hundreds of money-filled red envelopes on major holidays. He invited officials to his infamous "Red Mansion," a pleasure palace that provided food, liquor, entertainment, and women. From all reports, he was well liked and appreciated more than feared. Whereas elsewhere in this book I have described the CCP's efforts to co-opt private entrepreneurs, Shawn Shieh describes Lai Changxing as an example of a private entrepreneur co-opting the local state, in which "corruption became so extensive and organized that it created a parallel system of authority that challenged that of the Chinese Communist Party."[35] Once his smuggling ring was reported to the central government, however, a large-scale investigation involving thousands quickly began, and those involved were arrested. Over 300 local, provincial, and central party, government, and military officials were jailed or executed for their involvement with Lai's operations, but Lai himself escaped to Hong Kong and eventually Canada in 1999; as of April 2007, he was still fighting China's efforts to extradite him.

A peculiar form of bribery involves the sale of party and government offices. High-level positions are controlled by the *nomenklatura* system, the list of offices that require CCP approval. Some of these positions are subject to approval by higher levels or the local people's congresses, but many others receive less scrutiny, even though they can be quite lucrative for the people holding them. A mid-level official in Shaanxi was sentenced to 13 years in prison for accepting 1.6 million yuan from 27 officials seeking promotions between 2001 and 2004; the office seekers included officials in the party's Discipline Inspection Commission and Organization Department.[36] The price for an office was roughly commensurate with the amount of bribes a person could expect to receive in the course of a year. Offices were sold to incumbent officials who wanted to ensure their reappointment or sought a promotion, SOE managers who wanted promotions or executive positions, and even members of organized crime syndicates. According to Sun, office selling is most common in less developed inland provinces, where opportunities for rent-seeking in the economy are less abundant.[37] The sale of offices not only leads to incompetent and predatory local leaders but is also an easy way for organized crime to collude with the local government, creating what Minxin Pei terms "mafia states."[38]

---

[35] Shawn Shieh, "The Rise of Collective Corruption in China: The Xiamen Smuggling Case," *Journal of Contemporary China*, vol. 14, no. 42 (February 2005), pp. 67–91, quoted at p. 68. Shieh's article provides much of the information on the Lai Changxing case in this paragraph. See also Hannah Beach, "Smuggler's Blues," *Time*, October 7, 2002.

[36] "Zhang Gaiping's List of Office Buyers," *China Elections and Governance* (http://www.chinaelections.org).

[37] Sun, *Corruption and Market in Contemporary China*, pp. 145–148.

[38] Pei, *China's Trapped Transition*, pp. 159–165.

Not all bribes work. When businessmen offer bribes that are deemed too low, some officials may turn the bribe-givers over to the local discipline inspection office, which makes the officials look clean but exposes the businessmen to possible punishment.[39] In Beijing, deputy mayor Liu Zhihua was exposed after demanding a bribe from a foreign businessman in exchange for the rights to develop a piece of land; when Liu did not provide the land as promised, the businessman reported him to the authorities. What is ironic about this case is that the businessman was not upset about having to pay the bribe but about not getting what he paid for.

Whereas some forms of corruption were seen to be helpful to reform and economic growth in the 1980s by giving underprivileged firms and individuals access to the market, the types of bribes common in the 1990s distorted development. An increasing share of corruption cases, especially those involving bribery, involved SOE managers who used bribes to solidify their advantages rather than to create more equal competition. According to Sun, their aim was to "avoid regulatory burdens, sabotage fair competition, violate laws, and harm public interests." The collective costs included environmental damage, wasteful spending, dangerous construction projects (such as roads, bridges, and dams), shoddy products, and loss of tax revenue. The higher growth rate achieved after 1992 "has not meant a better or larger economic pie for all social groups, thanks partly to corruption. In fact, many groups have had it worse in [this] period."[40] As we will see in the next section, not only did income disparities rise in this period but corruption itself fueled and exacerbated the inequalities. Both the givers and receivers of bribes were already among the most powerful. Rather than corruption providing access to economic opportunities, in the post-1992 period it reinforced existing inequalities.

The CCP has tried to get these forms of corruption under control with new institutions and policies. According to Dali Yang, "The introduction of relatively standardized processes for competitive tendering and bidding, auctions, as well as the abolition of stock listing quotas appears to have helped improve the transparency and fairness of the bureaucratic processes and, if properly enforced, should help

---

[39] He, Zhou, and Zhu, "Quanneiren."
[40] Sun, *Corruption and Market in Contemporary China*, pp. 154, 203.

rein in corruption in those areas."[41] Melanie Manion also notes that China's leaders have begun to show "substantial interest in reorganization of procedures to lessen incentives for corrupt transactions."[42] These changes include reductions in the number of permits required by firms and the divestment from commercial interests by government, judicial, public security, and military units. Although new institutional arrangements are in place, old ways of doing business have not been eradicated, and public perceptions about the widespread and worsening nature of corruption have not diminished.

Summary

Although those convicted of corruption often face harsh punishments, including lifetime prison sentences and even execution, corruption seems to have become entrenched in China. As far back as 1979, party elder Chen Yun described corruption as a "matter of life and death" for the party. In the years after, similar statements continued to be made, and the phrase eventually became a formulaic way of describing the CCP's ongoing intent to address the problem of corruption. Instead of such dire predictions, it may be more accurate to view corruption as a chronic ailment plaguing the party: although it periodically flares up in acute cases, it is not by itself life threatening. However, combined with other widespread grievances, such as inequitable distribution of income and opportunity, it threatens to delegitimize the party, despite its record of rapid economic growth.

INEQUALITY

China has followed the East Asian model of export-led growth but has not been able to achieve the East Asian miracle of growth with equity. At the beginning of the reform era, China had one of the world's lowest levels of inequality, but that meant that most people were equally poor. As economic reforms produced rapid rates of growth, inequality also began to grow. The United Nations Development Programme

---

[41] Dali L. Yang, *Remaking the Chinese Leviathan: Market Transition and the Politics of Governance in China* (Stanford, CA: Stanford University Press, 2004), p. 23.
[42] Manion, *Corruption by Design*, p. 201.

estimates that China's Gini coefficient increased from .30 in 1982 to
.45 in 2002, a 50 percent increase in just 20 years; by 2005, the Chinese government estimated that its Gini coefficient had risen to .48 (the
Gini coefficient is a measure of inequality in which a score of 0 means
income is distributed completely equally and a score of 1 means one
individual controls all the wealth). Most of the increase in inequality
occurred during the early part of the reform era, and it increased more
gradually after 1995. However, the political significance of growing
inequality has continued to worsen as public awareness of the inequality and the state's complicity in it has widened over the years. In 2002,
out of 131 countries ranked from least to most unequal in terms of
income inequality, China placed 90th.[43] This trend was comprehensive: whether comparing urban and rural areas, coastal and inland
areas, incomes within cities or within the countryside, income inequality grew. By 2005, urban incomes were more than three times those in
rural areas. According to the National Bureau of Statistics, the richest
10 percent controlled 45 percent of China's wealth, whereas the poorest 10 percent controlled only 1.4 percent. The Ministry of Labor and
Social Security warned that "China's growing income gap is likely to
trigger social instability after 2010 if the government finds no effective
solutions to end the disparity."[44]

In part, this growing inequality is a common by-product of rapid
development and an inevitable outcome of China's development strategy, which privileged coastal areas and encouraged advantaged areas
and individuals to "take the lead in getting rich." Although Hu Jintao and Wen Jiabao have tried to redirect economic growth toward
inland provinces and rural areas, they have faced political resistance
from regional leaders. This was one of the main motivations behind
the removal of Chen Liangyu as party secretary of Shanghai and member of the Politburo. He openly resisted central efforts to slow growth
in Shanghai and ridiculed policies designed to create more balanced
growth. His ouster signaled to other local leaders that even powerful

---

[43] *China Human Development Report 2005* (Beijing: United Nations Development Pro-
gramme and China Development Foundation, 2005); see also Carl Riskin, Zhao
Renwei, and Li Shi, eds., *China's Retreat from Equality: Income Distribution and
Economic Transition* (Armonk, NY: M. E. Sharpe, 2001); Martin Ravallion and
Shaohua Chen, *China's (Uneven) Progress against Poverty* (Washington, DC: World
Bank, 2004).

[44] Agence France-Presse, August 23, 2005.

and well-connected leaders could not expect to defy the new Hu–Wen policy line. To also signal that Chen's ouster was not simply a power grab, he was replaced by another member of the elitist faction, Xi Jinping. However, efforts to reduce regional inequality by slowing growth along the coast and shifting resources inland did not achieve immediate success. During 2007, China's economic growth rate was over 11 percent, despite efforts by central leaders to slow the pace of development.

Beyond the objective measures of inequality, there was a growing perception that opportunities to succeed were also unequal. During the 1990s, the CCP under Jiang Zemin's leadership pursued an elitist strategy, focusing on private entrepreneurs and coastal areas. During the Jiang era, the number of red capitalists grew rapidly: by 2005, approximately 35 percent of entrepreneurs were party members. This increasingly close relationship between the party and the private sector has created the widespread perception that the benefits of economic growth are being monopolized by a small segment of the population while the rest are being left behind. Rising inequality has also been exacerbated by the corrupt behavior and personal ties among political and economic elites. According to a report from the Central Party School, a major reason for the inequality of wealth and opportunity was collusion between local officials and wealthy businessmen in "power-for-money deals."[45] Many people now believe that economic success is based on personal connections with party and government officials, not individual initiative or quality work. As people come to believe that the benefits of the reform and opening policies are unfairly distributed, the legitimacy of the party's policy of letting some get rich first is jeopardized, and the continuation and expansion of crony communism are also put in doubt.

Entrepreneurs who were already in the party before going into business have used their connections to convert their political privileges into economic wealth. As chapter 3 showed, the largest firms are run by these *xiahai* entrepreneurs. Their numbers are large and growing.[46] In addition, the spouses and children of high-ranking party and government leaders have used their husbands' and fathers' status to prosper in the private sector. According to a report by the Research Office of

[45] Xinhua, September 20, 2005.
[46] See also Gong, "Jumping into the Sea."

the State Council, the Research Office of the Central Party School, and the Chinese Academy of Social Sciences, 90 percent of China's richest people – those with personal wealth over 100 million yuan – are the children of senior officials.[47] These "princelings" include the sons and daughters of China's top leaders, who have at times prevailed on their children to either cut their business ties or maintain a low profile. Deng Pufang, son of Deng Xiaoping, ran the Kanghua Development Corporation, which developed a reputation for corrupt business deals. In the aftermath of the June 4 massacre, the Politburo announced a new campaign against corruption, including the closing of Kanghua and other firms staffed by relatives of senior leaders. This was a tacit acknowledgment that public anger over corruption, a main motivation for the 1989 demonstrations in Tiananmen Square and around the country, was justified.[48]

The offspring of China's fourth generation of leaders have also been deeply involved in private business. Hu Jintao's son Hu Haifeng runs a company called Nuctech, which controls 90 percent of China's market for airport security scanners. Its multimillion-dollar contract to provide baggage inspection equipment, including specialized scanners to detect liquids in luggage, was quietly canceled after high-level intervention.[49] Wen Jiabao's son Wen Yunsong allegedly received $900 million in stock shares from the Ping An Insurance Company just before its initial public offering in June 2004. The allegation against Wen Yunsong was first reported in the *21st Century Economic Herald* and carried on several prominent Web sites but then quickly removed. An investigation into the stock scandal reportedly cleared Wen Yunsong of wrongdoing.[50]

The integration of wealth and power in today's China is perhaps best symbolized by the sons-in-law of Hu and Wen. Hu's daughter Hu Haiqing married Daniel Mao, formerly chief executive officer of

---

[47] Reported in Hong Kong's *Singdao Daily* on October 19, 2006, available at http://financenews.sina.com/ausdaily/000–000-107–105/202/2006–10-19/ 1509124173.shtml.

[48] Tanner with Feder, "Family Politics, Elite Recruitment, and Succession in Post-Mao China," pp. 105–109.

[49] Shu-Ching Jean Chen, "China's First Son Keeps Low, Goes Global," *Forbes*, December 13, 2006; Edward Cody, "China's Crackdown on Corruption Still Largely Secret," *Washington Post*, December 31, 2006.

[50] Wang Xiangwei, "Anti-Corruption Drive Futile while 'Princelings' Thrive," *South China Morning Post*, November 29, 2004.

Sina.com, one of China's leading Internet companies. In keeping with her father's wish to keep a low profile, their wedding took place in Hawaii, away from Chinese and international media. Wen's daughter Wen Chunru is married to Xu Ming, who is president of the Shide Group investment company in Dalian and was ranked number 15 on the *Forbes* 2006 list of China's wealthy.[51]

Local leaders provide a variety of privileges to economic and social elites. The children of "big taxpayers" (who pay over 3 million yuan, approximately $375,000) in Zhangzhou, Fujian, can receive an extra 20 points on their high school entrance exams. Big taxpayers, investors, families where both husband and wife have PhDs, and returned overseas scholars are able to have a second child, despite the continued one-child policy, in Guangzhou. Entrepreneurs are allowed to evaluate cadres' performance, determining whether they will be reappointed or dismissed in Kunshan, Jiangsu, giving entrepreneurs tremendous influence over policy and personnel. In Qinyang, Henan, local officials offered the usual tax incentives to lure new investment from businessmen outside the region, plus a red booklet identifying them as "honorary citizens," which they could use to avoid traffic fines, receive discounts for medical care, and place their children in the best local schools. Public security officials in Chongqing provided personal security services for more than 100 entrepreneurs. In Hebei's county H, which was included in my survey project, local officials described how they appointed big taxpayers to political posts in order to encourage their cooperation and support. In each of these examples, local officials were forced to abandon these practices after media coverage brought attention to them.[52]

With economic wealth controlled by the already politically privileged, the notion that China's reform policies have provided everyone with an equal opportunity to prosper is discredited. This has been a prominent theme of "New Left" writers as well as mainstream economists. According to He Qinglian, those who succeeded on the

[51] "The Wen Dynasty," *The Age*, March 31, 2006, at http://www.theage.com.au/news/in-depth/the-wen-dynasty/2006/03/31/1143441318429.html.
[52] Sun Liping, "Giving Privileges to Rich People Hurts Social Justice," *China Daily*, August 21, 2006; Don Lee, "Putting Up Money Has Its Privileges: Entrepreneurs in Some Areas Receive Perks that Make Life a Little Easier," *Los Angeles Times*, May 14, 2007.

basis of their own hard work and initiative make up a small segment of entrepreneurs and are concentrated mostly in the high-tech sector.[53] Political activist Liu Xiaobo makes a similar claim: only 5 percent of China's wealthy obtained their wealth on their own merits, without the benefit of personal ties or corruption.[54] Sun Liping has denounced giving political and social privileges to the wealthy because it shakes "the very foundations of social life and does damage to social justice."[55] Liu Guoguang, an economist and former vice president of CASS, said that a market economy that develops in the absence of the rule of law and without an accompanying "socialist spirit of fairness and social responsibility ... is going to be an elitist market economy."[56] Wu Jinglian, an influential reform economist, argues that the "'inequality of opportunity' is the root cause of the income gap."[57] Scholars on different parts of the policy spectrum share concerns about the negative impact of reforms on society, though they may differ on preferred solutions.

More generally, the New Left challenges the assumption that a market economy leads inevitably to democracy and common prosperity. Although the "Old Left" warned that the rise of entrepreneurs would give them unequal and unfair influence over the party and government, the integration of wealth and power has now become official policy and practice, legitimized in the "Three Represents" slogan. The New Left, in turn, is less worried about ideological propriety than about basic social justice. Wang Hui, former editor of the influential journal *Dushu* (Reading), rejects the "all good things go together" argument often made by advocates of economic reform in China. He believes that unequal markets perpetuate and intensify economic and social inequality and provide a new rationale for authoritarian rule in China. "The hope that the market will somehow automatically lead to equity, justice, and democracy – whether internationally or domestically – is

---

[53] He Qinglian, "China's Listing Social Structure," *New Left Review*, vol. 5 (September–October 2000), pp. 72–75. This article was originally published in the March 2000 issue of the Chinese journal *Shuwu*.

[54] Pankaj Mishra, "China's New Left Calls for a Social Alternative," *New York Times Magazine*, October 13, 2006.

[55] Sun, "Giving Privileges to Rich People Hurts Social Justice."

[56] Interview with *Business Watch* magazine, quoted in Joseph Kahn, "A Sharp Debate Erupts in China over Ideologies," *New York Times*, March 12, 2006.

[57] Xinhua, September 20, 2005.

just another kind of utopianism."[58] The New Left rejects the notion that China's capitalists will be agents of democratization and even questions the presumed link between capitalism and democracy.

Whereas the New Left was ridiculed and marginalized during the 1990s, when the CCP pursued elitist, pro-growth policies under Jiang Zemin, they have been more influential and visible as the party has shifted toward a more populist agenda under Hu and Wen. Their critique of economic reform begetting inequality finds echoes in the populist policies promoted by Hu and Wen. To try to narrow the income gap and other residual problems stemming from rapid development, the CCP has attempted to slow growth in the urban areas and along the coast by diverting resources to rural areas and inland provinces. It has tried to raise rural incomes through direct income subsidies and lowering or eliminating certain taxes. One immediate effect of this initiative was a sudden labor shortage in some urban areas, as migrant workers returned to the countryside. Wen Jiabao has talked about the desirability of developing a "green GDP" index that would incorporate pollution and energy efficiency as well as growth. The government is also committed to strengthening welfare provisions, particularly access to education and medical care. It has promised greater transparency on policy and budget priorities at the local level. In April 2007, the government announced new regulations requiring local governments to make public information about government finances and economic plans, statistics, land development, environmental regulations, and many other policies.

All of this is being done under the umbrella of building a "harmonious society." The issue of inequality is not just a matter of social justice but is also about political stability. Chinese officials say that increased protests are to be expected in a country at China's level of development but also that the government cannot be passive about the threat of potential instability. It is adopting a variety of measures designed to alleviate poverty and inequality, as described earlier. Party leaders are betting that improved governance and common prosperity, more than fundamental political reform, will resolve the causes of instability and enhance party rule.

---

[58] Wang Hui, *China's New Order: Society, Politics, and Economy in Transition* (Cambridge, MA: Harvard University Press, 2003), p. 180.

But the pursuit of a harmonious society also has a dark side: the party is also developing the resources to forcibly suppress the protests that do arise. It has established rapid-response police teams to quickly put down protests when they occur and prevent them from spreading to other areas of the country. It has restricted access to the "letters and visits" (*xinfang*) system, in which citizens can petition the state for redress against alleged wrongdoing by local officials. It is engaged in an ongoing battle to monitor information being shared on the Internet in order to prevent politically sensitive communication while allowing economic information to flow. In recent years, it has monitored social organizations more stringently, limiting some activities and forcing some to close. This is done to preempt a "color revolution" in China similar to how social movements have engaged in political activities in former communist countries such as Georgia, Ukraine, and Kyrgyzstan. China's leaders are determined to maintain social harmony, if possible by alleviating some of the causes of instability but by force if necessary.

Summary

China's leaders have come to recognize that the elitist, pro-growth strategy of economic development pursued in the 1990s is not sustainable. Although it succeeded in achieving high rates of growth, it also led to unbalanced growth, an explosion of corruption, and rising inequality. These ripple effects threatened popular support for the CCP's reform agenda, in particular the integration of wealth and power that gave rise to crony communism. As the new leadership under Hu and Wen adopted more populist policies to balance rising inequality and the resulting political instability, the attention to social justice and social harmony gained greater credence. China's leaders are committed to regaining popular support but equally determined to prevent any challenges to their monopoly on power.

CHARITABLE WORK AMONG CHINA'S ENTREPRENEURS

To partially compensate for the popular resentment toward growing corruption and rising inequality, many of China's private entrepreneurs have done what wealthy capitalists have done in other countries: they give money to charity. This is done both to benefit the less fortunate in their communities and also to improve the reputations of China's new wealthy elites. Lai Changxing, the ringleader of the infamous smuggling operation in Xiamen in the late 1990s noted earlier, was not only a generous giver of bribes but also a popular philanthropist. He donated 1 million yuan to his hometown to build a school, and he received national honors for supplying food, supplies, and over 1 million yuan to flood victims in 1998.[59] As the Chinese government moved from the elitist approach of the Jiang Zemin era to the goal of building a harmonious society, charity work has also become an official priority. The importance of developing charitable organizations was included in prime minister Wen Jiabao's annual government work report to the NPC for the first time in 2005, reflecting the populist concern for those left behind by China's economic reforms.

According to a 2006 survey by the ACFIC, over 80 percent of China's private entrepreneurs donated to charity.[60] The ACFIC coordinates charitable work for the alleviation of poverty through its "Guangcai Promotion Association," which was created by a group of private enterprises to provide relief for areas stricken by poverty and natural disasters. Its work includes both domestic and international relief projects. Charitable giving is reportedly on the rise: the top 50 on the Hurun Report's list of philanthropists gave 3.75 billion yuan between April 2005 and March 2006, compared with 1.35 billion yuan in the two previous years combined. According to a report in the *Public Welfare Times* newspaper, charitable giving in 2005 was up 40 percent over the previous year. But other reports suggest as few as 1 percent of private firms made donations.[61] Moreover, most donations came from foreign sources. Of the 1.2 billion yuan (US$145 million) donated to the China Charity Foundation between 1996 and

---

[59] Shieh, "Rise of Collective Corruption in China," pp. 82–83; Beach, "Smuggler's Blues."

[60] "Entrepreneurs Charitable," *China Daily*, February 10, 2007.

[61] Tang Yuankai, "Underpinning Charity Work," *Beijing Review*, January 19, 2007; "Favorable Donation Policies Called to Help Bridge China's Wealth Gap," Xinhua, March 3, 2007.

2002, only 30 percent came from within China, with the rest from overseas.[62]

Charitable donations are generally low in China relative to other countries. According to one estimate, donations in China were only .05 percent of GDP, compared with 2.17 percent in the United States.[63] Several reasons account for low levels of giving in China. First, most firms are still relatively young, and the businessmen have not been in business for very long. They are still concerned with expanding their businesses and accumulating their wealth. Similarly, most Chinese entrepreneurs prefer to give their money to their children, not to charity. According to economist Ma Jinlong, "A philanthropist like [Andrew] Carnegie cannot be expected currently in China. Most of the Chinese rich are thinking more about their kids than donation."[64] Li Ka-shing, one of Hong Kong's wealthiest magnates and himself a significant charitable donor, encouraged other Chinese businessmen to abandon the traditional cultural practice of passing their wealth on to their children. "Even if our government structure is as yet not geared towards supporting a culture of giving, we must in our hearts see building society as a duty in line with supporting our children."[65]

Low levels of charitable giving are not simply a reflection of cultural expectations but also a response to minimal material incentives. China provides low tax incentives for charity. Deductions are limited to 3 percent of a firm's profits and 30 percent of an individual's income. The low limit on tax-deductible donations by firms in particular is routinely mentioned as an obstacle to higher levels of giving. China also lacks an inheritance tax, which has encouraged large donations in

---

[62] *China Business Times*, reported in *China Daily*, March 5, 2003 (http://www.china.org.cn/english/government/57374.htm). See also Cameron Dueck, "Business of Giving Can Do with a Little Help," *South China Morning Post*, October 9, 2006; Zhang Zhiping, "Making China Charitable," *Beijing Review*, January 19, 2007.

[63] "Favorable Donation Policies Called to Help Bridge China's Wealth Gap." In contrast, William L. Parish and Dali Ma argue that charitable contributions from Chinese firms as a percentage of pre-tax revenue were *higher* than in the United States; see William L. Parish and Dali Ma, "Tocquevillian Moments: Charitable Contributions by Chinese Private Entrepreneurs," *Social Forces*, vol. 85, no. 2 (December 2006), pp. 943–964.

[64] Theresa Miao, "Charity Begins at Home," *Shanghai Star*, May 12, 2005 (http://app1.chinadaily.com.cn/star/2005/0512/f04-1.html).

[65] Dueck, "Business of Giving Can Do with a Little Help." Li has promised to donate one-third of his fortune to charity.

the United States (although it is derided by some critics as the "death tax" because it goes into effect when the individual dies). Another material disincentive is the fear that publicity given to large donations will bring unwanted attention to donors' wealth, exposing them to pressure from officials to make new donations, potential extortion, and other threats. Because many of China's wealthy gained their wealth through questionable practices, large donations can also bring public scrutiny of how they made their money.

Another reason for low levels of giving concerns the charitable organizations themselves. China's charity organizations have been criticized for embezzling and diverting funds and illegal fund raising, as well as inefficiency and poor service.[66] Project Hope, China's best-known charity, with an emphasis on education for disadvantaged children, allegedly diverted 100 million yuan to a business in the city of Beihai.[67] The China Charity Foundation was defrauded of 17 million yuan in 1996 by the leader of the organization.[68] Even the best-known philanthropists are not immune from being swindled. Yu Pengnian, number one on the 2007 Hurun Report list of top Chinese philanthropists, complained that 10 ambulances he donated to a hospital were refitted and used by local officials.[69] Li Shufu, chairman of Geely Automobile Holding Company and number seven on the 2007 Hurun Report list, provided financial aid to let 1,000 poor students finish college only to find out that some of the recipients were the children of local officials.[70] According to Huang Daifang, an NPC delegate and president of Tellhow Sci-Tech Ltd., "China's charity agencies are slow to tell the public how they got the money and where the money has been used."[71]

---

[66] For a general overview of the problems facing charitable and other social organizations in China, see Yuanzhu Ding, Xunqing Jiang, and Xin Qi, "China," Background paper, Asian Pacific Philanthropy Consortium, APPC Conference, September 5–7, 2003 (http://www.asianphilanthropy.org/pdfs/conference/china1.pdf).

[67] The allegations were published in Hong Kong's *Ming Pao* newspaper in 2002. *Ming Pao* later reported that the CCP's Central Propaganda Department banned coverage of the story by China's media. See *Ming Pao*, March 22, 2002 and June 21, 2002, in *World News Connection*, March 22, 2002 and June 21, 2002, respectively.

[68] Ding, Jiang, and Qi, "China."

[69] Miao, "Charity Begins at Home." The Hurun Report's list of China's top philanthropists is a creation of Rupert Hoogewerf, who earlier assembled the *Forbes* list of the wealthiest Chinese; see http://www.hurun.net/indexen.aspx.

[70] Tang, "Underpinning Charity Work."

[71] "Favorable Donation Policies Called to Help Bridge China's Wealth Gap."

As a result, many philanthropists prefer to make direct donations instead of giving to charitable foundations.

The Chinese government is ambivalent about philanthropy. It recognizes that philanthropy can complement the government's development priorities and compensate for a lack of adequate resources, but it also fears it could lead to political activism. One-time donations to schools, hospitals, or roads benefit local communities and are in keeping with the government's objectives. But philanthropic programs are often tied to the priorities of the donor, which may not be in line with those of the government. As a result, the Chinese government is the main conduit for charitable donations. According to a report by the McKinsey Group, government-affiliated nonprofit groups account for 85 percent of all donations. At the local level, charity work is often under the control of local leaders. In Shanghai, Politburo member and vice premier Huang Ju's wife, Yu Huiwen, was vice president of the Shanghai Charity Association, described as having "a local monopoly on fund raising."[72] She was also reportedly closely involved in the pension fund scandal that led to the ouster of Chen Liangyu as Shanghai party secretary and Politburo member.

Most entrepreneurs in my two surveys reported making contributions to one or more types of charitable causes. Entrepreneurs were asked what types of public welfare projects their enterprises had contributed to in recent years, and cadres were asked a similar question about the donations of local entrepreneurs (see table 7.1). Slight majorities of entrepreneurs in both the 1999 and 2005 surveys reported that they had donated money for schools. This was the most common form of charitable giving in both years. Large percentages also reported they contributed money for the building and repair of roads, bridges, dams, wharves, and other infrastructure; social welfare projects; students with financial hardships; and local holidays and celebrations. Much smaller numbers contributed to temples, hospitals, or parks.

The surveys of local party and government officials provide some confirmation of the types of charitable contributions that were most popular. Compared with the entrepreneurs, a much higher percentage of officials reported that donations of all types were made, but that is

---

[72] James T. Areddy, "Beijing Tightens Grip on Economic Policy; Investors Feel Impact," *Wall Street Journal*, September 27, 2006.

TABLE 7.1. *Charitable Donations by Private Entrepreneurs (for entrepreneurs, percentage who made contributions for different types of projects; for cadres, projects for which entrepreneurs in their communities made contributions)*

	Entrepreneurs		Cadres	
	1999	2005	1999	2005
Schools	54.6	50.8	94.3	85.2
Roads, bridges, dams, etc.	42.6	32.7	76.7	70.4
Social welfare projects	42.4	45.5	75.8	70.0
Help students with financial hardships	29.8	37.9	80.2	87.8
Local holidays or other celebrations	26.5	32.8	54.2	65.6
Temples	9.9	9.2	22.9	25.2
Hospitals and medical facilities	4.6	3.8	26.9	22.6
Parks	3.5	2.4	13.2	18.5
None	10.8	15.7	1.8	2.5

to be expected: cadres were asked what kinds of projects entrepreneurs in their whole communities had contributed to, whereas entrepreneurs were asked about their personal contributions. With the single exception of aid to needy students, officials and entrepreneurs agree that schools were the most common recipients of entrepreneurs' charitable donations, that transportation projects, social welfare projects, and holidays and festivals were slightly less common, and that temples, hospitals, and parks were the least common.

Certain specific types of contributions were much more common in some regions than in others. For example, in the 2005 survey, 18.5 percent of entrepreneurs in Zhejiang and 16.1 percent in Hunan donated money for local temples, but only 3.9 percent in Hebei and 0.4 percent in Shandong did the same (there was a similar disparity in the 1999 data). In Shandong's city Z, contributions for transportation projects (roads, bridges, etc.) were well below average in both surveys: 5.3 percent in 1999 and 8 percent in 2005 (compared with averages of 42.6 percent and 32.7 percent in 1999 and 2005, respectively). In general, however, there was not much of a pattern in giving as a result of regional factors alone.

According to interviews with local officials, charity work is a key part of the work of business associations and party-building efforts in the private sector, and the 2005 survey data bear this out. Charitable contributions were more likely to come from those who were integrated into the state, both as members of the CCP and as members of the official business associations. In a multivariate analysis of charitable donations (an index where $0 =$ no donations, $1 =$ one type of donation, $2 =$ two types, etc.), entrepreneurs who were not party members and did not want to be were much less likely to make donations than other entrepreneurs (see table 7.2). Similarly, those who did not belong to any of the official business associations were even less likely to make donations. In contrast, entrepreneurs who had party organizations in their firms were more likely to donate than those who did not. These three variables – CCP membership, business association membership, and party organizations in firms – are all indicators of party building, and they all point in the same direction: charitable contributions are more common among those who are part of the crony communist system. In fact, when looked at individually, those who did not want to be party members, did not belong to any of the official business associations, or did not have party organizations in their firms were more than twice as likely than other entrepreneurs to make *no* donations.[73] A somewhat related variable is the source of investment capital: the more entrepreneurs relied on private sources of capital (including family, friends, or other social relations) for investment capital and the less they had loans from collective or state sources, the less likely they were to make donations. In short, the less dependent entrepreneurs were on the state, the less likely they were to make charitable contributions.

Donations were also more likely to come from relatively large-scale enterprises (measured by sales volume) and those who had been in business longer. These findings are quite intuitive: efforts to mobilize charitable donations would understandably focus on large and established firms. Not only are they more able to give, they may be more inclined to give something back to their communities. Those who reported higher levels of life satisfaction (measured by improving living standards and social status) were also more likely to make more

---

[73] The importance of party membership, business association membership, and party organizations was equally strong in the 1999 survey when looked at individually, but in a multivariate analysis, those who did not want to join the CCP and did not have party organizations in their firms were not statistically significant. See the text for further comparisons between the two surveys.

TABLE 7.2. *Multivariate Analysis of Charitable Donations, 1999
and 2005 (OLS regression coefficients with robust standard errors
in parentheses)*

	1999	2005
Political Factors		
Non-CCP, don't want to be	−.056	−.193*
	(.142)	(.091)
No business association	−.396**	−.331***
	(.137)	(.078)
Party cell in firm	.005	.261**
	(.039)	(.095)
Individual and Firm Characteristics		
Age	−.005	−.016**
	(.009)	(.006)
Gender	−.013	.033
	(.226)	(.100)
Level of education	.106	−.010
	(.060)	(.049)
Years in county	.001	.007
	(.007)	(.004)
Sales revenue (log)	.209***	.208***
	(.042)	(.023)
Years in business	.072***	.019*
	(.014)	(.004)
Share of capital from personal savings	−.005*	−.004**
	(.002)	(.001)
Cultural Factors		
Life satisfaction	.003	.105***
	(.052)	(.031)
Contextual Factors		
Level of development	−.003	−.001
(per capita GDP, 1,000 yuan)	(.052)	(.005)
Constant	1.105	.811*
	(.582)	(.371)
N	379	959
R^2	.217	.223

*$p < .05$; ** $p < .01$; *** $p < .001$.

donations. In other words, those who were successful in business and felt good about themselves were more likely to donate.

Most individual socioeconomic indicators were not significant: women were not more likely to donate than men, better-educated entrepreneurs were not more likely to donate than the less well educated, and length of residence did not motivate entrepreneurs to make contributions in their communities (all else being equal). Age was a factor, however: young entrepreneurs were more likely to donate than were older entrepreneurs.[74]

In their study of charitable giving, William Parish and Dali Ma concluded that entrepreneurs used donations to curry favor with officials and gain access to the political system: the more entrepreneurs contributed, the more likely they were to be members of local people's congresses. They further speculated that "institutionalized reciprocity between government and private business was possibly more stable than interpersonal clientelism based on corruption." Although the evidence for this direct exchange of charity for representation was circumstantial, survey data from the mid-1990s showed a strong correlation between charitable contributions and people's congress membership.[75] My argument is different: charitable donations are not given to gain access to the political system but are given by those who are already in the full embrace of the party. My survey data do not show the same correlation between charitable giving and people's congress membership, but that may be because of differences in how we measure the amount of charitable giving: Parish and Ma use the estimated monetary value of donations, whereas I base mine on the types of donations because I could not independently verify the value of the donations. My survey data provide some confirmation of the Parish and Ma argument: entrepreneurs who wanted to join the CCP had more charitable giving than did entrepreneurs who were not interested in joining. One way of demonstrating their commitment to the party's goals was to contribute to local projects. But my data point to a different conclusion: charitable contributions were the result of the CCP's party-building efforts rather

---

[74] This contrasts with other reports on charitable donations in China, which typically find that older entrepreneurs are more likely to make charitable donations than younger ones.

[75] Parish and Ma, "Tocquevillian Moments," quoted from p. 960.

than a means to gain political access. Red capitalists were more charitable than non-CCP entrepreneurs, and *xiahai* entrepreneurs more so than co-opted entrepreneurs. In other words, it was the entrepreneurs who were already the most privileged – and in particular those who had already been in the party before going into business – and those who were already integrated with the CCP who were most charitable. In order to show definitively whether charity was the cause or the effect of political integration, we would need to know whether the donations were made before or after they joined the local political elite. Further research will be needed to resolve this question.

Comparisons with the 1999 data are difficult because missing data on one or more variables caused more than 25 percent of the respondents to be omitted in the multivariate analysis. There are several similarities and differences that merit comment, however, even if they are not fully conclusive. In both the 1999 and 2005 surveys, being a member of an official business association is closely correlated with charitable giving. Even in the late 1990s, charity work was part of business associations' work. The sales volumes of the firms and the length of time they were in business were also positively correlated with donations. Similarly, the more the entrepreneurs' capital came from private sources, the less likely they were to donate. Gender, education, and length of residence also had the same statistically insignificant results. All of the variables that were statistically significant in the 1999 data were also significant in the 2005 data and had the same sign, meaning that the direction of the relationships, either positive or negative, was the same. Three variables – entrepreneurs who did not want to join the CCP, age, and life satisfaction – had the same sign but were only significant in the 2005 data. In short, the results from the two surveys were generally consistent, and the differences may result as much from missing data as from changed circumstances.

The vast majority of entrepreneurs claimed their charitable contributions were given voluntarily: 80.4 percent in 1999 and 87.0 percent in 2005 (see table 7.3). The party status of the entrepreneurs did not make much of a difference: co-opted entrepreneurs were most likely and those who do not want to join the party were least likely to report that their contributions were voluntary, but the more notable trend is that higher percentages of all types of entrepreneurs reported voluntary contributions in 2005 compared with 1999. There was little

TABLE 7.3 *Motivations for Charitable Donations by Private Entrepreneurs* *Q1: Did you provide charitable contributions voluntarily or were you under pressure? (Cadres were asked a similar question about private entrepreneurs' motivations.)*

	1999			2005		
	Voluntarily	Under pressure	Both	Voluntarily	Under pressure	Both
All entrepreneurs	80.4	1.7	17.7	87.0	1.1	11.9
Xiahai	80.2	0.9	19	85.7	1	13.4
Co-opted	87.9	0	12.1	91	1	8.4
Want to join CCP	80.3	3.2	16.5	87.4	0.4	12.2
Don't want to join CCP	77.3	2.1	20.6	85.4	2.5	12.1
All cadres	46.4	1.8	51.8	47.4	0.7	51.8
County	33.3	2.3	64.4	40.3	0	59.7
Township/village	64.2	1.1	34.7	52.9	1.3	45.8

Q2: If you were under pressure, what kind of pressure was it? (Cadres were asked a similar question about pressure on entrepreneurs.)

	1999				2005			
	Social	State	Both	Other	Social	State	Both	Other
All entrepreneurs	28.9	26.5	39.8	4.8	21.4	17.9	56.3	4.5
Xiahai	35.0	10.0	50.0	5.0	24.4	12.2	61.0	2.4
Co-opted	14.3	42.9	42.9	0.0	30.8	23.1	38.5	7.7
Want to join CCP	45.8	29.2	20.8	4.2	20.7	10.3	62.1	6.9
Don't want to join CCP	17.7	33.3	43.3	6.7	13.8	31.0	51.7	3.5
All cadres	32.4	9.5	57.1	1.0	23.8	7.0	69.2	0.0
County	30.1	9.6	58.9	1.4	22.5	7.0	70.4	0.0
Township/village	37.5	9.4	53.1	0.0	25.0	6.9	68.1	0.0

regional variation in motivations for giving: entrepreneurs in all counties reported similar levels of voluntary contributions. In contrast, there were sharp differences among cadres about the reasons for charitable giving. In the 1999 survey, township and village officials were almost twice as likely as county officials to believe that contributions were voluntary. In the 2005 survey, the gap narrowed considerably, but most township and village officials still believed contributions were voluntary, and most county officials believed that pressure played some part in the decision to make contributions. Overall, officials had a less charitable interpretation of entrepreneurs' motivations than did the entrepreneurs themselves.

For those who believed that pressure was at least a partial motivation, the smallest proportions said it was state pressure alone, more said it resulted from societal pressure, and the largest proportions said it was a combination of both societal and state pressure. The size of the proportions varied across subgroups and across the two surveys, but the rank orderings were generally the same.

Summary

Charitable donations by China's capitalists are given for a variety of familiar reasons: to improve reputations, to give back to the community, to curry favor with officials, and to fulfill a sense of obligation among the newly rich. Although some may give to charity in order to gain access to the political arena, most donations are made by those who are already integrated into the CCP and the crony communist system. Whether these charitable activities achieve their intended goals of helping those in need and improving the reputations of those who have taken the lead in getting rich, either by their own merit or by their connections with party and government officials, will help determine whether society at large will continue to support the party's economic reform agenda and by extension bolster the CCP's claim to legitimacy.

CONCLUSION

The CCP's reform and opening policies have had contradictory consequences for its claims of legitimacy. Although they have succeeded in producing sustained rates of rapid growth and national pride in China's growing international prominence, they have also produced political instability as resentment against corruption and inequality have triggered popular protests around the country. China's capitalists have been at the center of these problems. The tremendous levels of wealth and prosperity they have created provide both the means and the opportunity for rampant corruption among Chinese officials.

Although corruption has been a perennial cause of popular resentment, China's capitalists have shown little inclination to challenge the corruption that is inherent in crony communism. As Victor Shih puts it, "both the Yuanhua smuggling case [Xiamen] and the Shanghai real estate scandal show that private entrepreneurs are prone to use influence over officials for private gains rather than to lobby for policy changes."[76] Corruption has become accepted as a routine part of doing business in China. It allows businessmen to prosper through their connections with the state instead of relying on their competitive advantages and entrepreneurial skills. Corruption therefore exacerbates and perpetuates political and economic inequality: those who are most likely to prosper are the ones who are most closely tied to the state. Those who have taken the lead in getting rich have little incentive to change the system that has allowed them, their families, and their friends to prosper.

The party leadership under Hu and Wen has come to realize that this unalloyed pursuit of growth cannot be sustained. The elitist approach of the Jiang era created the severe social and economic tensions that resulted in growing political instability. The CCP has adopted a new set of populist policies designed to balance – but by no means replace – the pro-growth policies of the past. The efforts by Hu and Wen to balance growth with equity are a test of whether the CCP's survival can be based on the strategy of integrating wealth and power.

---

[76] Victor Chung-Hon Shih, *Factions and Finance: Elite Conflict and Inflation* (Cambridge: Cambridge University Press, 2007), p. 193.

8

Conclusion

The Chinese Communist Party has defied predictions of its imminent demise. From the start of the reform era, observers have anticipated the collapse of communism in China as a result of growing economic prosperity and the inherent contradictions between a market economy and a Leninist political system. One main line of thinking draws its inspiration from the insights of modernization theory, which notes the clear correlation between economic modernity and political democracy. As the size of China's economy grows and as individual incomes and quality of life increase, the prospects for democracy are said to increase correspondingly. A second line of thinking is based on the social changes that accompany economic development. As the economy shifts from agriculture to industry and services, and the population shifts from rural to urban areas, a middle class begins to grow and a civil society begins to emerge to organize people with similar interests. At the same time, these economic and structural changes lead to changes in basic political values, leading people to expect more political liberties to match their economic freedoms. Economic development in China has also entailed the gradual decline of the centrally planned economy and the commensurate increase in the market economy and the size of the private sector. This shift in economic activity has created a steadily growing number of private firms and private entrepreneurs. Because economic wealth not controlled by the state is an inherent threat to an authoritarian regime, China's growing private sector is seen as an indicator of declining CCP control and improved prospects for political change.

The emergence of private entrepreneurs in China represents a glaring anomaly in China's still nominally communist political system, which was initially created to eliminate capitalism but now embraces it. Rather than being threatened by the reemergence of capitalists in China, the CCP has been able to adapt its Leninist institutions enough to accommodate them. It has given ever-greater rhetorical and political support to the private sector, repeatedly revising the party constitution to reflect its evolving practices. This is not an arms-length relationship: the party has integrated itself into the private sector with party branches and officially sponsored business associations, encouraged its members, including party and government officials, to "plunge into the sea" of the private sector, and recruited growing numbers of successful entrepreneurs into the party. These red capitalists represent the integration of wealth and power that is at the heart of crony communism in China. This integration is also a key element of the so-called "Beijing consensus": the ability to achieve economic growth without accompanying political reform. Red capitalists own the largest firms and are more likely to participate in China's formal political institutions. As such, they are more inclined to support the status quo in which they have prospered than seek fundamental political reform. Indeed, red capitalists are part of the status quo, not challengers on the outside looking in. Most red capitalists were already in the CCP before joining the private sector, giving them an even stronger stake in the current political system. In short, the integration of political and economic elites in China may serve to sustain the existing authoritarian political system rather than pose a direct challenge to it. The CCP's strategy of integrating itself with the private sector, both by encouraging current party members to go into business and co-opting entrepreneurs into the party, continues to provide dividends. This is a key element of the CCP's strategy for survival, and so far it is working.

The results presented in this book reinforce the findings of my earlier study[1] and those of other scholars who have looked at the potential for China's private entrepreneurs to be agents of political change. David

---

[1] Bruce J. Dickson, *Red Capitalists in China: The Party, Private Entrepreneurs, and the Prospects for Political Change* (Cambridge: Cambridge University Press, 2003).

Wank and Kellee Tsai have shown how private entrepreneurs have employed different strategies toward the state in order to pursue their business interests, without showing much inclination to agitate for political change.[2] Similarly, my study showed how the party employed its own strategy of selectively integrating some entrepreneurs into the political system in order to solicit their support and preempt their potential opposition. In contrast to the popular perception that privatization is leading inexorably to democratization, and by extension that China's capitalists would prefer a democratic system, the findings presented here demonstrate that they are already part of the incumbent political system. In addition, on a variety of political questions, the views of entrepreneurs were remarkably similar to those of local party and government officials. This again suggests that the growing shared interests of China's communist officials and capitalist businessmen are creating an environment that supports the status quo rather than one in which capitalists are motivated to press for change.

The close relationship between political and economic elites has drawn the ire of those who feel that these ties are the cause of much of the corruption that plagues China today, who feel that the prospects for business success are skewed in favor of party members and communist cronies, and who feel that pro-business policies have led the party to abandon its commitment to the workers and farmers of the country. These sentiments are a reaction against Jiang Zemin's elitist strategy of the 1990s, in which the party courted newly emerging economic and social elites at the expense of workers and peasants. Although China's workers and farmers are the traditional base of the party, their interests were largely abandoned as the party pursued its pro-growth policies that favored urban economic elites. Current leaders Hu Jintao and Wen Jiabao have adopted more populist policies to quell dissatisfaction over high levels of inequality and cronyism, but they have not gone as far as abandoning the goal of rapid growth that led to the expansion of the private sector and the growing number of red capitalists. So long as the CCP sees high rates of economic growth

---

[2] David L. Wank, *Commodifying Communism: Business, Trust, and Politics in a Chinese City* (Cambridge: Cambridge University Press, 1999); Kellee S. Tsai, *Capitalism without Democracy: The Private Sector in Contemporary China* (Ithaca, NY: Cornell University Press, 2007).

as a foundation of its legitimacy, the party's embrace of the private sector is unlikely to loosen and the salience of crony communism is unlikely to decline.

PROSPECTS FOR CHANGE

What might cause China's capitalists to shift their support away from the CCP and favor democratizing reforms? Given that the political support of capitalists is contingent on their degree of state dependence and fears that mobilizing workers and farmers into the political system would harm their material interests,[3] several scenarios could lead China's capitalists to support democratization. The most obvious is a sudden decline in the pro-business policies of the party. If the party reduced the level of protection from foreign competition, enforced safety and environmental regulations that are already on the books, or adopted less repressive labor policies that resulted in increased wages, capitalists' support for the regime would likely decline. This is one reason why China has been reluctant to let its exchange rate drop as quickly as the United States and other trading partners would like. It recognizes that a sudden and dramatic change in the exchange rate would harm the interests of domestic firms, on whom the party relies for political support. Similarly, capitalists' support for the CCP would also decline if the pro-growth policies of the reform era were curtailed in favor of more populist policies that address the social welfare needs of the vast majority of the population, who have not prospered as much as economic elites. The challenge facing Hu and Wen is to satisfy popular demands for higher living standards and more equal opportunities to get rich while also maintaining the support of the capitalists by continuing to generate high rates of growth.

If new sources of investment became available that were not controlled by the state, this would also make the private sector less dependent on the state. For instance, the CCP requires public and private firms to obtain permission to list their shares on domestic and foreign stock exchanges, and some of the requirements for listing, such as the amount of fixed assets, clearly favor the largest firms, which

---

[3] Eva Bellin, "Contingent Democrats: Industrialists, Labor, and Democratization in Late-Developing Countries," *World Politics*, vol. 52, no. 2 (January 2000), pp. 175–205.

are also the most politically connected and often still in the public sector. If private firms could become listed without requiring official permission or if bank loans were given on the basis of creditworthiness instead of political calculations, dependence on the state would also decline.

The opportunity to be competitive and profitable without political protection would also reduce the tolerance for the endemic corruption that has characterized the reform era. Although many local governments actively support developmental policies, many others are more predatory in nature. If predatory demands were to outweigh the commitment to economic development and the accumulation of private wealth, China's capitalists might seek alternatives for investing both their political support and their economic capital. In other countries, dissatisfaction with corruption has contributed to a shift in capitalists' political loyalties away from the incumbent regime in favor of democracy.[4] Although some businessmen view bribes and other forms of official corruption as a regular part of doing business, others who are less able to afford the bribes and have less access to decision makers chafe under their unequal and unfair treatment at the hands of corrupt officials.

Capitalists' support for democracy might also increase if they were less worried that participation by a broader range of social groups in a democratic polity would harm their material interests. If poverty was significantly alleviated and the growing income gap narrowed, democratization might not introduce new commitments to social welfare spending that would reduce economic growth. However, because the overall level of development in China remains relatively low and the causes of poverty and inequality are as much structural as political, the fears that democratization would entail the mobilization of China's have-nots against the interests of China's capitalists are not likely to diminish anytime soon. As China's middle class expands, it is likely to seek greater protection of its property rights and predictability in governance, which would make it a natural ally of China's capitalists. As capitalists realize that their material needs do not require them to seek political favors from communist officials, they may come to favor the greater transparency and accountability that democratization entails.

---

[4] Bellin, "Contingent Democrats"; Stephan Haggard and Robert Kaufman, *The Political Economy of Democratic Transitions* (Princeton, NJ: Princeton University Press, 1995).

The subgroup of capitalists who are not in the CCP and do not want to be may be a potential threat to the CCP in this regard. These capitalists are less satisfied with the extent of local political reforms and are more pessimistic about the business environment they face than are red capitalists. Most of this subgroup are apolitical and prefer to limit their activities to the economic sphere. However, a portion of them are alienated from the CCP, seeing it as a corrupt and repressive party. They are least likely to have party organizations in their firms and least willing to have party members among their workforce. Because they have not been co-opted into the crony communist system, they may become a source of political pressure outside the party. But although they have the motive to press for change, they have limited opportunities to do so: their numbers are small, they are less likely to be members of business associations (including self-organized associations), and have lower perceived economic and social status. As a result, they face more severe collective-action problems. Nevertheless, the CCP will need to monitor this group if its strategy of embracing the private sector is to succeed.

In the short run, and for the foreseeable future, crony communism in China seems more likely to lead to a perpetuation of authoritarian rule, growing inequality, and the further integration of wealth and power. Three elements of the overall reform strategy fit together: first, the CCP needs to maintain a high rate of economic growth and therefore needs the support and cooperation of private entrepreneurs; second, rapid growth creates inequality, corruption, pollution, and other "externalities," which in turn lead to increased protests; and third, to preserve the stability needed for both continued CCP rule and economic growth, repression will increase along with protests. Hu and Wen hope that their populist policies will be able to break this cycle but they are prepared to use force if necessary in order to preserve stability, growth, and CCP rule. If generally seen as preserving political stability, strong leadership may prove to be popular, as it has for Vladimir Putin in Russia and Hugo Chavez in Venezuela, among other elected leaders.[5]

---

[5] On the popular basis for a strong state and suppression of civil liberties, see Fareed Zakaria, *The Future of Freedom: Illiberal Democracy at Home and Abroad* (New York: Norton, 2004).

At the same time, we must also realize that even if private entrepreneurs' support for the CCP diminishes, they may not necessarily favor democracy as an alternative. As the examples of other countries have shown, there are other options for regime change besides democratization. All the factors that could make entrepreneurs oppose the regime would exist and even be reinforced under a democratic system, under which labor interests would be more protected and "populist policies" would be strengthened as a result of politicians' need to attract support from voters as well as the business community. In addition, when private entrepreneurs withdraw their support for the current regime, they do not necessarily support democratization. It is quite possible that they would support a different type of authoritarian government as long as that government protects their interests.[6]

However, the very success of the close cooperation between the CCP and private entrepreneurs may lead to its undoing. The progrowth strategy favored by the CCP and business has also contributed to many of the social problems that have led to an increase in popular protests in recent years. Resentment against official corruption exacerbated by the cozy relations between the state and business, environmental degradation caused by rapid and unregulated growth, and rising economic, social, and political inequality have triggered protests throughout China, and as these problems fester and grow, they are likely to lead to even more protests in the future. Hu and Wen are trying to respond to those protests with a combination of carrots and sticks, accommodating many of the material demands while also punishing those who lead the protests. The durability of the current regime will depend largely on how effectively the CCP can limit the "externalities" of growth while still achieving rapid rates of growth.

The CCP's record of sustained growth may also present a challenge of a different kind in the long run. As Bruce Gilley has pointed out, rapid growth can itself de-legitimate an authoritarian regime as citizens come to expect more from their government than material benefits.

---

[6] For a discussion of the probability of different types of postcommunist regimes in China, see Bruce J. Dickson, "The Future of the Chinese Communist Party," in Jae Ho Chung, ed., *Charting China's Future: Political, Social, and International Dimensions* (Lanham, MD: Rowman and Littlefield, 2006).

This insight is an often-overlooked aspect of modernization theory: "Value change rather than performance failure is a more likely cause of legitimacy crisis in China given the regime's ability to remain effective and maintain strong growth."[7] In the coming years, scholars as well as the CCP will undoubtedly be looking for signs that changing values and normative expectations – for a cleaner environment, greater equality and social justice, and protection of rights and liberties – are creating new challenges for the regime.

THE FUTURE OF THE PARTY

What are the future prospects for the CCP and the perpetuation of communist rule in China? A variety of predictions have been made, often based on different assumptions about the adaptability of the party and the drivers of democratization.

One scenario entails a transition to democracy in the not-too-distant future largely resulting from the effects of continued economic development. As noted in the introduction, several scholars have made quite specific predictions about when such a transition will occur: Shaohua Hu has predicted China will become democratic by 2011, Henry Rowen by 2020, and Ronald Inglehart and Christian Welzel by 2025.[8] Other scholars are less precise but no less optimistic. Bruce Gilley does not give a precise timetable for a democratic transition but envisions an elite-led transition to a parliamentary democracy in the near future, based on the assumption that "the laws of social science grind away in China as they do elsewhere."[9] He argues that political change is not predicated on economic development alone but on the

---

[7] Bruce Gilley, "Legitimacy, Regime Survival, and Democratization in China," paper presented at the annual meeting of the Association for Asian Studies, March 22–25, 2007, p. 2.

[8] Shaohua Hu, *Explaining Chinese Democratization* (Westport, CT: Praeger, 2000); Henry S. Rowen, "The Growth of Freedoms in China," APARC Working Paper, Stanford University, 2001; Ronald Inglehart and Christian Welzel, *Modernization, Cultural Change, and Democracy: The Human Development Sequence* (Cambridge: Cambridge University Press, 2005).

[9] Bruce Gilley, *China's Democratic Future: How It Will Happen and Where It Will Lead* (New York: Columbia University Press, 2004), p. xiii. He is confident this transition will come sooner than later: "For the record, I would be surprised if this change were delayed beyond the year 2020" (p. 98).

accompanying changes in political values and social structure. Larry Diamond believes that "sooner or later" economic development will put pressure on the regime to make a transition to democracy.[10] All of these predictions have a common theme: economic development will eventually and inevitably be the basis on which democracy arrives in China.

The CCP has not passively watched these changes but has been actively involved in their development. Its policies were the underlying cause of these unfolding economic and social changes, and it has actively responded to them. Although the CCP has supported the expansion of the private sector, it has been less accommodating to other political challengers that have arisen in the post-Mao era. It aggressively defends its monopoly on political power by repressing efforts to create autonomous parties, unions, and other groups that may have political agendas. It is aware of how social movements have undermined authoritarian regimes in recent years (the "color revolutions") and has actively monitored and suppressed these potential threats by monitoring and closing nongovernmental organizations (NGOs), arresting activists, and limiting access to certain Web sites (with the cooperation of U.S. firms such as Yahoo!, Microsoft, and Google). In doing so, the CCP continues to show that democratization is not the natural and inevitable result of rapid and sustained economic and social change. The patterns of inclusion and exclusion in the CCP's survival strategy also demonstrate the importance of distinguishing between the economic and political realms of civil society when forecasting the likelihood of political change. The CCP has been willing to allow innovation in the economic realm – including the formation of grassroots organizations to promote shared business interests – because it is necessary for growth while continuing to suppress it in the political realm because it is a threat to the party's monopoly on power.

In contrast, other scholars are far more pessimistic about current trends in China and their implications for both the CCP and the political system as a whole. Andrew Walder describes how the transition to a market economy erodes the "institutional pillars" of a communist

---

[10] Larry Diamond, *Developing Democracy: Toward Consolidation* (Baltimore: Johns Hopkins University Press, 1999), p. 265.

system: the Leninist style of party organization and central planning over the economy. As the CCP's capacity to monitor and sanction economic and social behavior declines, so too does the stability of the political system.[11] Minxin Pei offers a more harsh evaluation of the effects of economic reform in China, arguing that China is unlikely to experience "a process of gradual political opening that parallels gradual economic reform" because the ruling elites enjoy a monopoly on political organization and coercive power, have strong incentives to defend their economic and political privileges, and employ a combination of strategic co-optation and selective repression to minimize threats to themselves. Instead, he believes China suffers from political paralysis that threatens the state's ability to provide basic public goods, such as education and health care, and sustain economic modernization. He believes that "the collapse of the CCP is a low-probability event" because of the absence of any credible opposition and that "political stagnation would accompany economic stagnation, with further erosion of state capacity, the decline of the CCP's legitimacy, and increases in lawlessness, corruption, and social disorder."[12] Gordon Chang and Jack Goldstone similarly note the decline in state capacity but offer more severe forecasts for China's political future. They argue that the decentralization of decision-making authority and the privatization of the economy have eroded the central state's authority. Whereas Rowen, Gilley, Diamond, and others see economic development leading directly or indirectly to democratization, Chang and Goldstone foresee a coming collapse into chaos. In contrast to those who contend that economic development is laying the foundation for an imminent and smooth transition to democracy, this perspective sees an extended period of decay and disunity, perhaps even leading to the breakup of China into separate countries.[13]

[11] Andrew G. Walder, "The Decline of Communist Power: Elements of a Theory of Institutional Change," *Theory and Society*, vol. 23, no. 2 (April 1994), pp. 297–323; see also Andrew G. Walder, "The Quiet Revolution from Within: Economic Reform as a Source of Political Decline," in Andrew G. Walder, ed., *The Waning of the Communist State: Economic Origins of Political Decline in China and Hungary* (Berkeley: University of California Press, 1995).

[12] Minxin Pei, *China's Trapped Transition: The Limits of Developmental Autocracy* (Cambridge, MA: Harvard University Press, 2006), pp. 25, 212.

[13] Gordon G. Chang, *The Coming Collapse of China* (New York: Random House, 2001); Jack A. Goldstone, "The Coming Chinese Collapse," *Foreign Policy*, no. 99 (Summer

In between these two extremes are predictions that party rule will remain the fundamental feature of Chinese politics for the foreseeable future. According to this middle position, fundamental political change, either transformation into a full-fledged democracy or a collapse into anarchy, is unlikely. Instead, the CCP is likely to survive because it is more adaptable than generally perceived. Its mechanisms for selecting top leaders and deciding policies have become more institutionalized and at least at the local level more transparent. It has abandoned the ideology of class struggle promoted by Mao Zedong in favor of economic modernization. It has led the economic transition from central planning to a market economy while still preserving its central role. Its criteria for party membership increasingly focus on professional skills and educational standards instead of political loyalty. As a consequence, the composition of the party has changed from the "three revolutionary classes" – workers, peasants, and soldiers – to economic and professional elites. It has welcomed new elites into the political arena, including membership in the party, participation in formal political institutions, and consultation in the policymaking process. The best examples of this inclusionary strategy are the red capitalists, who have gone from being pariahs to being welcomed as builders of socialism, the heart of the crony communist system.

Without question, China remains a decidedly authoritarian political system. The goal of political reforms enacted thus far is to allow the party to govern more effectively, not require it to govern more democratically. As Andrew Nathan has written, "Under conditions that elsewhere have led to democratic transition, China has made a transition from totalitarianism to a classic authoritarian regime, and one that appears increasingly stable."[14] The party strategically selects who will be allowed to enter the political arena, who will continue to be excluded, and who will be repressed for trying to create more political space for increased participation. In assessing Hu Jintao's intentions as party leader, Joseph Fewsmith has argued that Hu "seems determined to address the problems facing China by strengthening the Chinese

---

1995), pp. 35–52. See also Yasheng Huang, "Why China Will Not Collapse," *Foreign Policy*, no. 99 (Summer 1995), pp. 54–68, for a rejoinder to Goldstone.

[14] Andrew J. Nathan, "Authoritarian Resilience," *Journal of Democracy*, vol. 14, no. 1 (January 2003), p. 16.

Communist Party rather than adjusting the relationship between the party and society through greater openness."[15] All of this is being done to prevent the collapse of communism in China. As David Shambaugh has shown, the CCP has actively studied the experience of former communist parties in the former Soviet Union and Eastern Europe and adapted its ideology and organization in order to avoid their fate.[16]

Although my previous work has often been interpreted as predicting collapse, I put myself in the "adaptation" category. I am agnostic on the question of whether China will become democratic because the experience of previous democratizations suggests strongly that whether a country becomes democratic, and if that transition is successfully consolidated, is contingent on a variety of unknowable factors, including the strength of democratic attitudes among ruling elites and throughout society, the balance of power among elite groups, the international context, the sudden appearance of economic or social crises, and other factors. Although predictions of *when* China may democratize are not particularly useful, we have better tools for predicting *how* democratization may occur. In China's case, the answer to that question must begin with the role of the CCP. As I have argued in this book and in other works, it has adapted its policy agenda, its composition, and its interactions with key social groups. This survival strategy has allowed it to attract new supporters, preempt potential opponents, and in some cases forcibly repress those making demands for political change. Although not always subtle or nuanced, its strategy is effective enough and flexible enough to cope with the problems that have arisen so far. So long as China does not suffer from an unforeseen social or economic crisis, the CCP's limited adaptations may be sufficient to keep it in power indefinitely. If that is the case, then the corruption and inequality that are inherent in crony communism are likely to endure.

---

[15] Joseph Fewsmith, "China Under Hu Jintao," *China Leadership Monitor*, no. 15 (Spring 2005). His other writings in *CLM* and elsewhere stress the theme that the CCP is sponsoring political reforms at various levels in order to strengthen the party, not usher in democratization.

[16] David Shambaugh, *China's Communist Party: Atrophy and Adaptation* (Berkeley and Washington, DC: University of California Press and Woodrow Wilson Center Press, 2008).

The CCP is hoping it can continue to implement political reform gradually, much as it implemented economic reform over a period of decades. This may not be the best solution to China's problems, but as Andrew Walder and Jean Oi have noted, suboptimal solutions in the course of political reform may be the only available options. "In China, where the Communist Party is still firmly in power, and intent on staying there, change will come gradually, through myriad 'suboptimal' forms, if it comes at all."[17] Their comments were related specifically to the extension of property rights but are also relevant to the full sweep of political reforms. However, the experience of other countries suggests that a true democratic opening rarely occurs gradually, but often suddenly and without advance warning.[18] While noting that CCP rule in China is adaptable, resilient, and likely to survive indefinitely, we must also be mindful that unforeseen events can suddenly shatter the political equilibrium and bring with them new and previously unavailable options. Whether China's communist system will be replaced by a democracy, another form of authoritarianism, prolonged instability, or even military rule will depend on the sequence of events and constellation of actors that lead to political change.[19]

These different scenarios for the future of the CCP are not necessarily mutually incompatible. For example, although Walder had earlier described the decline of the party's monitoring capacity, in subsequent work he argued that this decline was not an insurmountable threat to party rule. Because current leaders are better educated, less trapped in the ways of the past, and more familiar with the experiences of other countries, it is "likely that the regime itself will generate creative solutions to political governance issues in much the way it has generated creative solutions to economic reform over the past 20 years."[20] While Gilley forecasts a future democratic turning point, he also sees

---

[17] Andrew G. Walder and Jean C. Oi, "Property Rights in the Chinese Economy: Contours of the Process of Change," in Jean C. Oi and Andrew G. Walder, eds., *Property Rights and Economic Reform in China* (Stanford, CA: Stanford University Press, 1999).

[18] Timur Kuran, "Now Out of Never: The Element of Surprise in the East European Revolution of 1989," *World Politics*, vol. 44, no. 1 (October 1991), pp. 7–48.

[19] For more on these points, see Dickson, "Future of the Chinese Communist Party."

[20] Andrew G. Walder, "The Party Elite and China's Trajectory of Change," in Kjeld Erik Brodsgaard and Zheng Yongnian, eds., *The Chinese Communist Party in Reform* (London: Routledge, 2006), p. 28.

the initiators of that change coming from within the party, tacitly recognizing the central role that the CCP will play in China's political future. Similarly, many scholars emphasize the party's monopoly on political power as one of its essential advantages but disagree on its consequences. Whereas some see stagnation and paralysis as the main result, others see signs of innovation and adaptation within the Leninist system. However, the result of the CCP's adaptability may lead to what Nathan calls a "more disturbing possibility: that authoritarianism is a viable regime form even under conditions of advanced modernization and integration in the global economy."[21] That is a scenario that many scholars, and even more policymakers, have not envisioned.

FUTURE IMPLICATIONS

This study leads to several implications for scholars and policymakers. Above all, it indicates that economic development by itself does not necessarily or directly lead to democracy. Even if social changes occur that would facilitate and support democratization, the state need not remain a passive actor. The CCP has shown how an effective strategy of survival can perpetuate authoritarian rule even in the midst of rapid economic and social change. In addition, this study reinforces the findings of others that the beneficiaries of economic reform need not support democratization. If they are able to pursue their business interests through patrimonial ties with the state, they are more likely to support the status quo than seek to change it. Expectations that China's capitalists will be natural supporters of democracy are based on a misreading of history. Barrington Moore's thesis on the role of the bourgeoisie in the emergence of democracy may have been true for feudal states but has little relevance for the cooperative relations between government and business in late developers. At best, these late developers are contingent democrats, willing to support authoritarian politics when their business success is dependent on official largesse and when they fear the potential instability that may accompany democratization. Crony

---

[21] Nathan, "Authoritarian Resilience," p. 16. For a general view of this scenario not limited to China, see Bruce Bueno de Mesquita and George W. Downs, "Development and Democracy," *Foreign Affairs*, vol. 84, no. 5 (September–October 2005), pp. 77–86.

communism is one consequence of the CCP's survival strategy and an important factor in creating political support for continued political rule. Although there is little trace of Marxism left in China, Leninism is alive and well. In that sense, China remains a distinctly communist country despite the presence of a market economy.

As a result, there is no way of predicting when democracy will occur, if it comes at all. As Adam Przeworski and Fernando Limongi have demonstrated, democratization can occur at all levels of economic development; similarly, authoritarian regimes can survive indefinitely provided they avoid an economic crisis.[22] Whether China remains authoritarian or becomes democratic may also have significant ripple effects on other countries. Larry Diamond has suggested that if China undergoes significant political liberalization, and in particular if it becomes an electoral democracy, "the diffusion effects throughout East Asia and beyond could be powerful enough to launch a fourth wave of global democratization."[23] Alternatively, if the CCP's survival strategy proves successful, it will become a model for other authoritarian regimes to emulate.

Monitoring the prospects for democratization in China rightly focuses on the political realm of civil society, but the CCP is watching, too. Democratization requires political actors, but China lacks a charismatic pro-democratic leader who commands widespread public support. There is no equivalent of Nelson Mandela, Vaclav Havel, or Aung San Suu Kyi in China; that is, someone who is widely recognized and respected as a voice for democracy. Leaders can emerge in the midst of a social movement, as did Lech Walesa, but in the absence of identifiable leadership and effective organizations, political movements against authoritarian rule can also lead to tragedy, as did China's popular demonstrations in 1989. The CCP has consistently shown it is willing and able to suppress any individual or organization that it believes poses a threat to its monopoly on political power. Finding a way to overcome these obstacles – the lack of public support and the party's repressive powers – remains a considerable challenge for any democratic movement in China.

[22] Adam Przeworski and Fernando Limongi. "Modernization: Theories and Facts." *World Politics*, vol. 49, no. 2 (January 1997), pp. 155–183.
[23] Diamond, *Developing Democracy*, p. 267.

Just as economic development does not automatically guarantee democratization, there is also no reason to expect that either trade with China or China's integration into the international economy will necessarily facilitate political change that leads to democracy. The policy of the United States toward China should be based on U.S. interests, not sold as a means of attaining other goals that are not as germane. Arguments for trade policy toward China should emphasize the economic interests at stake and not be based on expectations that increased trade will contribute to the economic modernization of China, which in turn will enhance the prospects for future democratization. These arguments have not been borne out so far and create disappointment and disillusionment when the promised political change does not occur.[24] If the United States wants to promote democratization in China or elsewhere in the world, other more direct approaches are available. Programs to support the continued development of the rule of law, improved governance and public policy performance, corporate responsibility, and other similar efforts in the long run may be more effective, even if progress is hard to chart. Building effective institutions would also facilitate the consolidation of democracy in China if and when a transition occurs.[25] This is an implicit theme of Dali Yang's argument on institution building in China. Although not explicitly about the potential for democracy in China, the administrative institutions being created to foster economic modernization and improve the governing capacity of the current regime would also enhance the prospects for the success and survivability of a new regime.[26]

---

[24] This is the central theme in James Mann, *The China Fantasy: How Our Leaders Explain Away Chinese Repression* (New York: Viking, 2007). Mann's book harshly criticizes the tendency of American leaders to promote greater economic and strategic interaction with China as a means to foster its democratization but stops short of offering answers to the question raised by his critique: how should the United States promote democracy in China, if indeed it should do so at all?

[25] Juan Linz and Alfred Stepan, *Problems of Democratic Transition and Consolidation: Southern Europe, South America, and Post-Communist Europe* (Baltimore: Johns Hopkins University Press, 1996).

[26] Dali L. Yang, *Remaking the Chinese Leviathan: Market Transition and the Politics of Governance in China* (Stanford, CA: Stanford University Press, 2004), especially chapter 9.

Although some have pondered the contradictions inherent in the CCP's embrace of capitalism, those alleged contradictions do not concern China's leaders as much. Although they no longer pursue the Marxist utopia in the economy, they remain committed to Leninist party rule in the political realm. The integration of wealth and power is not only the defining feature of crony communism but also summarizes the CCP's strategy of survival for now and the foreseeable future.

Appendix

Survey Design

The data used in this book come from two surveys, the first conducted in fall 1997 and spring 1999 and the second conducted between late 2004 and early 2005 (throughout the book, they are referred to as the 1999 and 2005 surveys, respectively). Four Chinese provinces were selected (Hebei, Hunan, Shandong, and Zhejiang), and within each province two counties or county-level cities were selected (in all, three counties and five county-level cities; one of the county-level cities had become a district of a prefecture-level city by the time of the 2005 survey). The counties were purposively selected in order to have different levels of economic development represented in the sample. The same eight counties made up the 2005 survey, regardless of their current level of development, allowing me to observe trends over time. Although the local rates of economic development varied, the rank ordering of the counties by level of development was nearly identical, with the exception of the sixth- and seventh-poorest counties, which reversed places.

The survey targeted two specific groups: the owners and operators of large and medium-scale private enterprises (those with over 1 million yuan in annual sales, although as noted below this standard had to be relaxed in several counties) and the local party and government cadres with either general executive responsibilities or particular authority over the private economy. In each county, entrepreneurs were selected from three townships and towns where the private economy was relatively developed for that particular county (in the 1999 survey, a fourth township had to be added for one of the counties in order to get the targeted number of entrepreneurs). A sampling pool was created using name lists of enterprises provided by the industry and commerce management bureau. From this pool, entrepreneurs were selected using a random start, fixed interval system. In both the 1999 and 2005 surveys, the strategy was to concentrate on relatively large-scale firms, but in practice, this had to be relaxed. In some counties, the size of the private sector was too small to make the 1 million yuan threshold a feasible criterion for inclusion; in other counties, the private sector was large but the size of the firms was small (only firms with eight or more workers were included in the sample), again making the 1 million yuan threshold occasionally impractical.

The second targeted group was local officials, specifically chosen based on their areas of responsibility: county-level party and government cadres, including the party and government leaders and those in charge of the relevant political, economic, and united front departments; township and town (*xiangzhen*) cadres from the places of the enterprises in the sample; and village-level cadres. In each county, approximately 30 cadres were selected for the 1999 survey and approximately 35 for the 2005 survey (more township and village cadres were included in the 2005 survey).

The design of the questionnaire and the sample was done in coordination with the Research Center for Contemporary China (RCCC) of Peking University, and the actual implementation of the survey itself was conducted by the RCCC. A series of meetings was held in the summer of 1997 to develop a set of specific questions that would be both relevant to the theoretical issues of the project and also appropriate to the political and economic context in China. Before the implementation of the 2005 survey, I met again with the RCCC team, and we agreed to keep the questionnaire largely unchanged in order to maximize the comparability of responses across the two surveys. At the same time, we agreed to broaden the scope of the sample to include a larger number of entrepreneurs. A survey team from the RCCC visited each county in advance of the survey work to seek the permission of local officials and plan the practical details of implementation.

Separate questionnaires were used for private entrepreneurs and local officials, but most questions were asked of both. In each county, the county, township/town, and village-level officials gathered in separate meetings to fill out the questionnaires. They received the questionnaire, filled it out, and returned it in the same room. During this process, a member of the survey team was present at all times to pass out the questionnaires, explain the requirements of the survey, answer questions from the respondents, and collect the completed questionnaires. This was done to protect the integrity of the survey. At the time of the survey, the RCCC team also conducted group discussions with the county-level officials and collected aggregate county-level data that are used in the analysis throughout this book. The entrepreneurs selected for the sample were invited by the county officials to attend meetings to fill out the questionnaire. The office that took charge of the implementation of the survey varied: in different counties, the main work was done by either the Organization Department, the propaganda department, the county party committee's work office, or the industrial and commercial bureau of the government. The questionnaires were self-administered under the supervision of the survey team, who also checked the identity of the respondents to be sure they were the actual owners of the enterprise and not a family member or manager. Additional efforts were made to contact the entrepreneurs who did not attend the group meetings. Members of the survey team went to individual enterprises in order to have them fill out the questionnaire. Members of the survey team checked each questionnaire filled out at group meetings or after direct contacts; those that did not have the proper status, had too few workers, or for other reasons were invalid were not included in the final dataset.

The 1999 survey included 524 entrepreneurs and 230 cadres, and the 2005 survey included 1,058 entrepreneurs and 279 cadres. The response rate for the entrepreneurs was around 85 percent in 1999 and 78 percent in 2005. Among local officials, the response rate was nearly 100 percent; the only officials who were selected for the survey but did not participate happened to be out of town when the survey team visited their county.

This is not a random sample of China's population and was not intended to be. Although the results may not be generalizable to the population as a whole, or even to the full range of private entrepreneurs in China, the respondents do represent the economic and political elites in their communities and are therefore of most relevance for the questions asked in this study.

Bibliography

Almond, Gabriel and Sidney Verba. *Civic Culture: Political Attitudes and Democracy in Five Nations*. Princeton, NJ: Princeton University Press, 1963.

Alpermann, Bjorn. "'Wrapped up in Cotton Wool': Political Integration of Private Entrepreneurs in Rural China." *China Journal*, no. 56 (July 2006), pp. 33–62.

Ao, Daiya. "Siying qiyezhu zhengzhi canyu yanjiu baogao" (Report on the Political Participation of Private Entrepreneurs). In Zhang Houyi et al., eds., *Zhongguo siying qiye fazhan baogao*, no. 6 (2005) (A Report on the Development of China's Private Enterprises). Beijing: Shehui kexue wenxian chubanshe, 2006, pp. 61–83.

Ash, Timothy Garton. *The Uses of Adversity: Essays on the Fate of Central Europe*. New York: Vintage, 1990.

Barnes, Andrew. *Owning Russia: The Struggle over Factories, Farms, and Power*. Ithaca, NY: Cornell University Press, 2006.

Baum, Richard. *Burying Mao: Chinese Politics in the Age of Deng Xiaoping*. Princeton, NJ: Princeton University Press, 1996.

Bellin, Eva. "Contingent Democrats: Industrialists, Labor, and Democratization in Late-Developing Countries." *World Politics*, vol. 52, no. 2 (January 2000), pp. 175–205.

Boix, Carles and Susan C. Stokes. "Endogenous Democratization." *World Politics*, vol. 55, no. 4 (July 2003), pp. 517–549.

Brook, Timothy and B. Michael Frolic, eds. *Civil Society in China*. Armonk, NY: M. E. Sharpe, 1997.

Bruun, Ole. *Business and Bureaucracy in a Chinese City: An Ethnography of Private Business Households in Contemporary China*. Berkeley: University of California, Institute of East Asian Studies, 1993.

Bueno de Mesquita, Bruce and George W. Downs. "Development and Democracy." *Foreign Affairs*, vol. 84, no. 5 (September–October 2005), pp. 77–86.

Burkhart, Ross E. and Michael A. Lewis-Beck. "Comparative Democracy: The Economic Development Thesis." *American Political Science Review*, vol. 88, no. 4 (December 1994), pp. 903–910.

Chalmers, Douglas A. "Corporatism and Comparative Politics." In Howard J. Wiarda, ed., *New Directions in Comparative Politics*. Boulder, CO: Westview Press, 1985.

Chan, Anita. "Organizing Wal-Mart: The Chinese Trade Union at a Crossroads." *Japan Focus* (http://japanfocus.org/products/topdf/2217), accessed September 26, 2006.

Chan, Anita, Richard Madsen, and Jonathan Unger. *Chen Village under Mao and Deng*. Berkeley: University of California Press, 1992.

Chang, Gordon G. *The Coming Collapse of China*. New York: Random House, 2001.

Chang, Yu-tzung, Yun-han Chu, and Frank Tsai. "Confucianism and Democratic Values in Three Chinese Societies." *Issues and Studies*, vol. 41, no. 4 (December 2005), pp. 1–33.

Chen, An. "Capitalist Development, Entrepreneurial Class, and Democratization in China." *Political Science Quarterly*, vol. 117, no. 3 (Fall 2002), pp. 401–422.

Chen, Guangjin. "1992–2004 nian de siying qiyezhu jieceng: Yige xin shehui jieceng de chengzhang" (Private Entrepreneurs between 1992 and 2004: The Emergence of a New Social Stratum). In Zhang Houyi et al., eds., *Zhongguo siying qiye fazhan baogao*, no. 6 (2005) (A Report on the Development of China's Private Enterprises). Beijing: Shehui kexue wenxian chubanshe, 2006, pp. 223–267.

Chen, Guidi and Wu Chuntao. *Will the Boat Sink the Water? The Life of China's Peasants*. New York: Public Affairs, 2006.

Chen, Hongyi. *The Institutional Transition of China's Township and Village Enterprises: Market Liberalization, Contractual Form Innovation, and Privatization*. Aldershot: Ashgate, 2000.

Chen, Jie. *Popular Political Support in Urban China*. Stanford, CA: Stanford University Press, 2004.

China Human Development Report 2005. Beijing: United Nations Development Programme and China Development Foundation, 2005.

Cho, Young Nam. "The Politics of Lawmaking in Chinese Local People's Congresses." *China Quarterly*, no. 187 (September 2006), pp. 592–609.

Chung, Jae Ho. "Reappraising Central–Local Relations in Deng's China: Decentralization, Dilemmas of Control, and Diluted Effects of Reform." In Chien-min Chao and Bruce J. Dickson, eds., *Remaking the Chinese State: Strategies, Society, and Security*. London: Routledge, 2001.

Dahl, Robert A. *Democracy and Its Critics*. New Haven, CT: Yale University Press, 1989.

    Polyarchy: Participation and Opposition. New Haven, CT: Yale University Press, 1971.

Diamond, Larry. *Developing Democracy: Toward Consolidation*. Baltimore: Johns Hopkins University Press, 1999.

"Rethinking Civil Society: Toward Democratic Consolidation." *Journal of Democracy*, vol. 5, no. 3 (July 1994), pp. 5–17.

Dickson, Bruce J. "The Future of the Chinese Communist Party." In Jae Ho Chung, ed., *Charting China's Future: Political, Social, and International Dimensions*. Lanham, MD: Rowman and Littlefield, 2006.

"Beijing's Ambivalent Reformers." *Current History*, vol. 103, no. 674 (September 2004), pp. 249–255.

"Dilemmas of Party Adaptation: The CCP's Strategies for Survival." In Peter Hays Gries and Stanley Rosen, eds., *State and Society in 21st Century China: Crisis, Contention, and Legitimation*. New York: Routledge, 2004.

Red Capitalists in China: The Party, Private Entrepreneurs, and Prospects for Political Change. Cambridge: Cambridge University Press, 2003.

Ding, X. L. "The Illicit Asset Stripping of Chinese State Firms." *China Journal*, no. 43 (January 2000), pp. 1–28.

"Who Gets What, How? When Chinese State-Owned Enterprises Become Shareholding Companies." *Problems of Post-Communism*, vol. 46, no. 3 (May–June 1999), pp. 32–41.

Ding, Yuanzhu, Xunqing Jiang, and Xin Qi. "China." Background paper, Asian Pacific Philanthropy Consortium, APPC Conference, September 5–7, 2003. http://www.asianphilanthropy.org/pdfs/conference/china1.pdf.

Fairbanks, Charles H., Jr. "Georgia's Rose Revolution." *Journal of Democracy*, vol. 15, no. 2 (April 2004), pp. 110–124.

Fewsmith, Joseph. "Chambers of Commerce in Wenzhou Show Potential and Limits of 'Civil Society' in China." *China Leadership Monitor*, no. 16 (Fall 2005).

"China under Hu Jintao." *China Leadership Monitor*, no. 15 (Spring 2005).

"The Sixteenth National Party Congress: The Succession that Didn't Happen." *China Quarterly*, no. 173 (March 2003), pp. 1–16.

China since Tiananmen: The Politics of Transition. Cambridge: Cambridge University Press, 2001.

Foley, Michael W. and Bob Edwards. "The Paradox of Civil Society." *Journal of Democracy*, vol. 7, no. 3 (July 1996), pp. 38–52.

Foster, Kenneth C. "Embedded within State Agencies: Business Associations in Yantai." *China Journal*, no. 47 (January 2002), pp. 41–65.

Gallagher, Mary Elizabeth. *Contagious Capitalism: Globalization and the Politics of Labor in China*. Princeton, NJ: Princeton University Press, 2005.

Gershenkron, Alexander. *Historical Backwardness in Historical Perspective*. Cambridge, MA: Harvard University Press, 1962.

Gilley, Bruce. "Legitimacy, Regime Survival, and Democratization in China." Paper presented at the annual meeting of the Association for Asian Studies, March 22–25, 2007.

China's Democratic Future: How It Will Happen and Where It Will Lead. New York: Columbia University Press, 2004.

Glassman, Robert M. *China in Transition: Communism, Capitalism, and Democracy.* New York: Praeger, 1991.

Gold, Thomas. "Bases for Civil Society in Reform China." In Kjeld Erik Brodsgaard and David Strand, eds., *Rconstructing Twentieth-century China: State Control, Civil Society, and National Identity.* Oxford: Oxford University Press, 1998.

"Urban Private Business and China's Reforms." In Richard Baum, ed., *Reform and Reaction in Post-Mao China: The Road to Tiananmen.* New York: Routledge, 1991, pp. 84–103.

Goldman, Merle. *From Comrade to Citizen: The Struggle for Political Rights in China.* Cambridge, MA: Harvard University Press, 2005.

Goldstone, Jack A. "The Coming Chinese Collapse." *Foreign Policy,* no. 99 (Summer 1995), pp. 35–52.

Gomez, Edmund Terence, ed. *Political Business in East Asia.* London: Routledge, 2002.

Gong, Ting. "Jumping into the Sea: Cadre Entrepreneurs in China." *Problems of Post-Communism,* vol. 43, no. 4 (July–August 1996), pp. 26–34.

The Politics of Corruption in Contemporary China: An Analysis of Policy Outcomes. Westport, CT: Praeger, 1994, pp. 135–147.

Goodman, David S. G. "The Interdependence of State and Society: The Political Sociology of Local Leadership." In Chien-min Chao and Bruce J. Dickson, eds., *Remaking the Chinese State: Strategies, Society, and Security.* London: Routledge, 2001.

"The New Middle Class." In Merle Goldman and Roderick MacFarquhar, eds., *The Paradox of China's Post-Mao Reforms.* Cambridge, MA: Harvard University Press, 1999.

Green, Stephen and Guy S. Liu, eds. *Exit the Dragon? Privatization and State Control in China.* London: Chatham House, 2005.

"Introduction." In Stephen Green and Guy S. Liu, eds., *Exit the Dragon? Privatization and State Control in China.* London: Chatham House, 2005, pp. 1–14.

"China's Industrial Reform Strategy: Retreat and Retain." In Stephen Green and Guy S. Liu, eds., *Exit the Dragon? Privatization and State Control in China.* London: Chatham House, 2005, pp. 15–41.

Groot, Gerry. *Managing Transitions: The Chinese Communist Party, United Front Work, Corporatism, and Hegemony.* New York: Routledge, 2004.

Guiheux, Gilles. "The Political 'Participation' of Entrepreneurs: Challenge or Opportunity for the Chinese Communist Party?" *Social Research,* vol. 73, no. 1 (Spring 2006), pp. 219–244.

Guo, Xiaoqin. *State and Society in China's Democratic Transition: Confucianism, Leninism, and Economic Development.* New York: Routledge, 2003.

Haggard, Stephan and Robert R. Kaufman. *The Political Economy of Democratic Transitions.* Princeton, NJ: Princeton University Press, 1995.

Hale, Henry E. "Democracy or Autocracy on the March? The Colored Revolutions as Normal Dynamics of Patronal Presidentialism." *Communist and Post-Communist Studies*, vol. 39, no. 3 (September 2006), pp. 305–329.

Hannan, Michael T. and John Freeman. *Organizational Ecology*. Cambridge, MA: Harvard University Press, 1991.

He, Baogang. "Authoritarian Deliberation: Deliberative Turn in Chinese Political Development." Paper presented at the annual meeting of the Association for Asian Studies, April 6–9, 2006.

"Intra-party Democracy: A Revisionist Perspective from Below." In Kjeld Erik Brodsgaard and Zheng Yongnian, eds., *The Chinese Communist Party in Reform*. London: Routledge, 2006.

The Democratic Implications of Civil Society in China. New York: St. Martin's Press, 1997.

He, Qinglian. "China's Listing Social Structure." *New Left Review*, vol. 5 (September–October 2000), pp. 69–99.

Heimer, Maria. "The Cadre Responsibility System and the Changing Needs of the Party." In Kjeld Erik Brodsgaard and Zheng Yongnian, eds., *The Chinese Communist Party in Reform*. London: Routledge, 2006.

Hellman, Joel S. "Winners Take All: The Politics of Partial Reform in Post-communist Transitions." *World Politics*, vol. 50, no. 2 (January 1998), pp. 203–234.

Hoffman, David E. *The Oligarchs: Wealth and Power in the New Russia*. New York: Public Affairs, 2002.

Hong, Zhaohui. "Mapping the Evolution and Transformation of the New Private Entrepreneurs in China." *Journal of Chinese Political Science*, vol. 9, no. 1 (Spring 2004), pp. 23–42.

Hu, Shaohua. *Explaining Chinese Democratization*. Westport, CT: Praeger, 2000.

Hu, Xiaobo. "The State, Enterprises, and Society in Post-Deng China: Impact of the New Round of SOE Reform." *Asian Survey*, vol. 40, no. 4 (July–August 2000), pp. 641–657.

Huang, Yasheng. *Inflation and Investment Controls in China: The Political Economy of Central–Local Relations during the Reform Era*. Cambridge: Cambridge University Press, 1996.

"Why China Will Not Collapse." *Foreign Policy*, no. 99 (Summer 1995), pp. 54–68.

Huntington, Samuel P. *The Third Wave: Democratization in the Late Twentieth Century*. Norman: University of Oklahoma Press, 1991.

"The Goals of Development." In Myron Weiner and Samuel P. Huntington, eds., *Understanding Political Development: An Analytic Study*. Boston: Little, Brown, 1987.

"Social and Institutional Dynamics of One-Party Systems." In Samuel P. Huntington and Clement H. Moore, eds., *Authoritarian Politics in Modern Society: The Dynamics of Established One-Party Systems*. New York: Basic Books, 1970.

Hutchcroft, Paul D. "Oligarchs and Cronies in the Philippine State: The Politics of Patrimonial Plunder." *World Politics*, vol. 43, no. 3 (April 1991), pp. 414–450.

Inglehart, Ronald. *Modernization and Postmodernization: Cultural, Economic, and Political Change in 43 Societies*. Princeton, NJ: Princeton University Press, 1997.

Inglehart, Ronald and Christian Welzel. *Modernization, Cultural Change, and Democracy: The Human Development Sequence*. Cambridge: Cambridge University Press, 2005.

Jennings, Kent. "Local Problem Agendas in the Chinese Countryside as Viewed by Cadres and Villagers." *Acta Politica*, vol. 38 (2003), pp. 313–332.

Johnson, Ian. *Wild Grass: Three Stories of Change in Modern China*. New York: Viking, 2005.

Jones, Leroy and Il SaKong. *Government, Business, and Entrepreneurship in Economic Development*. Cambridge, MA: Harvard University Press, 1980.

Jowitt, Ken. *New World Disorder*. Berkeley: University of California Press, 1992.

Kang, David C. *Crony Capitalism: Corruption and Development in South Korea and the Philippines*. Cambridge: Cambridge University Press, 2002.

Karatnycky, Adrian. "Ukraine's Orange Revolution." *Foreign Affairs*, vol. 84, no. 2 (March–April 2005), pp. 35–52.

Kennedy, Scott. *The Business of Lobbying in China*. Cambridge, MA: Harvard University Press, 2005.

"The Stone Group: State Client or Market Pathbreaker?" *China Quarterly*, no. 152 (December 1997), pp. 746–777.

Kojima, Kazuko and Ryosei Kokubun. "The 'Shequ Construction' Programme and the Chinese Communist Party." In Kjeld Erik Brodsgaard and Zheng Yongnian, eds., *Bringing the Party Back In: How China Is Governed*. Singapore: Eastern Universities Press, 2004.

Kuran, Timur. "Now Out of Never: The Element of Surprise in the East European Revolution of 1989." *World Politics*, vol. 44, no. 1 (October 1991), pp. 7–48.

Lan Shiyong. "1994–2004 nian de Zhongguo siying jingji" (China's Private Economy, 1994–2004). In Zhang Houyi et al., eds., *Zhongguo siying qiye fazhan baogao*, no. 6 (2005) (A Report on the Development of China's Private Enterprises). Beijing: Shehui kexue wenxian chubanshe, 2006, pp. 3–8.

Levy, Richard. "Village Elections, Transparency, and Anti-Corruption: Henan and Guangdong Provinces." In Elizabeth J. Perry and Merle Goldman, eds., *Grassroots Political Reform in Contemporary China*. Cambridge, MA: Harvard University Press, 2007.

Li, Cheng. "The New Bipartisanship within the Chinese Communist Party." *Orbis*, vol. 49, no. 3 (Summer 2005), pp. 387–400.

Li, Hongbin, Lingsheng Meng, and Junsen Zhang. "Why Do Entrepreneurs Enter Politics? Evidence from China." *Economic Inquiry*, vol. 44, no. 3 (July 2006), pp. 559–578.

Li, Hongbin and Scott Rozelle. "Privatizing Rural China: Insider Privatization, Innovative Contracts, and the Performance of Township Enterprises." *China Quarterly*, no. 176 (December 2003), pp. 981–1005.

Li, Lianjiang and Kevin J. O'Brien. "The Struggle over Village Elections." In Merle Goldman and Roderick MacFarquhar, eds., *The Paradox of China's Post-Mao Reforms*. Cambridge, MA: Harvard University Press, 1999, pp. 129–144.

Lieberthal, Kenneth. *Governing China: From Revolution through Reform*. New York: Norton, 2004.

Linz, Juan and Alfred Stepan. *Problems of Democratic Transition and Consolidation: Southern Europe, South America, and Post-Communist Europe*. Baltimore: Johns Hopkins University Press, 1996.

Lipset, Seymour Martin. "The Social Requisites of Democracy Revisited: 1993 Presidential Address." *American Sociological Review*, vol. 59, no. 1 (February 1994), pp. 1–22.

"Some Social Requisites of Democracy: Economic Development and Political Legitimacy." *American Political Science Review*, vol. 53, no. 1 (March 1959), pp. 69–105.

Liu, Yia-Ling. "Reform from Below: The Private Economy and Local Politics in the Rural Industrialization of Wenzhou." *China Quarterly*, no. 130 (June 1992), pp. 293–316.

Lu, Chunlong. "Democratic Values among Chinese People: Analysis of a Public Opinion Survey." *China Perspectives*, no. 55 (September–October 2004), pp. 40–48.

Lu Ruifeng, et al. "Shenzhen shi siying qiye dang de jianshe wenti yu duice" (Problems and Counter-measures in Party Building in Shenzhen's Private Enterprises). *Tequ lilun yu shixian* (Shenzhen) (December 1995), pp. 35–39.

MacFarquhar, Roderick. "Provincial People's Congresses." *China Quarterly*, no. 155 (September 1988), pp. 656–667.

Manion, Melanie. *Corruption by Design: Building Clean Government in Mainland China and Hong Kong*. Cambridge, MA: Harvard University Press, 2004.

"Chinese Democratization in Perspective: Electorates and Selectorates at the Township Level." *China Quarterly*, no. 163 (September 2000), pp. 764–782.

"The Electoral Connection in the Chinese Countryside." *American Political Science Review*, vol. 90, no. 4 (December 1996), pp. 736–748.

"Corruption by Design: Bribery in Chinese Enterprise Licensing." *Journal of Law, Economics, and Organization*, vol. 12, no. 1 (April 1996), pp. 167–195.

Mann, James. *The China Fantasy: How Our Leaders Explain Away Chinese Repression*. New York: Viking, 2007.

Maxwell, Sylvia and Ben Ross Schneider, eds. *Business and the State in Developing Countries*. Ithaca, NY: Cornell University Press, 1997.

Moore, Barrington. *Social Origins of Dictatorship and Democracy: Lord and Peasant in the Making of the Modern World*. Boston: Beacon Press, 1966.

Mulvenon, James. *Soldiers of Fortune: The Rise and Fall of the Chinese Military–Business Complex, 1978–1998*. Armonk, NY: M. E. Sharpe, 2001.

Nathan, Andrew J. "Authoritarian Resilience." *Journal of Democracy*, vol. 14, no. 1 (January 2003), pp. 6–17.

Nathan, Andrew J. and Tse-Hsin Chen. "Traditional Social Values, Democratic Values, and Political Participation." *Asian Barometer Working Paper Series*, no. 23 (2004).

Naughton, Barry. *The Chinese Economy: Transitions and Growth*. Cambridge, MA: MIT Press, 2007.

  Growing Out of the Plan: Chinese Economic Reform, 1978–1993. Cambridge: Cambridge University Press, 1995.

Nevitt, Christopher Earle. "Private Business Associations in China: Evidence of Civil Society or Local State Power?" *China Journal*, no. 36 (July 1996), pp. 25–43.

O'Brien, Kevin J. "Implementing Political Reform in China's Villages." *Australian Journal of Chinese Affairs*, no. 32 (July 1994), pp. 33–60.

  "Agents and Remonstrators: Role Accumulation by Chinese People's Congress Deputies." *China Quarterly*, no. 138 (June 1994), pp. 359–380.

O'Brien, Kevin J. and Lianjiang Li. "Selective Policy Implementation in Rural China." *Comparative Politics*, vol. 31, no. 2 (January 1999), pp. 167–186.

O'Donnell, Guillermo and Philippe C. Schmitter. *Transitions from Authoritarian Rule: Tentative Conclusions about Uncertain Democracies*. Baltimore: Johns Hopkins University Press, 1986.

Ogden, Suzanne. *Inklings of Democracy in China*. Cambridge, MA: Harvard University Asia Center, 2002.

Oi, Jean C. *Rural China Takes Off: Institutional Foundations of Economic Reform*. Stanford, CA: Stanford University Press, 1999.

  "Economic Development, Stability and Democratic Village Self-Governance." In Maurice Brosseau, Suzanne Pepper, and Shu-ki Tsang, eds., *China Review 1996*. Hong Kong: Chinese University Press, 1996, pp. 125–144.

  "The Role of the Local State in China's Transitional Economy." *China Quarterly*, no. 144 (December 1995), pp. 1132–1149.

O'Neil, Patrick H. "Revolution from Within: Institutional Analysis, Transitions from Authoritarianism, and the Case of Hungary." *World Politics*, vol. 48, no. 4 (July 1996), pp. 579–603.

Organisation for Economic Co-operation and Development. "Policy Brief: Economic Survey of China, 2005," *OECD Observer*, no. 251 (2005).

Ostergaard, Clemens Stubbe and Christina Pearson. "Official Profiteering and the Tiananmen Square Demonstrations in China." *Corruption and Reform*, vol. 6, no. 2 (1991), pp. 87–107.

Parish, William L. and Charles Chi-Hsiang Chang. "Political Values in Taiwan: Sources of Change and Constancy." In Hung-mao Tien, ed., *Taiwan's Electoral Politics and Democratic Transition: Riding the Third Wave*. Armonk, NY: M. E. Sharpe, 1996, pp. 27–41.

Parish, William L. and Dali Ma. "Tocquevillian Moments: Charitable Contributions by Chinese Private Entrepreneurs." *Social Forces*, vol. 85, no. 2 (December 2006), pp. 943–964.

Park, Chung-min and Doh Chull Shin. "Do Asian Values Deter Popular Support for Democracy? The Case of South Korea." *Asian Barometer Working Paper Series*, no. 26 (2004).

Parris, Kristen. "The Rise of Private Business Interests." In Merle Goldman and Roderick MacFarquhar, eds., *The Paradox of China's Post-Mao Reforms*. Cambridge, MA: Harvard University Press, 1999.

"Local Initiative and National Reform: The Wenzhou Model of Development." *China Quarterly*, no. 134 (June 1993), pp. 242–263.

Pearson, Margaret M. "China's Emerging Business Class: Democracy's Harbinger?" *Current History*, vol. 97, no. 620 (September 1998), pp. 268–272.

China's New Business Elite: The Political Consequences of Economic Reform. Berkeley: University of California Press, 1997.

"The Janus Face of Business Associations in China: Socialist Corporatism in Foreign Enterprises." *Australian Journal of Chinese Affairs*, no. 31 (January 1994), pp. 25–46.

Pei, Minxin. *China's Trapped Transition: The Limits of Developmental Autocracy*. Cambridge, MA: Harvard University Press, 2006.

"Is China Democratizing?" *Foreign Affairs*, vol. 77, no. 1 (1998), pp. 68–82.

Pfeffer, Jeffrey and Gerald B. Salancik. *The External Control of Organizations: A Resource Dependence Perspective*. New York: Harper and Row, 1978.

Polanyi, Karl. *The Great Transformation: The Political and Economic Origins of Our Time*. New York: Farrar and Rinehart, 1944.

Przeworski, Adam. "Some Problems in the Transition to Democracy." In Guillermo O'Donnell, Phillipe C. Schmitter, and Laurence Whitehead, eds., *Transitions from Authoritarian Rule*, vol. 3: *Comparative Perspectives*. Baltimore: Johns Hopkins University Press, 1986.

Przeworski, Adam and Fernando Limongi. "Modernization: Theories and Facts." *World Politics*, vol. 49, no. 2 (January 1997), pp. 155–183.

Putnam, Robert. *Making Democracy Work*. Princeton, NJ: Princeton University Press, 1993.

Ravallion, Martin and Shaohua Chen. *China's (Uneven) Progress against Poverty*. Washington, DC: World Bank, 2004.

Riskin, Carl, Zhao Renwei, and Li Shi, eds. *China's Retreat from Equality: Income Distribution and Economic Transition*. Armonk, NY: M. E. Sharpe, 2001.

Robison, Richard and Vedi Hediz. *Reorganising Power in Indonesia: The Politics of Oligarchy in an Age of Markets*. London: RoutledgeCurzon, 2004.

Rowe, William T. "The Problem of 'Civil Society' in Late Imperial China." *Modern China*, vol. 19, no. 2 (April 1993), pp. 139–157.

Rowen, Henry S. "The Growth of Freedoms in China." APARC Working Paper, Stanford University, 2001.

"The Short March: China's Road to Democracy." *The National Interest*, no. 45 (Fall 1996), pp. 61–70.

Rueschemeyer, Dietrich, Evelyne Huber Stephens, and John D. Stephens. *Capitalist Development and Democracy*. Chicago: University of Chicago Press, 1992.

Saich, Tony. "Negotiating the State: The Development of Social Organizations in China." *China Quarterly*, no. 161 (March 2000), pp. 124–141.

Schmitter, Philippe C. "Still the Century of Corporatism?" In Philippe C. Schmitter and Gerhard Lehmbruch, eds., *Trends toward Corporatist Intermediation*. Beverly Hills, CA: Sage, 1979.

Schneiberg, Marc and Elisabeth Clemens. "The Typical Tools for the Job: Research Strategies in Institutional Analysis." *Sociological Theory*, vol. 24, no. 3 (September 2006), pp. 195–227.

Selznick, Philip P. *TVA and the Grass Roots*. Berkeley: University of California Press, 1949.

Seymour, James D. *China's Satellite Parties*. Armonk, NY: M. E. Sharpe, 1987.

Shambaugh, David. *China's Communist Party: Atrophy and Adaptation*. Berkeley and Washington, DC: University of California Press and Woodrow Wilson Center Press, 2008.

Shi, Tianjian. "Economic Development and Village Elections in Rural China." *Journal of Contemporary China*, vol. 8, no. 22 (1999), pp. 425–442.

Political Participation in Beijing. Cambridge, MA: Harvard University Press, 1997.

Shieh, Shawn. "The Rise of Collective Corruption in China: The Xiamen Smuggling Case." *Journal of Contemporary China*, vol. 14, no. 42 (February 2005), pp. 67–91.

Shih, Victor Chung-Hon. *Factions and Finance: Elite Conflict and Inflation*. Cambridge: Cambridge University Press, 2007.

Solinger, Dorothy J. "Labour Market Reform and the Plight of the Laid-Off Proletariat." *China Quarterly*, no. 170 (June 2002), pp. 304–326.

"Why We Cannot Count the 'Unemployed.'" *China Quarterly*, no. 167 (September 2001), pp. 671–688.

"Urban Entrepreneurs and the State: The Merger of State and Society." In Arthur Lewis Rosenbaum, ed., *State and Society in China: The Consequences of Reform*. Boulder, CO: Westview Press, 1992.

Chinese Business under Socialism: The Politics of Domestic Commerce in Contemporary China. Berkeley: University of California Press, 1984.

Steinfeld, Edward S. *Forging Reform in China: The Fate of State-Owned Industry*. Cambridge: Cambridge University Press, 1998.

Stepan, Alfred C. *The State and Society: Peru in Comparative Perspective*. Princeton, NJ: Princeton University Press, 1978.

Sun, Laixiang. "Ownership Reform in China's Township and Village Enterprises." In Stephen Green and Guy S. Liu, eds., *Exit the Dragon? Privatization and State Control in China*. London: Blackwell, 2005, pp. 90–110.

Sun, Yan. *Corruption and Market in Contemporary China*. Ithaca, NY: Cornell University Press, 2004.

    The Chinese Reassessment of Socialism, 1976–1992. Princeton, NJ: Princeton University Press, 1995.

    "The Chinese Protests of 1989: The Issue of Corruption." *Asian Survey*, vol. 31, no. 8 (August 1991), pp. 762–782.

Tang, Wenfang. "Political and Social Trends in the Post-Deng Urban China: Crisis or Stability?" *China Quarterly*, no. 168 (December 2001), pp. 890–909.

Tanner, Murray Scot, with Michael J. Feder. "Family Politics, Elite Recruitment, and Succession in Post-Mao China." *Australian Journal of Chinese Affairs*, no. 30 (July 1993), pp. 89–119.

Tao Qing. "Feigong youzhi jingji zuzhi dangjian gongzuo de xianzhuang fenxi" (Analysis of the Current Status of Party Building in Nonpublic Enterprises). *Zhonggong Ningbo shiwei dangxiao xuebao* (CCP Ningbo City Party School Report) (February 2002), pp. 56–59.

Teiwes, Frederick C. "Establishment and Consolidation of the New Regime." In Roderick MacFarquhar, ed., *The Politics of China*, second edition. Cambridge: Cambridge University Press, 1997.

Tenev, Stoyan and Chunlin Zhang with Loup Brefort. *Corporate Governance and Enterprise Reform in China: Building the Institutions of Modern Markets*. Washington, DC: World Bank and International Finance Corporation, 2002.

Thelen, Kathleen. "How Institutions Evolve: Insights from Comparative Historical Analysis." In James Mahoney and Dietrich Rueschemeyer, eds., *Comparative Historical Analysis in the Social Sciences*. Cambridge: Cambridge University Press, 2003, pp. 208–240.

Thogersen, Stig. "Parasites or Civilisers: The Legitimacy of the Chinese Communist Party in Rural Areas." In Kjeld Erik Brodsgaard and Zheng Yongnian, eds., *Bringing the Party Back In: How China Is Governed*. Singapore: Eastern Universities Press, 2004.

Tismaneanu, Vladimir. *Reinventing Politics: Eastern Europe from Stalin to Havel*. New York: The Free Press, 1992.

Tong, Yanqi. "State, Society, and Political Change in China and Hungary." *Comparative Politics*, vol. 26, no. 3 (April 1994), pp. 333–353.

Tsai, Kellee S. *Capitalism without Democracy: The Private Sector in Contemporary China*. Ithaca, NY: Cornell University Press, 2007.

    "Capitalists without a Class: Political Diversity Among Private Entrepreneurs in China." *Comparative Political Studies*, vol. 38, no. 9 (November 2005), pp. 1130–1158.

    Back Alley Banking: Private Entrepreneurs in China. Ithaca, NY: Cornell University Press, 2002.

Tsai, Lily Lee. *Accountability without Democracy: Solidary Groups and Public Goods Provision in Rural China*. Cambridge: Cambridge University Press, 2007.

"Cadres, Temple and Lineage Institutions, and Governance in Rural China." *China Journal*, no. 48 (July 2002), pp. 1–28.

Unger, Jonathan. "'Bridges': Private Business, the Chinese Government and the Rise of New Associations." *China Quarterly*, no. 147 (September 1996), pp. 795–819.

Unger, Jonathan and Anita Chan. "Corporatism in China: A Developmental State in an East Asian Context." In Barrett L. McCormick and Jonathan Unger, eds., *China after Socialism: In the Footsteps of Eastern Europe or East Asia*. Armonk, NY: M. E. Sharpe, 1996.

Wakeman, Jr., Frederic. "The Civil Society and Public Sphere Debate: Western Reflections on Chinese Political Culture." *Modern China*, vol. 19, no. 2 (April 1993), pp. 108–138.

Walder, Andrew G. "The Party Elite and China's Trajectory of Change." In Kjeld Erik Brodsgaard and Zheng Yongnian, eds., *The Chinese Communist Party in Reform*. London: Routledge, 2006.

"Local Governments as Industrial Firms: An Organizational Analysis of China's Transition Economy." *American Journal of Sociology*, vol. 101, no. 2 (September 1995), pp. 263–301.

"The Quiet Revolution from Within: Economic Reform as a Source of Political Decline." In Andrew G. Walder, ed., *The Waning of the Communist State: Economic Origins of Political Decline in China and Hungary*. Berkeley: University of California Press, 1995.

"The Decline of Communist Power: Elements of a Theory of Institutional Change." *Theory and Society*, vol. 23, no. 2 (April 1994), pp. 297–323.

Walder, Andrew G. and Jean C. Oi. "Property Rights in the Chinese Economy: Contours of the Process of Change." In Jean C. Oi and Andrew G. Walder, eds., *Property Rights and Economic Reform in China*. Stanford, CA: Stanford University Press, 1999.

Wang, Hui. *China's New Order: Society, Politics, and Economy in Transition*. Cambridge, MA: Harvard University Press, 2003.

Wang, Shaoguang. "The Rise of the Regions: Fiscal Reform and the Decline of Central State Capacity in China." In Andrew G. Walder, ed., *The Waning of the Communist State: Economic Origins of Political Decline in China and Hungary*. Berkeley: University of California Press, 1995.

Wank, David L. *Commodifying Communism: Business, Trust, and Politics in a Chinese City*. Cambridge: Cambridge University Press, 1999.

"Private Business, Bureaucracy, and Political Alliance in a Chinese City." *Australian Journal of Chinese Affairs*, no. 33 (January 1995), pp. 55–71.

Wedeman, Andrew H. "The Intensification of Corruption in China." *China Quarterly*, no. 180 (December 2004), pp. 895–921.

From Mao to Market: Rent Seeking, Local Protectionism, and Marketization in China. Cambridge: Cambridge University Press, 2003.

White, Gordon. "Democratization and Economic Reform in China." *Australian Journal of Chinese Affairs*, no. 31 (1994), pp. 73–92.

White, Gordon, Jude Howell, and Shang Xiaoyuan. *In Search of Civil Society: Market Reform and Social Change in Contemporary China.* Oxford: Oxford University Press, 1996.

Whiting, Susan H. *Power and Wealth in Rural China: The Political Economy of Institutional Change.* Cambridge: Cambridge University Press, 2001.

Whyte, Martin King. "Urban China: A Civil Society in the Making?" In Arthur Lewis Rosenbaum, ed., *State and Society in China: The Consequences of Reform.* Boulder, CO: Westview Press, 1992, pp. 79–80.

Wiegle, Marcia A. and Jim Butterfield. "Civil Society in Reforming Communist Regimes: The Logic of Emergence." *Comparative Politics*, vol. 25, no. 1 (October 1992), pp. 1–23.

Wright, Teresa. "Contesting State Legitimacy in the 1990s: The China Democracy Party and the China Labor Bulletin." In Peter Hays Gries and Stanley Rosen, eds., *State and Society in 21st Century China: Crisis, Contention, and Legitimation.* New York: Routledge, 2004.

Wu, Jinglian. *Understanding and Interpreting Chinese Economic Reform.* Singapore: Thomson/South-Western, 2005.

Xue Fei. "Feigong youzhi qiye dangjian de teshuxing fenxi jiqi zhidu chuangxin" (The Special Nature of Party Building in Nonpublic Enterprises and Its Institutional Innovations). *Tansuo* (Exploration) [Zhejiang edition] (January 2002), pp. 36–40.

Yang, Dali L. *Remaking the Chinese Leviathan: Market Transition and the Politics of Governance in China.* Stanford, CA: Stanford University Press, 2004.

You Dehai. "'Sange daibiao' tichu de jingguo yi fabiao de beijing" (The Process of Raising and Background of Issuing the 'Three Represents'). *Xuexi yu shijian* (Wuhan) (September 2000), pp. 18–20, 45.

Young, Susan, *Private Business and Economic Reform in China.* Armonk, NY: M. E. Sharpe, 1995.

Yusuf, Shahid, Kaoru Nabeshima, and Dwight Perkins. *Under New Ownership: Privatizing China's State-Owned Enterprises.* Palo Alto, CA, and Washington, DC: Stanford University Press and World Bank, 2006.

Zakaria, Fareed. *The Future of Freedom: Illiberal Democracy at Home and Abroad.* New York: Norton, 2004.

Zhang, Houyi. "Siying qiyezhu jieceng chengzhang de xin jieduan" (The New Era of Growth of Private Entrepreneurs). In Ru Xin, et al., eds., *2006 nian: Zhongguo shehui xingshi fenxi yu yuce* (Blue Book of China's Society 2006: Analysis and Forecast on China's Social Development). Beijing: Shehui kexue wenxian chubanshe, 2006.

"Kuaisu chengzhang de Zhongguo siying qiyezhu jieceng" (The Rapid Growth of China's Private Entrepreneurs). In Ru Xin, et al., eds., *2005 nian: Zhongguo shehui xingshi fenxi yu yuce* (Blue Book of China's Society 2005: Analysis and Forecast on China's Social Development). Beijing: Shehui kexue wenxian chubanshe, 2005.

"Jinru xin shiqi de Zhongguo siying qiyezhu jieceng" (Chinese Private Entrepreneurs Enter a New Era). In Ru Xin, et al., eds., *2004 nian: Zhongguo shehui xingshi fenxi yu yuce* (Blue Book of China's Society 2004: Analysis and Forecast on China's Social Development). Beijing: Shehui kexue wenxian chubanshe, 2004.

Zhang Hui and Yuan Yue. "2005 nian Zhongguo jumin shenghuo zhiliang diaocha baogao" (Survey Report on the Quality of Life of Chinese Residents in 2005). In Ru Xin, et al., eds., *2006 nian: Zhongguo shehui xingshi fenxi yu yuce* (Blue Book of China's Society 2006: Analysis and Forecast on China's Social Development). Beijing: Shehui kexue wenxian chubanshe, 2006.

Zhang Wenyuan, et al., "Cong Ningbo shi shehui jieceng bianhua kan feigong youzhi jingji zuzhi dangjian gongzuo" (Viewing Party-building Work in Nonpublic Enterprises from Social Structural Changes in Ningbo). *Zhonggong Ningbo shiwei dangxiao xuebao* (CCP Ningbo City Party School Report) (January 2002), pp. 54–59.

Zheng, Yongnian. *Will China Become Democratic? Elite, Class, and Regime Transition*. Singapore: Eastern Universities Press, 2004.

Zheng, Yongnian and Lye Liang Fook. "Elite Politics and the Fourth Generation of Chinese Leadership." *Journal of Chinese Political Science*, vol. 8, nos. 1 and 2 (Fall 2003), pp. 65–86.

Zhongguo siying jingji nianjian, 1996 (China's Private Economy Yearbook, 1996). Beijing: Zhongguo gongshang lianhe chubanshe, 1996.

Zhongguo siying qiye fazhan baogao (1978–1998) (Report on the Development of China's Private Enterprises, 1978–1998). Beijing: Shehui kexue wenxian chubanshe, 1999.

Zhou Linghua and Zheng Hefu. "Siying qiye: Dangjian luohou de yuanyin ji duice" (Private Enterprises: The Causes and Policies toward Sluggish Party Building). *Dangzheng luntan* (Shanghai) (January 1995), pp. 29–30.

Zweig, David. "Undemocratic Capitalism: China and the Limits of Economism." *The National Interest*, no. 56 (Summer 1999), pp. 63–72.

Index